MUHAMMAD
Prophet of God

MUHAMMAD
Prophet of God

Daniel C. Peterson

WILLIAM B. EERDMANS PUBLISHING COMPANY
GRAND RAPIDS, MICHIGAN / CAMBRIDGE, U.K.

© 2001, 2007 Wm. B. Eerdmans Publishing Company

First published 2001 as part of *The Rivers of Paradise*
This edition published 2007 by
Wm. B. Eerdmans Publishing Co.
2140 Oak Industrial Drive N.E., Grand Rapids, Michigan 49505 /
P.O. Box 163, Cambridge CB3 9PU U.K.

Printed in the United States of America

11 10 09 08 07   7 6 5 4 3 2 1

Library of Congress Cataloging-in-Publication Data

Peterson, Daniel C.
Muhammad, prophet of God / Daniel C. Peterson.
p.   cm.
Includes bibliographical references and index.
ISBN 978-0-8028-0754-0 (pbk.: alk. paper)
1. Muhammad, Prophet, d. 632 — Biography.   I. Title

BP75.P42   2007
297.6'3 — dc22
[B]

2006036407

www.eerdmans.com

To my parents-in-law,

Ruth and Keith Stephens,

acknowledging (though scarcely repaying)
their many years of kindness and generosity

Contents

Acknowledgments

I should like to thank Professors David Noel Freedman and Michael J. McClymond for their comments on an earlier draft of this book. I should also like to thank Alison V. P. Coutts for her vital computer expertise and my wife, Deborah, for her help at various stages.

Foreword

The events of 9/11, along with President Bush's declaration of the war against terror and the targeting of primarily Muslim countries as belonging to an axis of evil, created a demand for knowledge about Islam. Universities and colleges started offering more courses on Islam, and authors bombarded the public with books about the religion. Several writers have portrayed Islam as a religion that is intensely anti-Western and bent on world domination, willing to achieve this end by terrorism or any means possible. According to the majority of these writers, the war in Iraq and Afghanistan and the Pakistani and Iranian forays into nuclear technology all set the stage for a clash of civilizations. Another set of writers, clearly in the minority, have sought to present Islam as a thoroughly misunderstood religion that, far from being bellicose and retrogressive, is in fact a recipe for progress and that the religion should not be judged by the actions of a misguided few.

The fact of the matter is that truly objective works on Islam exist for the most part in academic circles, largely inaccessible to the general public. And even in such works, the focus on 9/11 often fails to properly analyze Islam as a religion, presenting the culture and politics of the Arab Muslim Middle East as representative of a monolithic Islam. There still exists a dire need for material that genuinely seeks to understand Islam, far removed from polemic or apologetic perspective.

Professor Daniel Peterson's book answers this need. It initially appeared as his contribution to a larger volume, *The Rivers of Paradise,* edited by noted scholars of religion, Professors David Noel Freedman and Michael J. McClymond (Grand Rapids: Wm. B. Eerdmans, 2001). That book had been prepared just before 9/11, and while discussing many of the tensions and developments of the Muslim world, was free from the taint of *ex post eventu* ruminations. The idea was to present five religions that were based on great religious founders, analyzing these historical personalities and faiths under several rubrics, including origins, development, history, size, geography, and importance in world affairs.

Professor Peterson has approached his work as the consummate academic, starting with a look at the conditions in the Arabia to which Muhammad made his appearance. He blends the historical and critical analyses well with the traditional reports, seeking to make the religion truly understandable. While some authors have tried to portray the Islamic concept of the Divine as distinct from the Judeo-Christian idea and based on a moon-god, he shows the common origins of the Hebrew and Arabic terms for God.

This irenic piece of scholarship does not target any particular author for censure, but carefully debunks some of the old assumptions. Professor Peterson shows that the Christianity of Muhammad's time was not that of the modern mainstream views now accepted, but was highly variegated. In this light, it can be understood why people were not unwilling to convert from the harsh Byzantine interpretations to the religion of the Arab Muslims. Unlike some revisionist authors who have sought to question even the actual existence of Muhammad or the importance of Mecca, Professor Peterson provides details on the early life of Muhammad and shows that even from the second century Mecca was mentioned in Greek writings.

This admirable book comes with copious footnotes and is written in a clear, fluid style that makes it suitable for both the scholar and non-scholar. It is improbable to assume that any one book that presents a summary view of Islam will be accepted by all and sundry without critique. Some scholars may critique Professor Peterson's reliance on primarily Western orientalist material instead of original Arabic sources. Yet, to rely on Arabic sources only presents a monolithic Islam, instead of the many versions that actually exist. Muslims who view Islam only from a faith-based approach may not appreciate some of the opinions expressed— although those opinions are extrapolated from the reports of Muslim scholars. The questions that may be raised regarding this book all aid in bringing forth the goal of the original publication: to create dialogue.

Renowned theologian Hans Kung, in writing the Foreword to *The Rivers of Paradise*, noted that there would be no peace between religions without a dialogue between religions. Such dialogue, he noted, must create trust by specifically

- Clearing up misunderstandings
- Healing traumatic memories
- Dissolving hostile stereotypes
- Coming to terms with conflicts caused by guilt in societies and individuals
- Breaking down hatred and destructiveness
- Reflecting on what is held in common
- Offering positive models

Even if it had fulfilled only one of those requirements, this book would have been a welcome addition to the field of religious and Islamic studies. Somehow, Professor Peterson has managed to achieve all of the recommended objectives. I recommend this work most highly.

KHALEEL MOHAMMED
San Diego State University
October 2006

Overture

On the eve of the birth of Muhammad and the rise of Islam, in the seventh century of the common era, two great empires, the Byzantine and the Sassanid, faced each other — as they and their predecessors had for centuries — across an unstable border. That border ran from north to south across Mesopotamia but continued thereafter to separate the relatively fertile lands of the eastern Mediterranean coast and its immediate hinterlands from the vast and arid deserts of the Arabian Peninsula. Although the Byzantines exercised seemingly firm control over greater Syria and the Sinai to the west, Arabia had eluded control by either of the two rival states.

There may have been a vague awareness of other great cultures beyond the Byzantines and the Sassanids. Tang China was far away to the east, as were the kingdoms of India, Burma, Indonesia, and the empire of the Khmers. Even farther away was the mysterious island nation of Japan. Still, for the world between the Nile and the Oxus Rivers, only the "Romans" and the Persians really counted. Both empires were deeply ideological, verging on the theocratic. The Byzantine Empire, which controlled the Balkans up to the Danube, Anatolia, Syria, Egypt, and (to varying extents) Italy and North Africa from its great capital of Constantinople, was passionately Christian. The Byzantines' dominant language was Greek, although Latin continued to play an important role in the official documents of this continuation of the ancient Roman Empire.

The Sassanid Empire, to the east, had its base in the rich river lands of Iraq and extended eastward across modern-day Iran to Afghanistan and the banks of the Oxus River. It was equally passionate in its commitment to

1

Mazdaism, or Zoroastrianism. Its language was Persian, an Indo-European tongue attested from Old Testament times whose greatest literary achievements were still in the future. The ideological loyalties of the two empires added fire to a rivalry that was, at its base, simply one of shared but indistinct and uncertain borders. The Persian rulers, however, confronted an ethnic and religious diversity within their domain that far exceeded the problems of their Byzantine rivals. Their Magian or Zoroastrian religion remained very much a matter for the ruling class, and there is little evidence that it ever became rooted among the Persian masses. Although they were officially Zoroastrian, their subjects included large numbers of Jews, Nestorian and Monophysite Christians, Manichaeans, Gnostics (Marcionites and proto-Mandaeans), and pagans. In fact, at least in late Sassanian Iraq, aggressive and successful Christian proselytizing became such a threat that apostates from Zoroastrianism were subject to capital punishment.[1] The Persians' diversity presented them with a real problem of social incoherence (which probably contributed, in the mid–seventh century, to the rather swift collapse of the Sassanid state before the armies of Islam) and, by rendering them somewhat insecure, heightened their religious aggressiveness.

Geopolitical conflict between the Persians and the "Romans" had been ongoing for many centuries, and it must have seemed to most contemporaries in what M. G. S. Hodgson has called the Nile-to-Oxus region that the two empires were permanent fixtures of the political scene. A third-century rabbi named Samuel predicted that the Roman and Persian Empires would remain until the advent of the Messiah, and little in the intervening centuries had suggested that he was wrong.[2] Indeed, the tendencies of the age were centralizing and urbanizing, and both the Sassanid and Byzantine states increasingly sought to govern their huge domains through a centralized bureaucracy based on political doctrines of absolute monarchy. Each sought economic mastery. Each sought to control the trade routes by which the products of East Asia, particularly silk, came to the West. The Byzantines wanted to reconquer Armenia and Mesopotamia, which their Roman predecessors had governed in the days of Trajan. The Persians, on the other hand, remembered the old days of Darius when they had owned Syria and Egypt, and dreamed of their return. The

---

1. Michael G. Morony, *Iraq after the Muslim Conquest* (Princeton: Princeton University Press, 1984), pp. 298-300.

2. Cited by Morony, pp. 326-27.

Byzantines and the Sassanids seemed strong, and growing stronger. But neither empire was as solid, by Muhammad's lifetime, as it appeared.

For one thing, the form of Christianity enforced by Byzantium in greater Syria and Egypt was unpopular among their peoples, who felt oppressed and alienated from imperial authority. "Adherence to completely incomprehensible dogmas, like the espousal of the Monophysite doctrine by great masses of people in the Orient and in Egypt," Max Weber observed, "was the expression of an anti-imperial and anti-Hellenic separatist nationalism. Similarly, the monophysitic Coptic church later preferred the Arabs to the Romans as overlords."[3]

Christendom was richly variegated then, as it is now. We in the West are perhaps inclined to see its history through the "mainstream" church. But much more was going on in Christian circles than merely the orderly working out of the creeds. In the philosophically sophisticated though not purely cerebral politics of the great ecumenical councils, schisms repeatedly arose among those who found themselves outvoted. In Judaism, too, the rather coolly rational spirit of the two fifth-century Talmuds, although it was and is immensely influential, should not be mistaken for the whole of the religion.[4] In both faiths the old apocalyptic imagination was still very much awake, and it testifies eloquently if indirectly of social dislocation and political dissatisfactions. The *Apocalypse of Peter,* for example, although it seems to have originated in Palestine early in the second century, was popular up to the eighth or ninth century in Egypt and perhaps elsewhere in the Near East.[5] But new works of quasi scripture were still being created as well. The *Apocalypse of Sedrach,* a Jewish text that underwent a later Christian redaction, may have been written as late as the fifth century, while the Hebrew *Apocalypse of Enoch,* or *3 Enoch,* seems to have originated in the fifth or sixth century in either Palestine or Babylonia. The *Vision of Ezra* may have been composed as late as the seventh century, during or after the lifetime of Muhammad, as were also the *Sibylline Oracles,* which seem to have originated mainly in Egypt, but also in Syria, Asia Minor, and elsewhere in the Near East. The *Revelation of Ezra,* a Christian work, was written sometime prior to the ninth century, while the *Greek Apocalypse of Ezra* may date

---

3. Max Weber, *The Sociology of Religion,* trans. Ephraim Fischoff (Boston: Beacon Press, 1993), pp. 70-71.

4. The final redaction of the Babylonian Talmud was completed around 540 C.E.

5. J. K. Elliott, *The Apocryphal New Testament* (Oxford: Clarendon, 1993).

somewhat later still. The *Apocalypse of Daniel* was probably written at the very beginning of the ninth century, in Palestine or perhaps Egypt.[6]

One of the great divisions in the Near East on the eve of Islam's advent, as today, was that between urban and rural areas. The socioeconomic distinctions that always exist between town and country were exacerbated by linguistic dissimilarity. In the eighth and seventh centuries B.C.E., the Assyrians had, by military conquest, spread a single high culture throughout the region. Its vehicle was the Aramaic language, which, owing to the social prestige of the new masters, gradually replaced the earlier languages and became the mother tongue of Syria and Iraq. It remained so, essentially, until the time of the Arab conquests. By means of the subsequent victories and colonial enterprises of the ardent Hellenizer Alexander the Great, however, Greek culture had been imposed upon the area, which thus entered the Hellenistic period. But it was the cities that absorbed Hellenism far more than the largely untouched countryside. The educated classes now frequently knew Greek, as well as the philosophy, science, and general ideals that it carried. But Aramaic was still the basic language of much of the Near East (including its Christian form, called Syriac), and would provide an excellent and easy bridge for transition to Arabic (a related Semitic language) following the rise of Islam. In Egypt it was Coptic, a form of the ancient Egyptian language that had adopted a modified Greek alphabet and some Greek vocabulary, that formed the daily speech of the hinterlands beyond Greek-speaking cities such as Alexandria. And the great church capitals of Alexandria, Rome, and Constantinople had Syriac-speaking counterparts in the episcopal sees and theological schools of such cities as Edessa and Antioch.

On the Sassanid side of the border, Khusraw I Anushirvan ("he of the immortal soul"), perhaps the greatest of the shahs, attempted to centralize power even more directly in the sixth century by taking it from the landowning gentry class, thus leaving them sullen and disaffected, and imported bedouin Arabs from Arabia for use in his army.[7] Both sides, in fact, had re-

---

6. Information on dating and provenance for these apocryphal materials has been drawn from James H. Charlesworth, ed., *The Old Testament Pseudepigrapha*, vol. 1, *Apocalyptic Literature and Testaments* (Garden City, N.Y.: Doubleday, 1983).

7. The centralization continued under his eventual successor, Khusraw II Parviz (d. 628), with very probably fatal consequences for the dynasty. (Muslim armies conquered Persia before the middle of the seventh century.) It was during this period, and as a result of this process, that the semiautonomous administrative structures built up by Babylonian Jewry were suppressed or destroyed. Khusraw I Anushirvan seems also to have presided over the writing

sorted to using bedouin mercenaries to patrol their borders in the far distant and very unpleasant areas along the Arabian and Iraqi frontiers. The
Ghassanids, in and near Syria, and the Lakhmids in the vicinity of Iraq effectively formed client states for the Byzantines and Sassanids, respectively,
protecting the interests of the two empires and occasionally providing soldiers for the imperial armies. In the Sassanian realm, however, some Arabs
became so powerful that they were able to interfere in the royal succession.

The partial Arabization of the Sassanid army would have consequences
that no Persian military planner could possibly have foreseen at a time when
the notion of a military threat from a disorganized rabble of camel nomads
would surely have been dismissed as laughable. The alienation of powerful
segments of their subject populations ultimately facilitated the lightning-
paced Arab conquests that sharply reduced the Byzantine lands and eliminated the Sassanids altogether, not long after the death of Muhammad. During Muhammad's lifetime, in the early seventh century, the Sassanians and
the Byzantines fought an extremely destructive war that at first seemed to
achieve for the Persians what they had dreamed of: Syrian Antioch fell to
them in 611, followed by the fall of the holy city of Jerusalem on May 5, 614.
The patriarch of Jerusalem and the inhabitants of the city were taken captive,
its churches were burned, and the sacred relic of the True Cross, upon which
Christ had been crucified, was removed to the Sassanid capital amidst great
ceremony. In 615 and again in 626 Persian forces seized the city of Chalcedon,
famous for the ecumenical council that had been held there and strategically
crucial because it lay across the strait from the Byzantine capital of Constantinople. Between 617 and 619 the Persians occupied Egypt, which had long been
the granary of the Roman Empire and, in particular, of the capital.

But a new and resourceful leader, Heraclius, had come to the throne
in Byzantium. In February of 628, as he was advancing on the Sassanid
capital of Ctesiphon, the Persian generals and nobles overthrew and executed the shah and placed on the throne a new ruler who sued for peace. In
March 630 Heraclius made a solemn pilgrimage to Jerusalem, bringing
with him the True Cross. Thus the war ended in a decisive victory for Constantinople. But it proved to be a rather Pyrrhic one that left both empires
financially, militarily, and politically exhausted. Islam arose and expanded
in the relative vacuum of effective political power resulting from that war.

---

down of the Avesta and the Zand, two scriptural documents of the Zoroastrian tradition — a
conservative act that was probably designed to buttress the authority of Magian priests.

The Arabian *Jahiliyya*

The Arabian Peninsula, nearly a third the size of Europe, lay at the juncture of the two great empires. It was and is an arid land, sparsely populated because of its low rainfall and lack of water. (In some areas there may be no rainfall for a decade or more.) Vast lava fields occasionally come to surface, but the most picturesque feature of the region is its sand dunes, some of which rise higher than six hundred feet and are several miles in length. One particularly desolate region, the so-called Empty Quarter, is the size of France. Culture there and most everywhere else could not be agrarian. Rather it was bedouin based, resting on camel nomadism. (One nineteenth-century Orientalist famously described the Arabs as parasites on camels.) There were lesser herds of sheep and goats and some oases with wells, which permitted the cultivation of date palms.

On the north the peninsula bordered on the scattered territories in Mesopotamia and Syro-Palestine often referred to as the Fertile Crescent. Here migrant Arabs searching for better living conditions came into contact with the settled civilizations of the wider world, imbibing influences from them and occasionally influencing them as well. The Nabateans, for example, were Aramaicized Arabs who interacted with Rome from their famous capital of Petra until their territory was absorbed under the emperor Trajan in 105 C.E. and designated the provinces of Palaestina Tertia and Arabia. A common name among Nabatean rulers was Aretas, which appears also in 2 Corinthians 11:32. (This is simply a Hellenized form of the Arabic masculine name *Harith* or *Haritha*, from a root relating to the tilling of the soil.) In the first half of the third century C.E., at least two Arabs actually ruled the Roman Empire for brief periods. One, Elagabalus (218-

22), had been the high priest of the sacred black stone of Syrian Emesa, and upon his accession to the imperial dignity he had the stone transported to Rome and enshrined within a temple there. The second, Philip, sat on the throne in 244 C.E., the year of Rome's millennial celebrations. Just after his death another Aramaicized Arab kingdom, Palmyra, arose, first as a Roman client state dominating the trade route between Damascus and Mesopotamia and then, briefly but famously, as an independent would-be empire under its rebel queen Zenobia.[1]

The great sixth-century Byzantine emperor Justinian appointed Harith, of the Monophysite Christian Arab tribe Banu Ghassan, king of the East and commander of the empire's Arab auxiliary forces. The fighting between the Byzantines and their predecessors the Romans, on the one hand, and the Parthians and Sassanids, on the other, had been going on for centuries and was fierce but desperately hopeless. Justinian, however, desired to focus his attention on the lands in Europe and North Africa that the empire had lost when the barbarians overran the imperial armies there in the fifth century.[2] He was more than happy to turn the conduct of the eastern wars over to Arab mercenaries. So, for that matter, were his Persian rivals. They, too, had more pressing concerns than the old and fruitless border wars of the Syrian and north Arabian steppes, and consequently designated the Banu Lakhm tribe to do their fighting there for them.[3]

On the south and on the east, the peninsula's boundary was formed by the Indian Ocean and the Persian Gulf, while the Red Sea provided its perimeter to the west. The southwestern corner of the peninsula, the Yemen, was mountainous but relatively well supplied with water, which facilitated the rise of fairly advanced monarchical societies based on intensive terraced cultivation and irrigation. It produced a rich crop of incense, myrrh, and other perfumes and aromatic substances for sale to the Medi-

1. Her name in Arabic was Zaynab. She proclaimed her son Athenodorus — whose name in Greek denotes the "Gift of Athena" and probably reflects an underlying Arabic *Wahballat* ("Gift of Allat") — Caesar Augustus of the Near East.

2. Byzantium seems simply to have been unable to fight successfully on both fronts at once. See Maxime Rodinson, *Mohammed,* trans. Anne Carter (Harmondsworth: Penguin Books, 1971), p. 34, for the sixth century.

3. It is not clear which appointment came first. The Lakhmids are said, at one point, to have massacred four hundred Christian nuns in honor of the goddess al-Uzza, and some have speculated that this outrage impelled Justinian to appoint Harith and the Ghassanids as his agents and policemen.

terranean basin, and was a major transit point for trade from India and East Africa. Pearls, ivory, silk, cotton, textiles, rice, pepper, slaves, monkeys, gold, and even ostrich plumes could be found in its markets and warehouses. Not surprisingly, Yemen's culture was quite distinct from that of the rest of Arabia. Its people did not call themselves Arabs, and they spoke a language that was distinct from but related to Arabic. Their rich temples and elaborate priesthood were without parallel elsewhere in Arabia.

Travel in the peninsula was difficult but not impossible, given the right combination of skills and a knowledge of the watering holes. Several trade routes crisscrossed the region, notable among them a course running from the ports of the Red Sea and the border outposts of Syria-Palestine and Transjordan, or even directly from Gaza and Damascus, down along the coast of the Red Sea to the Yemen. Dating to at least the time of Alexander the Great and his successors, and probably back to the time of the domestication of the camel, this route has in more recent years served the Hijaz railway.

Rome's commercial relationships with the East began in the days of its early empire, when its increasing hunger for luxuries turned its attention to the raw goods and exotics that could be had via the customs stations first of the Parthians and then of the Sassanids. But the Arabian land route also grew in importance. Seafaring merchants who had mastered the monsoons brought goods from India and elsewhere to the Yemen, whence other entrepreneurs carried them overland. Not content to serve as transit points, however, the kingdoms of south Arabia also produced rich crops of frankincense and myrrh to feed the funeral pyres and the temple liturgies of the Mediterranean basin. With the massive influx of wealth that such trade brought, the Yemen earned its classical reputation as Arabia Felix, "Arabia the Blessed."[4]

For reasons easily grasped, Roman/Byzantine and Persian rulers were very interested in this route. The Sassanids wanted to control it for its profits; the Byzantines sought to control it in order to escape the tariff duties

4. Classical authors by the time of Ptolemy (second century c.e.) had divided Arabia into perhaps four parts. They were somewhat familiar with Arabia Petraea (the area surrounding the spectacular rock-hewn city of Petra, in modern Jordan) and with the coastal regions. Of Arabia Felix and the much larger interior Arabia Deserta they had, at best, spotty and inaccurate notions. Solid treatments of the subject include G. W. Bowersock, *Roman Arabia* (Cambridge: Harvard University Press, 1983), and Fergus Millar, *The Roman Near East: 31 BC–AD 337* (Cambridge: Harvard University Press, 1993).

imposed on them by their hereditary enemies along the other trade route. The Romans had sent a large expedition into Arabia in 24 B.C.E., but it proved a disaster. In the middle of the fourth century C.E., their Byzantine successors sent a Christian bishop to the Yemen in an effort to counteract Persian political activity there by preaching the ideology of the Byzantine state, Christianity. Likewise, just across the narrow strait of today's Bab al-Mandab, the new Christian power of Abyssinia (Ethiopia) cast envious and greedy eyes on the riches of the Yemenis. Early in the sixth century the Byzantines encouraged their fellow Christians in Abyssinia to occupy Yemen as a way of heading off further Sassanid inroads.[5]

The remainder of the Arabian Peninsula, however, seemed far removed from the interests of the great powers. Bedouin culture is much less stratified than that of societies based on an agricultural surplus. There might be transient concentrations of wealth, perhaps, but no lasting class divisions. The herdsman or nomad cannot be exploited like the rooted peasant, who is, from the bedouin perspective, a slave to his fields and hence to others. The nomad has his pride, and he is, by definition, mobile. If the situation is not to his liking, he can simply strike his tent and move away.

Tribal organization was, and is today, based first on extended families and then, in ever larger circles, on conglomerations of groups known as "clans" and "tribes." At least in theory, the basis of these groupings was common kinship, based on descent — real or fictional — from a shared ancestor. Elaborate genealogies served both as an ideological prop for the system and, under early Islam, as tools for political analysis. (Muhammad's lieutenant and successor, Abu Bakr, was famous for his genealogical expertise.) Each group possessed a recognized pastureland in which to wander. There were limits and boundaries, but they were fluid and changed constantly in intertribal conflict. Each tribe was sovereign and was led by a chief, or *shaykh,* who was chosen partly on the basis of descent but partly also on the basis of proven valor and wisdom.

Under such circumstances, obviously, although lineage and group loyalties were intense, there could be no authoritarian political forms. Thus the political culture of Arabia — if there could truly be said to be one

---

5. The Abyssinians were Monophysites while the Byzantines termed themselves "Orthodox," but that did not prevent them from regarding each other as Christians — nor from recognizing common political interests.

— was quite opposite that of the Sassanians. Indeed, there was really no Arabian concept of a "state" at all, except perhaps among the Lakhmids and Ghassanids to the north (who had come into contact with the settled regimes of Iran and the Mediterranean basin) and among the sedentary and quite distinct culture of Yemen to the south. The bedouin chief had no authority to coerce. He was, rather, obliged to entreat his followers by generosity and kindness and, no doubt, by leading them in directions that he could sense they had already chosen to travel. The very notion of kingship or even political authority was abhorrent to the nomads of Arabia. Bernard Lewis puts it well when he says that the Arabian ideal was "a maximum of freedom of action and a minimum of public authority."[6]

However, another factor in Arabian life needs to be taken into account, one far less well known and clearly understood: There existed, in Arabia, professional men of religion who came to their role by family inheritance and served as interpreters of customary law.[7] These were, in effect, holy families, certainly priestly families, and they were generally associated with a sacred enclave or sanctuary. In modern south Arabia this enclave is called a *hawta;* in ancient Arabia it was known as a *haram* — the term still used for the Meccan sanctuary of the Ka'ba, which is the sacred center of the Muslim world. In the Yemen, for example, the sanctuary of a god named Dhu Samawi was set within a sacred enclave that was apparently surrounded by boundary stones just like those in Mecca.[8] As the leading scholar of the subject has observed,

> In a society where war is the norm of existence, a neutral territory is a necessity for reasons religious, political, and economic. The hawtah is such an area, often situated at a natural road junction, where tribes meet, perhaps an important market. A saint, it is often recorded, in his

6. Bernard Lewis, *The Arabs in History,* rev. ed. (New York: Harper & Row, 1967), p. 35.

7. See R. B. Serjeant, "Ḥaram and Ḥawṭah, the Sacred Enclave in Arabia," in *Mélanges Taha Husain, publiés par Abdurrahman Badawi* (Cairo, 1962), pp. 41-58; and R. B. Serjeant, "The Saiyids of Ḥaḍramawt" (inaugural lecture at the School of Oriental and African Studies of the University of London, 1956). Both papers are now available in R. B. Serjeant, *Studies in Arabian History and Civilization* (London: Variorum Reprints, 1981). As Serjeant, "The Saiyids of Ḥaḍramawt," p. 6 n. 1, observes, the religious aristocracy of pre-Islamic Arabia seems, after the coming of Islam, to have distinguished itself in jurisprudence.

8. Serjeant, "Ḥaram and Ḥawṭah," p. 52. The name of the god seems to suggest astral worship, or something of the sort. It means, roughly, "he of the heavenly [things]."

own lifetime will demarcate a ḥawṭah with whitewashed pillars. After death his holiness and power are embodied in his tomb, now become a sanctuary, which his successor, known as Manṣab, and his posterity administer. The essential political factor herein is that the saint induces the tribes or [in Islamic times] sulṭāns to contract agreements with him to maintain the inviolability of the ḥawṭah and define penalties for its infringement. . . . The ḥawṭah and the Meccan ḥaram are institutions identical in essence.[9]

Early Muslims described the period before the rise of Islam in Arabia as the time of *Jahiliyya,* generally translated into English (and understood in modern Arabic) as the "Age of Ignorance."[10] The obvious point of the name — as was the point of the Enlightenment's rather misleading invention of the "Dark Ages" — was to heighten the contrast between the bad old days and the presumably better days that had followed.

The religious views of the pre-Islamic Arabians have been described as a kind of "tribal humanism."[11] There was, according to this reading, little faith in an afterlife and little real concern for the gods among the inhabitants of Arabia before the coming of Islam. Given no economic basis for a feudal or aristocratic society, Arabian life was egalitarian and unstratified, but everything was viewed in tribal terms. Group solidarity — what the later Arab social theorist Ibn Khaldun (d. 1406) labeled *asabiyya* — was the fundamental premise of bedouin life and its chief tool of survival. Fissiparous tendencies were limited, however, by the consideration that, if one struck out on one's own, one lost all claim to protection and support from one's kinsfolk and, in the absence of any kind of "government," could be attacked with impunity. On the other hand the threat of costly and de-

9. Serjeant, "The Saiyids of Ḥaḍramawt," pp. 14-15.

10. Although it would probably be translated more accurately as the "Age of Barbarism." See the argument of Ignaz Goldziher, "What Is Meant by 'al-Jāhiliyya?" in Ignaz Goldziher, *Muslim Studies,* ed. S. M. Stern, trans. C. R. Barber and S. M. Stern (Albany: State University of New York Press, 1967), pp. 201-8.

11. The phrase is associated with W. Montgomery Watt, upon whose reconstruction of pre-Islamic Arabian social processes the following discussion is substantially dependent. For the phrase see W. Montgomery Watt, *Muhammad: Prophet and Statesman* (London: Oxford University Press, 1974), p. 51. For the social malaise of Mecca in the period just prior to the advent of Islam, see Watt, pp. 38, 43-55; Rodinson, pp. 65-66. On pp. 16-18 Rodinson echoes the notion of pre-Islamic Arabia as a rather irreligious place.

bilitating blood feuds maintained a rough-and-ready intertribal peace. Vengeance was meted out by groups to groups, for the simple reason that the group was the basic unit of society rather than the individual, who had rights and obligations only as a member of his or her tribe or clan. As a poet named Durayd b. Simma put it, speaking of his own tribe,

I am of Ghaziyya: if she be in error, then I will err;
And if Ghaziyya be guided right, I go right with her.[12]

The virtues most highly prized among the pre-Islamic Arabs included bravery in battle, patience in misfortune, persistence in revenge, protection of the weak, defiance of the strong, honor, and generosity. They were very much like the qualities that some scholars have identified as characteristic of "heroic" cultures such as Homeric Greece, pagan Scandinavia, and early Sumer.[13] In this context it is significant that the early Arabic term equivalent to the English "virtue" is *muruwwa,* or "manliness."[14] Much of the pre-Islamic Arabian moral ideal might be expressed in the vow that Tennyson ascribes to his Ulysses, "To strive, to seek, to find, and not to yield."

Revenge was an important element of that ideal. Here is one early Arab commenting on his kinsfolk who had refused to help him against the raiders who had stolen his camels:

For all their numbers, they are good for naught,
My people, against harm however light:
They pardon wrong by evildoers wrought,
Malice with lovingkindness they requite.[15]

12. Cited by Reynold A. Nicholson, *A Literary History of the Arabs* (Cambridge: Cambridge University Press, 1969), p. 83. All of the translations of pre-Islamic poetry cited here are from Nicholson. The abbreviation "b." represents the Arabic word *ibn* (son [of]).

13. Following the classic statement of the idea in H. Munro Chadwick, *The Growth of Literature,* 3 vols. (Cambridge: Cambridge University Press, 1932-40), discussed most fully in vol. 1. See also Albert B. Lord, "Homer, Parry, and Huso," *American Journal of Archaeology* 52 (1948): 34-44; Samuel Noah Kramer, "New Light on the Early History of the Ancient Near East," *American Journal of Archaeology* 52 (1948): 156-64. In my opinion, accordingly, Nicholson is not far off when he labels Antara b. Shaddad, the dashing hero of a pre-Islamic Arabian romance, "the Bedouin Achilles." See Nicholson, p. 114.

14. Of course, the English word itself is derived from the Latin *vir,* or "man."

15. Nicholson, p. 92.

The ancient Arabs were fond of the story of Shanfara of Azd, an ideal hero who, as a child, had been captured from his tribe and raised by the Banu Salaman. Years later, when he had grown up, he returned to his own tribe and vowed to extract vengeance from his onetime captors — a nice illustration of the power of blood kinship even over the ties of acquaintance and perhaps affection. He swore an oath that he would kill a hundred men of the Salaman. He was so successful that he managed to kill ninety-eight when he was caught in an ambush by his infuriated enemies. During the struggle that ensued, one of his hands was severed by the stroke of a sword. Shanfara grabbed the severed hand with his other hand and threw it with such force into the face of one of his opponents that it killed the man. This brought him to within one victim of fulfilling his vow of vengeance. Unfortunately, though, the Banu Salaman killed him and left his body to rot in the desert. Sometime later, however, one of them was passing by the spot and saw Shanfara's skull lying on the sand, bleached out by the intense desert sun. He could not resist the temptation to kick it. But that was a bad move. A splinter of bone from the skull went into his foot and, when the wound mortified, he died. Even after death Shanfara, the consummate Arabian hero in this regard, had completed his vow of revenge.[16]

Honor was another important pre-Islamic virtue. Even into the Islamic period, Arabs related the story of a Jewish Arab named al-Samawal b. Adiya, who owned a castle north of the agricultural oasis of Yathrib. According to this story, the great poet Imru al-Qays took refuge with al-Samawal while fleeing toward Syria from some of his many enemies. When he continued on his journey, he left five coats of mail, heirlooms of his family, with his host for safekeeping, intending to pick them up again on his return. But he never came back, for he died on the way home from an audience with the emperor in Constantinople. In the meantime the enemies of Imru al-Qays besieged al-Samawal in his fortified dwelling, demanding that he surrender the coats of mail he had promised to preserve for the poet. This he would not do. And when the besiegers captured his son, who had gone out of the castle to hunt, and threatened to kill him if his father did not yield up the armor, al-Samawal responded that they must do as they saw fit, for he could not in

16. The story is told at Charles James Lyall, *Translations of Ancient Arabian Poetry* (New York: Columbia University Press, 1930), p. 83.

honor renege on his obligation to Imru al-Qays. At that, the enemies outside slew the boy and lifted the siege.[17]

Finally the pre-Islamic Arabs venerated the ideal of generosity. The model figure in this regard was a man named Hatim of Tayyi, who has served to illustrate the lavish generosity of the perfect Arab chieftain for many centuries.[18] To his wife, Mawiyya, he remarked:

> The guest's slave am I, 'tis true, as long as he bides with me,
> Although in my nature else no trait of the slave is shown.[19]

When Hatim's mother was pregnant with him, so the story goes, she had a dream in which she was asked whether she would prefer to bear a generous son or ten strong and brave warriors. She chose the first. When Hatim grew up, it became his custom to throw away his food if he could find nobody with whom to share it. Such prodigality irritated his father, who gave him a slave girl, a mare, and a foal and sent him out into the middle of nowhere to herd the family's three hundred camels, the core of their wealth. True to form, when it came time to eat Hatim looked desperately for someone with whom to share his food. Finally, just as he was about to cast it away, he saw three riders in the distance and went out to meet them. They asked him for something to eat, and he slaughtered three camels for them. The riders — who, as it happened, were a trio of well-known poets from diverse regions of the peninsula — protested that a drink of milk would have been enough for them and said that, at the most, he might have butchered merely a young she-camel for their refreshment. Hatim responded that he could tell that they came from various places, and that he had gone to such lengths in order to ensure that his reputation for generosity would be carried to their different homes. Obligingly they thereupon composed and recited verses in praise of his extravagance. But this only served, as Hatim saw it, to put him in their debt, and he insisted that they come forward and divide his camel herd among them. They did, and each left with ninety-nine camels. When Hatim's father heard what had been done, he was furious. But Hatim assured him — quite accurately, as it

17. Nicholson, pp. 84-85, provides an easily accessible translation of the story from al-Isbahani's classical collection *Kitab al-Aghani*.

18. He is mentioned, for example, in Omar Khayyam's famous twelfth-century Persian poem, the *Rubaiyat*.

19. Nicholson, p. 87.

turned out — that his generosity had now assured for both of them ever-lasting fame and honor, seeing that it would be celebrated in poetry across Arabia and beyond forever. The camels were a good investment for such a return.[20]

Ancient Arabs made the same connection between expert horseman-ship and the cluster of values associated with "chivalry" and "knighthood" — virtues such as heroism, nobility, and valor — that later peoples of western Europe made. Indeed, the Arabs used the same word, *furusiyya* (lit. "horsemanship"), for both.[21] "Knight-errantry, the riding forth on horseback in search of adventures, the rescue of captive maidens, the suc-cour rendered everywhere to women in adversity — these were essentially Arabian ideas, as was the very name of *chivalry,* the connection of honour-able conduct with the horse-rider, the man of noble blood, the cavalier."[22]

Muhammad was a native of Mecca, a small oasis town dominated by an Arab tribe known as the Quraysh, who controlled its economy and politics and enjoyed immense religious prestige in connection with the local shrine known as the Ka'ba. This shrine was an object of pilgrimage venerated by people throughout Arabia. The ancient frankincense trail passed near or through Mecca, and caravans of all types constantly plied the route, which ensured at least a measure of acquaintance, on the part of the town's inhabitants, with cultures and religions beyond Arabia. It would seem that the residents of Mecca originally hired themselves out as guides or as guards for the caravans that moved through their territory — in the latter case, their "guardianship" may have been little more than the demanding of protection money — but that, somewhere in the sixth cen-tury C.E., they began actually to take control of the trade and to outfit their own caravans. This led to a rapid increase in wealth, and to the rise

20. The story is translated, again from the *Kitab al-Aghani,* at Nicholson, pp. 85-86. The father, by the way, was not mollified by Hatim's reasoning and disowned him, leaving him alone in the desert with his slave girl, his mare, and her foal.

21. It is very likely, in fact, that the western European notion derives from the Arabs, who occupied substantial portions of the Iberian Peninsula for nearly eight centuries and occasionally ruled other portions of southern Europe as well. The historical association of horsemanship with certain ideals is well attested in various European languages, where we speak, for example, of "chivalry," "caballeros," "cavalry," and a "cavalier attitude." Beyond the Romance languages, the same equation can be seen in the German *Ritter* (knight), cognate with the German verb *reiten,* "to ride."

22. Nicholson, p. 88.

of class divisions within the formerly rather undifferentiated population of the town.

Especially in the years just prior to the revelation, when unprecedented wealth was flowing into Mecca, the leaders of the tribe of Quraysh saw themselves as having achieved just about all there was to be achieved. In the late sixth century both the Lakhmids and the Ghassanids had abruptly lost their official status as clients of, respectively, the Sassanids and the Byzantines.[23] No Arabian power now stood to rival the ambitions of the Quraysh. Their wealth was certainly to be enjoyed for its own sake, but it also enabled them to live out the ideal of Arab generosity in a way that perhaps had never been known before. By means of wealth a man could be powerful and could further strengthen his situation by arranging marriages with other families of wealth and status. Thus he could be a protector of the weak and a sought-after ally. On a daily basis he could be a lavish host and a giver of gifts, not because of some religious precept or out of hope for a transcendent reward in a life to come, but because of the praise it would bring him. Perhaps he could even hope for a kind of immortality in the words of some poet, who could be brought to praise him either out of honest admiration or, failing that, through a relatively modest transfer of wealth.

Poetry was the sole medium of literary expression among the Arabs of the pre-Islamic period. Indeed, since it took no space in a saddlebag and was easily portable, it was by far the most important artistic form developed by the bedouin nomads. The earliest extant Arabian poems date from about 500 C.E., but, since the first poets of whom we know are consummate masters working within conventions that seem already set, there is good reason to believe that the poetic tradition extends backward considerably further. Many scholars think the earliest poetic or poetrylike compositions were created in *saj'*, a style of elevated prose in which the lines have no meter but their final words rhyme. This was also the rhetorical form in which the pre-Islamic Arabian seers or soothsayers known as *kahins* delivered their oracles.[24] (Significantly, perhaps, it is likewise the style of the Qur'an.) The pre-Islamic poet was thought to be a sort of wizard, in league with and inspired by the jinn or even the *shayatin* (satans). The *jinn* (sing. *jinni*), creatures that ancient Arabian thinking ranked

---

23. On the Lakhmids and Ghassanids, see Rodinson, pp. 26-28.
24. Compare the Hebrew *kohen,* "priest."

above humans but below angels, could be either good or bad (hence the "satans") but tended to be mischievous and unreliable.

Poetry was immensely popular among the masses of Arabs, and not merely among an elite — which, in Arabia, was essentially nonexistent in any event. It is thus not surprising that among a people obsessed with words and in a culture that has been called "language intoxicated," the distinction between prophet and poet should have been so uncertain. And indeed, prophethood is not easy to distinguish from that ancient sense of the vocation of the poet, for the prophet is by definition someone who speaks the word of another, not himself. He or she is literally an "enthusiast," having the god or *theos* within, and can fittingly be described, at the moment of the reception of revelation, as "possessed."[25] In ancient Greece and Israel, as in pre-Islamic Arabia, prophet and poet were originally one.[26] In the Bible Moses, Miriam, and Deborah are all termed "prophets," and specific poetry is attributed to each of them. Indeed, most of the canonical prophets of the Bible delivered oracular speeches that are, by most standards, poetic, even if the larger parts of such books as Jeremiah and Ezekiel are written in prose.

A story from the early Islamic period will serve to illustrate the pre-Islamic passion for poetry, which survived into at least the early years of the new religion but was, as the story shows, clearly under attack. There was a great and often bitter rivalry between two poets named Jarir and Farazdaq, and each poet had an enthusiastic and multitudinous following. One day during the civil wars that rent the Islamic community after the death of Muhammad, the governor of Khurasan, who was marching forth with an army to do battle with a sect of purist Muslim schismatics called the Azariqa, heard the noise of an upheaval in his camp. When he inquired about its cause, he learned that his soldiers had been arguing passionately about the respective merits of the two poets. They decided to submit the question to him for adjudication. The governor declined to enter the dispute, but suggested that they take their question to the Azariqa, who not only clung to the simple, fierce, and rather anarchic ways of the desert but retained a deep passion for poetry. Thus, on the following day, when the ar-

25. G. van der Leeuw, *Phänomenologie der Religion,* 4th ed. (Tübingen: J. C. B. Mohr [Paul Siebeck], 1977), pp. 244-45; compare pp. 457-63.

26. See the discussion of David Noel Freedman, "Pottery, Poetry, and Prophecy: An Essay on Biblical Poetry," *Journal of Biblical Literature* 96, no. 1 (1977): 5-26; also van der Leeuw, pp. 244-45, 250. Compare Plato, *Apology* 22.

mies had faced off against one another and one of the Azariqa had stepped forward to issue the traditional challenge to single combat, a warrior in the governor's army accepted the challenge but demanded to know, first, whether Jarir or Farazdaq was the better poet. "God confound you!" cried the rebel champion. "Are you asking me about poetry instead of studying the Qur'ān and the law?" Nonetheless, the dissenting warrior proceeded to cite a verse by Jarir and to give judgment in that poet's favor.[27]

Poetry unified the Arabs. Across the peninsula it was composed in the same dialect, following the same rules of composition. This made it, in modern terms, a powerful public relations tool. A poet praised his tribe and vilified its rivals. If he was good, if his verses were memorable, his praise or his ridicule could stick to his subject for many years.

> When there appeared a poet in a family of the Arabs, the other tribes round about would gather together to that family and wish them joy of their good luck. Feasts would be got ready, the women of the tribe would join together in bands, playing upon lutes, as they were wont to do at bridals, and the men and boys would congratulate one another; for a poet was a defence to the honor of them all, a weapon to ward off insult from their good name, and a means of perpetuating their glorious deeds and of establishing their fame for ever. And they used not to wish one another joy but for three things — the birth of a boy, the coming to light of a poet, and the foaling of a noble mare.[28]

The early Islamic poets Jarir and Farazdaq figure in another story that will illustrate the power of poets and poetry — as well as the power that was thought to lie behind them — in ancient Arabia and that continued on for some years beyond the life of the Prophet. There was a rather well-known poet called as "the Camel-Herd," a member of the tribe of Banu Numayr, who had been very vocal in his opinion that Farazdaq was a better poet than Jarir, despite the fact that Jarir had been known to praise the Banu Numayr while Farazdaq had sometimes attacked them in his verse. One day Jarir ran into the Camel-Herd near the new city of Basra and an argument arose. The Camel-Herd, whose son Jandal had accompanied him, was riding a mule. Young and impatient, Jandal suddenly burst

27. Nicholson, p. 239, retells this story from the invaluable *Kitab al-Aghani*.
28. Ibn Rashiq, quoted in Lyall, p. 17.

out, "Why are you stopping before this dog of the Banū Kulayb, as if you had anything to hope or to fear from him?" Saying so, he lashed the mule with his whip, and the surprised animal kicked Jarir, who was standing nearby. Picking up his cap, which had fallen to the ground, Jarir brushed it, put it back on his head, and said, in spontaneous verse,

O Jandal! What will Numayr say of you
When my dishonoring shaft has pierced your father?

Jarir was coldly furious. He returned to his home, performed the evening prayer, called for a lamp and some date wine, and then proceeded to plot his poetic revenge. An old woman in the house heard the sound of muttering coming from his room and, climbing the stairs to see what the problem was, discovered him crawling, naked, on his bed. She ran downstairs, shouting that he was "mad" (*majnun;* lit. "jinn-possessed") and describing to the others in the house what she had seen. But they seem to have been wiser about the ways of poets than she was. "Go away," they said. "We know what he is up to." By dawn the following morning, Jarir had composed a devastating eighty-verse satire of the Banu Numayr, and he signaled his triumphant satisfaction with a shout of *Allahu akbar!* (God is most great!). He immediately rode to meet the Camel-Herd and his friends, including Farazdaq himself. He said nothing to any of them, but proceeded directly to recite his poem. Farazdaq, the Camel-Herd, and their friends listened in horrified silence as the lethal satire unfolded.

Jarir closed his poem with an insult against the entire tribe ("Cast down your eyes for shame! For you are of Numayr — no peer of Ka'b nor even of Kilāb"), and the Camel-Herd, now agonizingly aware of the evil he had brought upon them all, hurried back to the camp of his tribesmen. "Saddle up!" he cried. "Saddle up! You cannot stay here any longer, for Jarīr has disgraced you all!" They left as soon as they could strike their tents, and they never forgave the Camel-Herd for the shame he had called down upon their heads. Centuries later his tribe still lamented what he had done, and in fact, his story and his shame are preserved to this day in the great Arabic poetic anthology known as the *Kitab al-Aghani,* or "Book of Songs."[29]

---

29. The story is retold at Nicholson, pp. 245-46. The early Arabs often compared *hija'* (satire) to arrows. They believed in the intrinsic power of words to "cast a 'spell.'" The story of Balaam in Num. 22–24 may reflect similar notions.

Although the view of pre-Islamic Arabia as a society dominated by a "tribal humanism" has much to recommend it, we should be careful not to exaggerate its allegedly secular character. As Tor Andrae observes of Muhammad, "Every sentence of his discussions with his countrymen shows that they clung to the pagan gods and customs with a devout loyalty which possessed an unmistakably religious colouring."[30] For many years scholars have pointed to the striking lack of religious feeling in extant *jahili* poetry, and to the rarity of its allusions to the pagan deities of the peninsula, as evidence that the pre-Islamic Arabians were largely irreligious. This seems to me unjustified.

The ancient Arabian *qasida,* or ode, was not an organic whole, but rather something like a series of paintings by the same artist or, as the Arabs themselves liked to describe it, a necklace of pearls that differed in size and quality. Each line was a separate unit, a complete thought. The ancient Arabs did not employ the technique of enjambment, continuing a sentence on into a following line. This means that modern editors and scholars frequently disagree over the proper order of the lines in early poems, and it means, furthermore, that lines can easily disappear completely. It is thus altogether possible — and, I would say, likely — that expressly pagan lines disappeared from these poems in the early and zealous days of Islam. One's suspicion that this might be so is strengthened when one considers the transmission history of the poems. They were orally composed and, for many years, orally transmitted. Although the oldest of the poems claim to date from the beginning of the sixth century, they were not reduced to writing and anthologized, in many cases, until the close of the eighth century. That allows abundant time for editing.[31]

And who preserved the poetry? As Islam spread with lightning speed beyond what was then the rather small world of Arabic speakers, into Mesopotamia and Syria and Persia and across North Africa, new converts to

30. Tor Andrae, *Mohammed: The Man and His Faith,* trans. Theophil Menzel (New York: Harper & Row, 1960), p. 119; compare pp. 120-21. See, too, the materials quoted by F. E. Peters, *Muhammad and the Origins of Islam* (Albany: State University of New York Press, 1994), pp. 172-73.

31. In fact, the great Egyptian scholar and writer Taha Husayn suggested, in his famous book *Fī al-shiʿr al-jāhilī* (On Jāhilī Poetry), that the entire corpus of pre-Islamic poetry is a late fraud. However, I would judge that the consensus view is that, although he raised important issues, he went too far.

the faith found the language of their holy book, the Qur'an, formidably difficult. To help them, an array of commentators and lexicographers stepped forward with linguistic guidance. Quite predictably they turned to the great repository of Arabic, its poetry, for help in explaining difficult terms, just as modern dictionaries use illustrative sentences to clarify the meanings and usage of terms under discussion. Thus, when the old patronage networks that had promoted poetic composition had broken down because of the religious revolution of Islam and the dispersion of Arabia's native sons from the peninsula to Iberia on the west and the borders of India on the east, it was the religious scholars who preserved tag lines of the poetry for philological reasons. But these, of course, would be the most likely people of all to omit lines paying tribute to pagan deities or expressing explicitly polytheistic religiosity.

We should be wary of exaggerating the gulf between pre-Islamic and Islamic religiosity, large though it undoubtedly is. It is abundantly clear from the Qur'an, for example, that Muhammad felt no need to introduce Allah to his Arabian audience. Allah was already known to them.[32] Thus, for instance, when an early revelation given to him called on the people of Mecca to "worship the Lord of this House" — i.e., of the Ka'ba — no need was felt to explain who the "Lord of this House" *was*.[33] Still, Allah was what historians of religion have sometimes termed a *deus otiosus* — a deity so distant and transcendent that he was of little practical relevance to the lives of the people. Their attentions seem to have been focused more on his three purported daughters — Manat, Allat, and al-Uzza — and on the quasi-divine beings known collectively as the jinn, than on Allah.[34] (Both Tor Andrae and Bernard Lewis term pre-Islamic Arabian religion "poly-

---

32. The word *Allah* is cognate with the name of the old Semitic high god *El* and the biblical *Elohim*. It is not so much a name as a title, a contraction of the Arabic *al-ilah* ("the god"), and is simply the Arabic equivalent for the English "God." As such, it is used by Arabic-speaking Jews and Christians as well as Muslims, and is the term employed in the Arabic Bible. It is derived from the same root as Hebrew *'lh* (= *'eloah*, the rare singular form of the very common plural [of majesty?] *Elohim*). The use of the definite article *al-* in the Arabic is equivalent to the Hebrew *ha-'eloah* or *ha-'elohim*, which would mean "the god" or, perhaps, "God himself." For a discussion of pre-Islamic attitudes toward Allah, see Peters, *Muhammad*, pp. 107-8, 117.

33. Qur'an 106:3. In citations from the Qur'an (hereafter Q), the number preceding the colon indicates the sura, or chapter; the number following the colon specifies the verse(s). All translations from the Qur'an are mine.

34. For a good brief summary, see Rodinson, pp. 16-17.

21

daemonism.")[35] These deities and demigods lived in or were represented by trees, fountains, and most particularly certain sacred stones.[36] (Recall the Arabo-Roman emperor Elagabalus and his sacred stone from Emesa, in Syria.) The jinn, in particular, seem to have originated as personifications of natural forces — often malevolent, seldom better than puckishly indifferent to human interests. They sometimes had to be bought off, but they seem never to have made moral claims or propounded moral law. There were a few fixed shrines (of which the Meccan Ka'ba was the most important), but the sacred objects may often have been — as is appropriate to the life of nomadic peoples — portable, rather like the biblical ark of the covenant or the tabernacle of Moses. In any event, whatever the religious situation in Arabia on the eve of the rise of Islam may have been, early Muslims insisted that the peninsula had once been an important center for the worship of the true and only God, linked inextricably to the sacred history of the Bible itself.

According to Islamic tradition, when Abraham cast Hagar and her son Ishmael out of his presence, they were led southward to a distant and barren valley in the Arabian Peninsula, some forty camel-days distant from the land of Canaan.[37] This valley, fifty miles inland from the Red Sea, was called Becca. It lay along a great caravan route, often called the "frank-

35. Andrae, *Mohammed*, p. 13; Lewis, p. 30. Our lack of clarity on the early Arabian religious situation is mirrored in the fundamental disagreements about it among Western Orientalists: Watt, p. 26, thinks pre-Islamic paganism was a polytheistic system that was moving in the direction of monotheism; Peters, *Muhammad,* p. 118, sees an "emerging henotheism"; Andrae, *Mohammed*, p. 16, says "the ancient paganism of Arabia may in general be regarded as an undeveloped polytheism, in which a development had just barely begun which would have gradually produced a pantheon consisting of a hierarchy of gods." Perhaps even more completely than the Deuteronomistic reform among the Hebrews, the Islamic "reform" of Arabian religion suppressed the evidence of earlier theological concepts.

36. For interesting information on ancient Semitic litholatry, see Andrae, *Mohammed*, pp. 13-14; Peters, *Muhammad,* pp. 12-13.

37. The sources of Islamic tradition upon which this essay depends for its basic narration of Muhammad's life include the chronicle of al-Tabari and, preeminently, the *Sira* or biography of Ibn Hisham. The English translation of the former, by various scholars, is now virtually complete from the State University of New York Press. The latter is readily available in translation as A. Guillaume, *The Life of Muhammad: A Translation of Ibn Ishaq's "Sīrat Rasūl Allāh"* (Karachi: Oxford University Press, 1967). These sources and others have been conveniently blended, without scholarly comment or analysis, in Martin Lings, *Muhammad: His Life Based on the Earliest Sources* (New York: Inner Traditions International, 1983).

incense trail," whose origins are enshrouded in the very ancient past but along whose length perfumes and incense and other goods were brought to the great templed cities of the eastern Mediterranean basin.

Becca was, perhaps even more than the rest of Arabia, an arid place, oppressively hot and dusty, and it was not long before Hagar and her son were in a desperate condition. Indeed, she feared that the boy was dying. As he lay in the sand, weakened by terrible thirst, she climbed up to a rock for a better view, to see if anybody was around to offer help. There was no one. Nearly hysterical, Hagar ran to another elevated location, but still could see nobody. Seven times she ran from the one place to the other, and then she sat down in despair. It was at this point, according to Arab tradition, that an angel spoke to her the words recorded in Genesis 21:17-19: "God heard the cry of the boy, and an angel of God called to Hagar from heaven and said to her, 'What troubles you, Hagar? Fear not, for God has heeded the cry of the boy where he is. Come, lift up the boy and hold him by the hand, for I will make a great nation of him.' Then God opened her eyes and she saw a well of water. She went and filled the skin with water, and let the boy drink."[38] The water gushed forth from the sand at Ishmael's heel, and he and his mother were saved. In the years that followed, the well became known as Zamzam and, because of the excellence and abundance of its water in parched Arabia, the valley of Becca emerged as a popular halt for the caravans that plied the ancient trail.

In fact, Abraham himself eventually came to visit his son at Becca where, according to the Qur'an, God showed him the precise location, adjacent to the well of Zamzam, where he and Ishmael were to build a sanctuary. The site had already been chosen by Adam, who had built an earlier shrine there that had subsequently been destroyed in the flood of Noah. God also gave the patriarch instructions on exactly how that sanctuary was to be constructed, as an earthly replica of a heavenly prototype.[39] It was

---

38. Gen. 21:17-19 JPS. Gen. 21:14, 21 seems to locate these events in "the wilderness of Beer-sheba," near "the wilderness of Paran," rather than in distant Arabia.

39. See Peters, *Muhammad*, pp. 4-6; Geo Widengren, *The Ascension of the Apostle and the Heavenly Book* (Uppsala and Wiesbaden: A.-B. Lundequistska Bokhandeln and Otto Harrassowitz, 1950), pp. 33, 33 n. 1; Geo Widengren, *Muḥammad, the Apostle of God, and His Ascension* (Uppsala and Wiesbaden: A.-B. Lundequistska Bokhandeln and Otto Harrassowitz, 1955), p. 97 n. 1. For cross-cultural perspectives on temples in general — phenomenologically, the Ka'ba is clearly an instance of the ancient temple type — and on the heavenly temple prototype, see various items by John M. Lundquist, including "Studies

built roughly as a cube — its name, Ka'ba, indicates its shape — with its four corners directed toward the four cardinal directions of the compass.[40] In its eastern corner is a meteoric stone that was brought to Abraham by an angel from a nearby hill. "It descended from Paradise whiter than milk," the Prophet would later teach his followers, "but the sins of the sons of Adam made it black." When the Ka'ba was completed, God again spoke to Abraham and told him to institute a regular pilgrimage to Becca and its shrine: "Behold, we provided for Abraham the place of the House, [saying] Do not associate anything with me, and sanctify my house to those who circumambulate it, or stand, or prostrate themselves. And proclaim the pilgrimage [al-hajj] among the people. They will come to you on foot and on every lean camel, coming from every deep mountain pass."[41] Included in the rituals of the pilgrimage would be a sevenfold run between Safa and Marwah, as the two locations were now called, commemorating Hagar's desperate search for help that resulted in the revelation of the spring of Zamzam.

When all was done, Abraham presented the Ka'ba to God and asked God's blessing on what had been accomplished in the once-barren and uninhabited area: "Our Lord, I have caused some of my posterity to dwell in a valley barren of cultivation at thy holy House, in order, O our Lord, that they might establish ritual prayer. So incline the hearts of the people toward them and provision them with fruits so that they might give thanks."[42] And indeed, Becca did become a major center and object of pil-

---

on the Temple in the Ancient Near East" (Ph.D. diss., University of Michigan, 1983); "The Common Temple Ideology of the Ancient Near East," in *The Temple in Antiquity*, ed. Truman G. Madsen (Provo, Utah: Brigham Young University Press, 1984), pp. 53-76; "What Is a Temple? A Preliminary Typology," in *The Quest for the Kingdom of God: Studies in Honor of George E. Mendenhall*, ed. H. B. Huffmon, F. A. Spina, and A. R. W. Green (Winona Lake, Ind.: Eisenbrauns, 1983), pp. 205-19; *The Temple: Meeting Place of Heaven and Earth* (New York: Thames & Hudson, 1993).

40. F. E. Peters, *Allah's Commonwealth: A History of Islam in the Near East, 600-1100 A.D.* (New York: Simon & Schuster, 1973), p. 44, says the Ka'ba was constructed in the second century C.E. However, since no archaeological excavation is permitted at the site, and since contemporary literary sources are utterly lacking, it is difficult to see how such a judgment can be made with any confidence.

41. Q 22:26-27.

42. Q 14:37. It is significant that the Qur'an never feels any need to argue for the association of Abraham with the Ka'ba. This suggests that the legend of its founding was probably widely known and accepted, even among the pagans.

grimage that united all of the peoples of the Arabian Peninsula.[43] Furthermore, say the early Muslim authorities, in those first years it remained a center of pure monotheism and its intimate link with the family of Abraham was retained in the people's remembrance. Adjoining the northwest wall of the Ka'ba is a small enclosure, called the Hijr Ismail because the tombs of Ishmael and his mother Hagar are thought to lie beneath its paving stones. Islamic writers have connected Becca and its Ka'ba with the otherwise unidentified valley celebrated in Psalm 84:

> How lovely is Your dwelling-place,
>   O Lord of hosts.
> I long, I yearn for the courts of the Lord;
>   my body and soul shout for joy to the living God. . . .
> Happy are those who dwell in Your house;
>   they forever praise You.
> Happy is the man who finds refuge in You,
>   whose mind is on the [pilgrim] highways.
> They pass through the Valley of Baca,
>   regarding it as a place of springs,
>   as if the early rain had covered it with blessing. . . .
> Better one day in Your courts than a thousand [anywhere else];
>   I would rather stand at the threshold of God's house
>   than dwell in the tents of the wicked.[44]

But the worship at the shrine of Becca did not remain pure. As Ishmael's posterity multiplied, they were soon far too numerous to be accommodated in the valley of Becca, and many had to seek other places to

---

43. In this regard, the legend may well reflect real history. Mircea Eliade observed correctly that "from its beginning Mecca was a ceremonial center around which a city progressively arose." See Mircea Eliade, *A History of Religious Ideas,* vol. 3, *From Muhammad to the Age of Reforms,* trans. Alf Hiltebeitel and Diane Apostolos-Cappadona (Chicago: University of Chicago Press, 1985), p. 64. For a theoretical and comparative perspective on analogous phenomena, largely in East Asia, see Paul Wheatley, *The Pivot of the Four Quarters: A Preliminary Enquiry into the Origins and Character of the Ancient Chinese City* (Chicago: Aldine, 1971). Scholars of Mesoamerican archaeology have occasionally debated whether the large but diffuse settlements of that region, which were clearly "ceremonial centers," could accurately be termed "cities" at all.

44. Ps. 84:2-3, 6-7, 11 JPS.

dwell. Necessarily, too, given the aridity and sparse vegetation of Arabia, they had to remove themselves to considerable distances. Still, they wished to retain their connection to the sacred site in the valley established by their patriarchal ancestors. So, as they moved away, they carried with them stones from the sacred precinct of the Ka'ba shrine and performed rituals to honor those stones in their far-flung settlements. Gradually, though, the stones became idols, and the memory of the pure doctrine and ritual established by Abraham grew dim. Finally the apostasy became virtually complete as the idolaters returned for pilgrimage and placed the objects of their worship within the sacred shrine itself. A god named Hubal became the divine lord of the Ka'ba and the patron deity of the inhabitants. Moreover, through intrigue and confusion the location of the well of Zamzam was itself forgotten and the spring covered over, though by now the burgeoning population had located other water sources in the adjacent area, and the loss of the original spring — though symbolically significant — was not economically crucial.

Many long centuries passed. Even though God sent prophets to Arabia such as Hud, Salih, and Shuayb, the period from Abraham to Muhammad's call in the early seventh century c.e. was, on the whole, a time of complete pagan apostasy. But there were changes. By about 400 c.e. an Arabian tribe called the Quraysh had taken control of the settlement in the valley, now called Mecca, and had assumed guardianship of the Ka'ba sanctuary.[45] The custodianship of the sanctuary was entrusted now, if it had not already been, to a hereditary succession of guardians who functioned as a quasi priesthood. The ruler of the Quraysh collected a tax from the people of the valley, with which he was to feed pilgrims too poor to provide for themselves. Arabian tradition says it was at this time, too, that the tents of the keepers of the sanctuary began to be replaced by permanent dwellings. The lord of the Quraysh himself — at the beginning of the fifth century a man named Qusayy — resided in a relatively spacious building known as the House of Assembly. Customary law banned all violence from the immediate vicinity of the shrine, as well as from Mecca itself for a distance of several miles.

Thus, although its shrine was much more ancient, Mecca — in the sense of a real town with permanent residences and a secular economy — was less than two centuries old at Muhammad's birth. After all, it was not

---

45. Mecca appears in Greek materials of the second century c.e. as *Makoraba*, which may reflect an Old South Arabic or Ethiopic word denoting a sanctuary. The word *quraysh* means "shark," and probably derives from an ancient tribal totem.

an inviting place. There was very little water, and not a blade of grass. Its soil was not especially good. It was suffocatingly hot and afflicted with swarms of irritating flies. For many long years only the holiness of the place drew the attention of the Arabs. And, as that holiness must in some way be accounted for, perhaps the traditional story of Abraham's connection with the site will serve as well as any other explanation.

Qusayy's grandson, Hashim, appears in the historical traditions as a pivotal figure, and his clan, the Hashimites, has enjoyed considerable prestige in the Arabic and Islamic world ever since. It was he, says the tradition, who established the two great annual caravans from Mecca in the latter half of the fifth century — the Caravan of Winter, southward to the Yemen, and the Caravan of Summer to the northwestern portion of the Arabian Peninsula and beyond to Byzantine-ruled Palestine and Syria. The religious prestige of Mecca's Ka'ba was probably a major factor in the establishment of this trade, as the inviolability of the sanctuary was transferred to the caravans operating under its patronage.[46]

Both caravan journeys followed the ancient frankincense road, on which Mecca sat at about the midpoint between the Yemen to the south and the Byzantine depots in Gaza and Damascus to the north. Thus no caravans traveled the entire distance from the Mediterranean to the far corner of Arabia, and the Meccans, equipped with their unique knowledge of the landscape and its water sources, came to exercise virtually total control of the trade along the frankincense trail.[47] Whatever hopes the Byzantines and Sassanids had once entertained of dominating that trade were now quite obviously vain.

One of the first halts of the summer caravan to the northwest was in an agricultural oasis known as Yathrib, which lay a journey of eleven camel-days due north of Mecca. At one point the oasis had been dominated by Jews, and they were still an important and prosperous presence in the settlement.[48] But an Arabian tribe of south Arabian origin was now in

---

46. See Serjeant, "Ḥaram and Ḥawṭah," pp. 54-55. Serjeant cites inscriptional evidence suggesting that caravans to the north and south, *Yaman wa-Sham* ("to Yemen and Syria"), were under way much earlier than the days of Hashim.

47. See Rodinson, pp. 35, 39-40. Peters, *Muhammad*, pp. 69-70, 72, 74, 75, 92-93, offers some cogent criticism of what he sees as exaggerations of the volume and importance of Meccan trade.

48. There were substantial Jewish populations in Yathrib and in all of the major oases to its north, which some have seen as evidence of a migration of Jews southward from Pales-

control of Yathrib, though it had divided into two groups known as the Aws and the Khazraj. Hashim's younger brother, Muttalib, married a girl of the Khazraj, and she bore him a son. She and her boy continued to live in Yathrib for several years, until Muttalib convinced them that the son, who would come to be called Abd al-Muttalib, ought to come and dwell with him in Mecca, eventually to take over the guardianship of the Ka'ba and the provisioning of the pilgrims as if he were a Meccan (which, in a sense, he was).

Abd al-Muttalib, who survived until roughly 580, did indeed become the master of the Ka'ba. During his time, and even into the days of Muhammad, the Ka'ba was probably a fairly humble structure, made of wood, unroofed, a little taller than a man's head, surrounded by crude mud huts, with its sacred meteoric stone embedded in one of its corners. Nevertheless, Abd al-Muttalib is said to have loved and reverenced the shrine so much that he sometimes spent the night in the Hijr Ismail adjacent to it. (It is said by the ancient Muslim authorities that he never prayed to Hubal, but rather to the true God, Allah — although modern scholars tend to mistrust this claim as too obviously apologetic in its intent.) During a period of sleeping there, he received instruction in a series of dreams that enabled him to rediscover and to reexcavate the well of Zamzam. Since he was already in charge of the Ka'ba and responsible for feeding and watering the pilgrims who came to it from across Arabia, it was only natural that he likewise assumed control of the waters of the holy spring.

His role as guardian of the sacred precinct established him as an important figure for all the tribes and clans of Arabia, who were united, if in little else, by their veneration of the Ka'ba and its meteoric stone. This required a certain diplomacy, and he was responsible to see that pilgrims from the entire peninsula, with their accompanying gods, felt welcome in the sanctuary and during the sacred seasons. Perhaps this was difficult for him, if his theology was really as distinct from the then-regnant Arabian religion as tradition says it was, or perhaps he had come to see Allah as symbolized, even if imperfectly, in the idols and gods of his kin.

Blessed as he was, though, Abd al-Muttalib was deficient, by Arabian

---

tine. But it could just as easily indicate the radiation of Palestinian Jewish influence on preexisting Arab populations. Some legends have Moses and Aaron themselves coming to Arabia, with Aaron dying there and being buried on Mount Uhud. More typically the legends say the Jews fled to Arabia in the sixth century B.C.E. when the Babylonians destroyed the temple in Jerusalem.

standards, in one of the blessings most important to his people. He had only one son. However, God had just given him Zamzam, and no doubt encouraged by this striking sign of divine favor, he prayed for more sons, vowing that if he were given ten sons who grew to manhood, he would, when the appropriate time came, sacrifice one of them to God at the Ka'ba. (This story would certainly suggest that, even if he were a monotheist, Abd al-Muttalib's religion had not entirely escaped influence from the pagan practices surrounding him.) The blessing came. Nine more sons were born to him. Naturally delighted with them, Abd al-Muttalib was nonetheless a man of his word. By means of a traditional Arabian rite of arrow divination, he determined that the one chosen of God was none other than his youngest and favorite son, Abd Allah ("Servant of God").[49]

Abd al-Muttalib immediately headed with his son toward the place determined for the sacrifice, but, no doubt to his own relief, other members of the family intervened and prevented him from carrying out his vow. He agreed, instead, to go to a well-known wise woman in Yathrib to discover from her whether it was possible to find a way out of his vow in this matter, and if so, to determine what that way might be. When he and those with him had reached Yathrib, however, they found that the seeress had moved to Khaybar, a wealthy Jewish settlement in a fertile valley almost a hundred miles away. Finally they found her. Her advice was to place Abd Allah to one side and ten camels, the customary Arabian fine for the shedding of blood, to the other side, and then to cast lots between them, if necessary increasing the number of camels until the lot fell upon them rather than the young man. Abd Allah was finally delivered by the sacrifice of a hundred camels — a considerable ransom in the camel-based economy of bedouin Arabia.

Abd al-Muttalib was not alone in worshiping Allah apart from the received idols, if indeed he did so. There were others in pre-Islamic Arabia who held to a kind of monotheism. They seem to have believed, as Muslims now also do, that idolatry was an innovation in Arabia and at Abraham's sanctuary, an innovation that had illegitimately supplanted the worship of the one true God, Allah. These people, known as the *hunafa* (sing. *hanif*) — the term *hanif* might not inappropriately be rendered "generic monotheist" (as opposed to the "brand-name monotheists" of Christian-

---

49. On Arabian arrow divination, see Toufic Fahd, *La divination arabe: études religieuses, sociologiques et folkloriques sur le milieu natif de l'Islam* (Leiden: Brill, 1966).

ity, Judaism, and later, Islam itself) — constituted nothing so specific and organized as a movement.[50] Rather they represented a tendency. They rejected the idols as a profanation and a pollution of the pure religion of God, as well as of the Ka'ba itself. The contact of the caravan traders with Christianity, Judaism, and Zoroastrianism during their travels had led some of them to wonder why Arabia had no comparable (and comparably sophisticated) revelation. These were people who sought a more demanding and more intellectually satisfying religion than that offered by Meccan paganism.

The surge in Meccan wealth in the generations immediately preceding Muhammad's call had evidently precipitated something of a social crisis. Meccan paganism was not sufficiently robust, not ethically demanding enough, to deal with the social strains created by the new class distinctions. The *hunafa* were appalled by what they viewed as the moral drift of Meccan society, which was undergoing a jarring transition from the heroic tribal ideals of a not-so-distant nomadic past to the not-yet-evolved ethics of a more individualistic mercantile lifestyle. And some of them were not particularly shy in expressing their opinions, which undoubtedly led to their being marginalized to the fringe of Meccan society. Yet, although they recognized the poverty of Arabian paganism and the superiority of the more developed religions they had encountered in their trading journeys, the *hunafa* seem to have been reluctant to take sides in the rivalry of the great Byzantine and Sassanid powers, which becoming Christian or Zoroastrian would have obliged them to do.[51]

Among them was a man named Waraqa b. Nawfal, a relative of Abd al-Muttalib (which does suggest that the notion of the latter's pre-Islamic monotheism need not be mere pious sanitizing). Waraqa had indeed become a Christian. Christianity was far from unknown to the pre-Islamic Arabs, and the inhabitants of the peninsula manifestly enjoyed some basic knowledge of the major biblical stories.[52] There were well-established Christian communities to the south, in Najran and in the Yemen, and the annual caravan to Syria had brought the Arabs into close contact with the venerable Christian culture of that region. In fact, the Ghassanids and the Lakhmids,

50. For a discussion of the term and its etymological origins in Syriac, see Andrae, *Mohammed*, pp. 109-10. Rodinson, pp. 36-37, offers a useful discussion of the *hunafa*.

51. In rather the same way, probably, as becoming a Marxist during the Cold War would have allied one with the Soviet Union.

52. See Rodinson, pp. 28-29.

the onetime Arab client tribes on the Byzantine-Sassanid frontier to the north, were themselves Christians of a sort. (The Lakhmids had converted late in the sixth century.) Additionally, there was a strong Jewish presence in the Lakhmid territories, including even a small rabbinical academy established there in 588 or soon thereafter, when Sassanian attempts to centralize and control Persian society disrupted the Jewish institutions that had existed for centuries elsewhere.[53]

It is even said that Christians occasionally came to the Ka'ba, to honor the sanctuary constructed by the prophet and patriarch Abraham, and that, in the ecumenical spirit of the place, they were made welcome.[54] In fact, an icon of the Virgin Mary and the infant Jesus had been painted on the inside wall of the Ka'ba, where it remained somewhat incongruously among the 360 idols that tradition says rested in or near the shrine. (It was probably this ecumenism, or syncretism, that made Mecca so little susceptible to the exclusivizing attractions of Christianity or Judaism. What was the icon, in the eyes of the Quraysh, but one more idol among very many?)

Waraqa seems to have been literate. And while it is almost certainly going too far to suggest that he was a student of the scriptures (let alone of "theology"), Waraqa does seem to have known something of Jewish and Christian belief.[55] Among those beliefs, at least in the folk Christianity of the peninsula, was the notion that an Arabian prophet was soon to come. The Jews, naturally, expected that he would be an Arabian of Jewish descent, as all the earlier prophets had been Jews. The Christians, by contrast, had no such ethnically limiting notion.

It was into this environment, religiously complex and suffused with a sense of spiritual anticipation, that the Prophet of Islam would be born.

53. See Morony, pp. 307, 309, 319-20, 322. The Jewish population in Iraq seems to have peaked early in the fifth century, and then, for various reasons, to have declined even as Jewish institutions were marginalized or demolished.

54. They had no problem in recognizing Allah as "the Lord of the House." Even today, *Allah* is the term for God employed in Arabic translations of the Bible.

55. There seems little if any trace, in the Judaism of the pre-Islamic Arabian Peninsula, of the ideas of the third–fifth century *amoraim* of Babylonia and Palestine, which eventually culminated in the Talmuds.

The Birth and Childhood
of Muhammad

Now that Abd Allah had been spared, his father, Abd al-Muttalib, set about to find a wife for the boy. He chose a girl named Amina, who was destined to become the mother of the founder of Islam. As is appropriate for so important an event, the birth of Muhammad and the occurrences leading up to it have been surrounded by numerous legends and embellishments, some of which I will relate in the narrative that follows.

On the day appointed for the wedding, Abd al-Muttalib took the young man by the hand and set off with him. En route they encountered Qutayla, the sister of their Christian kinsman Waraqa b. Nawfal. She was standing at the entrance of her house as they passed by, and she was deeply smitten by the son of Abd al-Muttalib. He was, the sources agree, a strikingly handsome fellow, but that isn't what intrigued her. His face glowed with radiance. She offered herself to him on the spot. But he declined, informing her that he was on his way to his wedding, which had been arranged by his father and could not properly be delayed or avoided. (She very likely knew this already.)

After the marriage had taken place, Abd Allah stayed with his new wife in the house of her guardian for several days. One day, though, he needed to return to his own house to fetch something, and he again passed by Qutayla. This time, though, she did not offer herself to him, and he inquired as to why. She replied that the light that had been with him on that earlier day had left him. "Today," she said, "you cannot fulfill the need that I had for you." The marriage of Abd Allah and Amina took place in 569. It was in the next year, according to most traditional sources, that the birth of Muhammad occurred.[1]

It is necessary and appropriate here to offer a parenthetical word about the sources available to us for reconstructing the life of the Prophet of Islam. Even counting the New Testament Gospels, Muhammad is the only founder of a major world religion for whom we possess a detailed and complete biography. Unfortunately, no extant form of that biography was committed to writing until decades — probably 125 years — after his death, and what we have bears all the marks of hagiography and folklore.[2] Apparently, for his disciples as for the followers of the biblical prophets, "it was more important to preserve knowledge of the prophet's sayings than to recall a record of his life. The charisma was not important in itself; it mattered only in relation to the social and religious changes which the charismatic individual brought about."[3] Only relatively late did people somewhat removed from Muhammad in time begin to think seriously about gathering and writing down the scraps of biographical information that were circulating about him in the by-now far-flung Islamic empire. The one source for the Prophet's life that is generally accepted as reliable and authentic is the Qur'an itself, but unfortunately it is allusive, fragmentary, and often enigmatic, and its interpretation for biographical purposes is fraught with daunting difficulties. In the biographical sketch presented here, we shall rely on the traditional narratives, accompanying them with commentary but feeling free to omit such portions as seem obviously tendentious and folkloric — although even these will be discussed when they shed useful light.[4] If we were to restrict ourselves entirely to the undisputed facts of Muhammad's biography, we would run out of information after only a few pages. After his emigration to Medina, the chronology of his life steps onto more-or-less secure ground; prior to that, we are left essentially to guesswork.

1. The year of Muhammad's birth is disputed, because the Arabs before Islam had no fixed annual dating system, but it must have been roughly 570 or 571 C.E.

2. See Peters, *Muhammad*, pp. 263-66.

3. Ronald E. Clements, "Max Weber, Charisma and Biblical Prophecy," in *Prophecy and Prophets: The Diversity of Issues in Contemporary Scholarship*, ed. Yehoshua Gitay (Atlanta: Scholars Press, 1997), p. 98.

4. Although the approach taken here is rather different from Montgomery Watt's, it still resembles his in the sense that "in the attempt to make a coherent story, [I] will give [the traditional sources] a more dogmatic form than is strictly justified" (Watt, p. 56).

Muhammad was born into a religiously aristocratic Meccan family, albeit into a faction of it that had fallen on hard economic times and had perhaps lost out in certain squabbles and conflicts with other factions. While his religious authority obviously did not derive solely from his family background — Qurayshi prophets were not an everyday event, after all — it is very doubtful that he would have been able to advance his prophetic claim so successfully had he not come from the lineage that he did.[5] In the Qur'an itself, the concept of a family or a kinship group that is uniquely endowed with spiritual power is explicitly present. "The Prophets were in all cases the lineal descendants of former Prophets," observes R. B. Serjeant. "To Muḥammad it is natural that spiritual qualities should reside exclusively in certain families and be inherited, just as trades were hereditary in other family groups."[6]

Muhammad's birth was, as it would turn out, by far the most important event of the year 570 in Arabia. But it was an eventful year in many ways, and things happened in the course of it that, in the short term, loomed far larger. At that period the Yemen was under the control of the Christian ruler of Abyssinia, or Ethiopia, known as the Negus.[7] The Abyssinian governor of the Yemen was a man named Abraha, who was determined to replace the purportedly Abrahamic but now clearly pagan shrine of Mecca with something overtly Christian. To this end he built a magnificent church in Sanʿa, intending that it supplant the Kaʿba as the chief object of Arabian pilgrimage. And it was truly a remarkable building. He constructed it, we are told, of marble taken from one of the ruined palaces of the ancient Queen of Sheba, and filled it with crosses made of gold and silver and pulpits made of ebony and inlaid ivory. But his ambitions for the building, quite freely proclaimed, irritated the Arabs of the Mecca region

5. Serjeant, "Ḥaram and Ḥawṭah," pp. 42, 53, 55; Serjeant, "The Saiyids of Haḍramawt," pp. 6-7.

6. Serjeant, "The Saiyids of Haḍramawt," p. 7 n. 3. See, for example, Q 4:54 (where Serjeant correctly notes that *hikma*, or "wisdom," very likely connotes "the ability to arbitrate — a very important function of Saiyids"); 57:26; also 10:83. It is not difficult to see how Shi'ism, which earlier generations of Orientalists, misled by its relatively recent dominance in Persia as well as by their own racialist misconceptions, sometimes imagined to be an "Indo-European" reaction to "Semitic" Islam, could easily have arisen, with its veneration of the *ahl al-bayt*, the "people of the house," on completely Arabian soil.

7. There had been an earlier Abyssinian invasion of the Yemen in roughly 513 C.E., but it did not last.

mightily, and one of them entered the church by night and deliberately defiled it.

Abraha was furious, and vowed to destroy the Ka'ba in revenge. Accordingly, he organized a large army and set off toward Mecca to carry out his plan. Accompanying the army was a large, armored elephant, in memory of which the year of Muhammad's birth has ever afterward been known as "The Year of the Elephant." Abraha's preliminary activities in the environs of Mecca went as he had planned, and so he summoned a representative of Mecca to his camp in order to give to him the ultimatum: Allow us to destroy the Ka'ba and there need be no shedding of blood. The chosen representative of Mecca was, not surprisingly, Abd al-Muttalib. When he entered the presence of Abraha, the Abyssinian vice-regent, no doubt attempting to strike a conciliatory posture, asked if there were any personal favor that he could render to the Meccan leader. Yes, replied Abd al-Muttalib. Two hundred of his camels had been seized by the Yemeni army, he explained, and he wanted them back. When Abraha expressed shocked disappointment that, at a time of such crisis, Abd al-Muttalib was thinking of his camels rather than of the religion that Abraha had come to destroy, the Qurayshi leader is supposed to have replied, "I am the lord of the camels, and the shrine likewise has a lord who will defend it." "He cannot defend it against me," asserted Abraha. "We shall see," responded Abd al-Muttalib. "But give me my camels." And Abraha did in fact order that the camels be returned.

Abd al-Muttalib went back to Mecca and the Quraysh, and advised them to withdraw to the hills that surround the town. He and his family and a few others then went to the Ka'ba and prayed for its deliverance, before they too retreated to the hills. The next morning Abraha and his troops prepared to enter Mecca and destroy its shrine. They led the richly caparisoned elephant before the soldiers. But rather than marching into the town, the elephant, which was facing Mecca, kneeled toward the Ka'ba (possibly, some demythologizing historians suggest, at the urging of an Arab guide who had been unwillingly pressed into service). No amount of prodding or torture could induce the animal to move, except in a direction away from the sacred valley and back toward the Yemen. Abraha should have taken the portent and gone home. But he repeatedly attempted to turn the army around. Suddenly the sky grew dark with birds, each one carrying a rock in its beak and one in each of its talons. The birds swooped over the Yemeni army, hurling the stones at it and killing many, and the army fled in disarray back in the direction from which it had first come. Abraha died soon after his arrival back in the Yemen.[8]

Abd Allah, the husband of Amina, was away from Mecca at the time. And in fact, he would never return, for he became ill and died in the home of his relatives in Yathrib while journeying back from a trading expedition to Syria and Palestine. His young wife was left a widow, and expecting a child. But it was to be no ordinary child. Muslim lore says a light shone forth from her womb so brightly that she was able to see the castles of Bostra in distant Syria. And a supernatural voice said to her, "You carry in your womb the lord of this people; and when he is born, say, 'I place him beneath the protection of the One, from the evil of every envier'; then name him Muhammad."

A few weeks later the boy was born. When Abd al-Muttalib was informed, he took his grandson in his arms and went with him to the sanctuary. He brought him into the Kaʿba itself, the holy house, and presented the infant to God, offering a prayer of thanks for the gift of this boy as a substitute for his dead son. It was customary among the families in the towns of Arabia to send their sons into the desert soon after birth, to be suckled by a bedouin wet nurse and to spend at least some portion of their childhood among the desert tribes. In fact, certain of the tribes seem almost to have advertised their services in this regard, and would come at regular intervals into the towns seeking babies to care for. Since Mecca had a reputation for epidemics and a high infant mortality rate, parents were eager to avail themselves of these services. But it was not only for health reasons that it was thought desirable to send a young son into the desert. The people of Mecca were themselves only a few generations removed from their nomadic past. Their "urbanism," such as it was, was of recent minting. It had only been in the days of Qusayy, at the beginning of the fifth century, that they had traded in their tents and begun to build permanent houses around Zamzam and the Kaʿba. And there still lingered, in their minds, the sense that the older way of life was the nobler. As previously noted, a nomad cannot be oppressed in the same way that a sedentary city dweller or an agriculturally rooted peasant can be, for he can simply move away. He is free. And, then as now, it was felt that the language of the bedouins was better, their diction and vocabulary richer. For pre-Islamic Arabia, living

8. Peters, *Allah's Commonwealth*, p. 28, is typical of Western scholars in ascribing the failure of Abraha's expedition to an outbreak of smallpox.

in its "heroic age," resembled the Greece of the Homeric period in its conception of the ideal hero as someone not merely equipped with courage and ability with weapons, but also endowed with eloquence and wisdom in council. And these attributes, it was thought, resided in their purity with the bedouins of the desert rather more than with their debased (if wealthier and more comfortable) cousins of the towns.[9] Sometimes the sons of the Quraysh would spend as many as eight years in the boarding school of the desert before they were allowed to return to their families at Mecca.

Amina, too, wanted her son to have the benefits of the desert. But she was at a disadvantage. Bedouin wet nurses did not expect direct payment for their services; to have demanded money for nursing and caring for a baby would have been considered a breach of good form. But they and their families certainly anticipated benefits from the people with whom they were, in the ancient Arabian view, cementing something very like a bond of kinship. Ultimately they expected an alliance with the boy, who would grow up as a quasi son and quasi brother to them. But that prospect was years away, and in the meantime they generally received some benefits from the father. Muhammad, however, had no father. And his economic outlook was not particularly bright. Abd Allah had died too early in his career to have amassed much wealth, and he left his son only five camels, a small flock of sheep and goats, and the services of one devoted slave girl. It was not much by the standards of the leading families of Mecca. Muhammad entered life, therefore, as the scion of a distinguished family, but poor — rather like a penniless aristocrat.

It took some time, therefore, for Amina to locate a bedouin woman named Halima who was willing to take Abd Allah's son. The traditional stories report, however, that economic benefits and the blessings of God immediately began to rest upon the foster parents, so that they not only never regretted their acceptance of the boy but eagerly sought to prolong his stay with them. His sojourn in the bedouin finishing school may also have benefited Muhammad's credentials as a future prophet. He is reported, much later, to have remarked that, like every prophet, he had been

9. The idea survived for many years even after the rise of Islam. The famous fourteenth-century *Muqaddima* of Ibn Khaldun, which drew on the author's North African experience to elaborate a philosophy of history and historical process, places crucial emphasis on the perceived contrast between the toughness and discipline of the desert nomads, on the one hand, and the decadence of the urban dwellers, on the other.

a shepherd.[10] But a far more spectacular sign of his preordained role has also been attributed to Muhammad's time in the desert:

One day, according to a story attributed to Halima, the future prophet and his foster brother were behind a tent, playing with some of the family's lambs. Suddenly the other boy came running to his parents, reporting with understandable alarm that two men, clothed in white, had come and laid Muhammad out on the ground. They had opened up his chest and, the boy continued, were stirring about in it. The two bedouins ran to see what was happening. They found Muhammad standing, apparently unharmed but very pale. He confirmed what his foster brother had said, but, though they searched diligently, Halima and her husband, Harith, could find no trace of the men nor any blood or wound on Muhammad that would confirm the story. Later on Muhammad is supposed to have supplied more details, telling of two men, dressed in white, who had come to him with a gold basin full of snow. When they split open his chest, they removed his heart and, opening it up, took out of it an ugly black clot which they threw away. Then they used the pure water of the melting snow to wash his heart and his breast, and restored him to his perfect physical condition.[11]

Mircea Eliade quite correctly notes that the cleansing of Muhammad's breast is reminiscent — indeed, events very like it are characteristic — of shamanic initiations around the world. And, since shamanic initiations also typically involve celestial ascents, this event should perhaps be connected with the ascension of Muhammad into the heavens that will be discussed below.[12]

Muhammad had remained perhaps three years with Halima and Harith in the desert. Not surprisingly, though, the experience with the two mysterious men unnerved the two bedouins, and they decided it was time to return their young charge to his mother. He lived with her in Mecca for

10. Widengren, *Muḥammad*, pp. 199-200, cites the parallels of Krishna, Cyrus, Faridun, and David.

11. There may be a reference to this event in Q 94:1-3. A similar story is told of Umayya b. Abi al-Salt. See Ignaz Goldziher, *Abhandlungen zur arabischen Philologie* (Leiden: Buchhandlung und Druckerei vormals E. J. Brill, 1869-99), 1:213.

12. Eliade, *History of Religious Ideas*, 3:63 n. 2; compare Andrae, *Mohammed*, p. 36. For a more complete discussion of shamanism in general, see Mircea Eliade, *Shamanism: Archaic Techniques of Ecstasy*, trans. Willard R. Trask (Princeton: Princeton University Press, 1964).

another three years, and then he and Amina traveled to Yathrib to visit some of his relatives there. It was apparently an enjoyable time for the young boy, for he later recalled learning to swim in a pool that belonged to some of his Khazraj kin and being taught how to fly a kite. Unfortunately, though, his mother fell ill not far into the return journey; she died and was buried just outside of Yathrib. Later legends say the jinn themselves wept at the news of her death, so good a woman was she.

So his grandfather Abd al-Muttalib, who was eighty years old, took charge of Muhammad, the son of Abd Allah, his favorite. According to the traditional accounts, they were very close. Abd al-Muttalib would even take the young boy with him when he went to discuss important matters in the assembly with the most influential men of Mecca.

Still, Muhammad was now completely an orphan, and the situation of orphans in late sixth-century Mecca was even more undesirable than it normally would have been. Under the old unwritten code of nomadic values, clan or family chiefs were expected to care for the weaker members of their groups, for the widows and the orphans, and for the poor. "But at Mecca in a mad scramble for more wealth every man was looking after his own interests and disregarding the responsibilities formerly recognized. Muḥammad's guardians saw that he did not starve to death, but it was difficult for them to do more for him, especially as the fortunes of the clan of Hāshim seem to have been declining at this time. An orphan, with no able-bodied man to give special attention to his interests, had a poor start in a commercial career; and that was really the only career open to him."[13] Max Weber says "a distinctive concern with social reform is characteristic of Israelite prophets."[14] It would also become a characteristic of Muhammad and the Qur'an, and many have seen the impoverished widowhood of his mother and his own orphaned status as contributors to that reformist tendency.

For the hammer of fate was by no means done raining its blows upon the young boy. Two years after the death of his mother, his grandfather too died. While on his deathbed, Abd al-Muttalib entrusted Muhammad to his son Abu Talib, who was the full brother of Muhammad's father, Abd Allah. Abu Talib treated the boy very kindly. But reversion into the family of Abd

---

13. Watt, p. 8.

14. Weber, p. 50. "This concern is all the more notable," he says, "because such a trait is lacking in Hindu prophecy of the same period."

al-Muttalib and then of Abu Talib did not improve Muhammad's material prospects. For, although the family had considerable prestige, the grandfather's fortunes had declined a great deal in his later years, and Abu Talib too was poor. In fact, the entire clan of Hashim had seen its wealth and influence decline in the recent period, particularly when compared to the rival clan of Makhzum. So Muhammad spent many of the days of his youth pasturing sheep and goats on the hills around Mecca. No doubt the solitude helped him to develop a habit of reflection. But his uncle and surrogate father also took the boy on his commercial journeys. The importance of such expeditions, and of the opportunities they would have provided for an intelligent young man to observe varying cultures and religious traditions, would be difficult to overstate — although, as Montgomery Watt observes, while the journeys gave Muhammad experience, they did not give him the capital with which to profit from that experience commercially.[15]

Muhammad is said to have been *ummi,* which virtually all Muslims take to mean "illiterate."[16] The apologetic purpose of this is immediately apparent: an illiterate Muhammad renders the miraculous nature of the Qur'an more dramatically evident. The claim is an old one. The last neo-Babylonian ruler, Nabonidus, claimed to be a visionary and, as proof that his heavenly wisdom came through unmediated divine inspiration, also claimed to be ignorant of the art of writing.[17]

Western scholarship, on the other hand, has seen it as unlikely that a person deeply involved in the caravan trade would not be able, at least, to keep accounts and to reach a level of literacy that was not uncommon among the Meccans of Muhammad's day. But all agree that Muhammad was not a scholar of the Christian scriptures, and most probably had no direct acquaintance with them.[18] Arabian culture was an oral one, with little

15. Watt, p. 8.

16. Q 7:157.

17. See the discussion and references offered at Geo Widengren, *Religions-phänomenologie* (Berlin: Walter de Gruyter, 1969), pp. 547-48.

18. See, for example, Peters, *Muhammad,* pp. 141-42. Western Orientalists have frequently argued that the Qur'an betrays an incomplete or even inaccurate grasp of the character of the Bible, pointing to such things as the fact that Jesus is said to have "received" the Gospels as a revelation from God to him (as at Q 3:58; 5:46; 57:27), and that believers are advised that the Gospel should be "observed" as Jews observe the Torah (Q 5:66, 68). They have also pointed as an error to the Qur'an's apparent claim (at Q 48:29) that Muhammad and his followers are described in the Gospels.

or no experience of book learning. (In this sense the word *ummi,* which derives from the Arabic term *umma,* or "community," may be lexically close, as it is etymologically analogous, to the English word "lay" or "layman.")[19] Qur'an 21:150 features a quotation from the Psalms of the Hebrew Bible, but it is the only indubitable biblical quotation in the Qur'an.[20] Muhammad's enemies said he had foreign teachers.[21] It is more likely, if he can be said to have had any human sources at all (a proposition that orthodox Muslims would vigorously deny), that his contacts were with midrashic and apocryphal works, probably via oral transmission, than with the biblical text itself. There are several accounts of the birth and childhood of Jesus in the Qur'an, for instance, that have parallels in the so-called infancy narratives.[22] The Qur'an's account of the death of Jesus has parallels among both the Manichaeans and the Basilidean Gnostics.

Muhammad could have observed Christianity and Judaism at first hand during his own travels, or from speaking with caravans returning from Syria or Mesopotamia, or with those returning from trade by sea with Abyssinia/Ethiopia,[23] or from contacts with Arabian businessmen visiting the great markets of Mecca and elsewhere. Christianity had appeared in Arabia itself among some of the tribes, and Christians participated in the annual pilgrimage to Mecca.[24] Indeed, in Mecca itself there were not only captive Christians taken in raids, but immigrant Christian

19. "Lay," "layman," and "laity" all derive from the Greek *laïkos,* "of the *laos* or people." For a discussion of the term *ummi,* see A. J. Wensinck, "Muhammad und die Propheten," *Acta Orientalia* 2 (1924): 191-92. See also Peters, *Allah's Commonwealth,* pp. 50-51; Rodinson, p. 49.

20. The Qur'an does not appear to know the Psalms as a part of a larger entity, the Hebrew Bible (see Q 17:55). The reference in Q 7:40 to the camel and the eye of the needle does not appear to indicate direct knowledge of the New Testament. Nevertheless, the Qur'an knows, and relates at length and in detail, the story of the patriarch Joseph (Q 12), and speaks repeatedly of such biblical characters as Adam, Noah, Abraham, Moses, Mary, Joseph, Zechariah, and John the Baptist.

21. As at Q 16:103; 25:4ff.; 44:14. Q 16:103 certainly doesn't refute this claim.

22. E.g., Q 19:22ff.; 3:36; 5:110ff.

23. Contacts with Ethiopia are evident from Ethiopic loanwords in the Arabic of the period. See Theodor Nöldeke, "Neue Beiträge zur arabischen Sprachwissenschaft," *Beiträge und Neue Beiträge zur semitischen Sprachwissenschaft: Achtzehn Aufsätze und Studien* (Strassburg: n.p., 1904-10), p. 47. Andrae, *Mohammed,* pp. 38-39, argues against Muhammad's having been to Syria, but I am not convinced.

24. On the pilgrimage, see the evidence gathered in Christiaan Snouck Hurgronje, *Het Mekaansche Feest* (Leiden: E. J. Brill, 1880), pp. 28, 128, 159.

believers from among the Ghassanid clients of the Byzantines along the Syrian frontier. Jews were settled in Medina and the oases to the north.

One of his trips to Syria occurred when Muhammad was either nine or twelve. The caravan halted, as was customary, near Bostra, an important crossroads (adjacent to what is known today as the Jabal al-Druze) that was not only the capital of Roman Arabia but an ancient Christian center. It had come to be occupied by semisedentary ethnic Arabs, who formed what F. E. Peters calls a "bedouin suburb" around it.[25] Nearby was an anchorite's cell where a Christian hermit lived. The traditions suggest that the cell was occupied by one monk after another, in succession, always alone, each new inhabitant inheriting not only the cell but also certain cherished ancient writings. Included in these writings, say the accounts, was the prediction of a prophet to the Arabs.[26] Bahira, the current occupant of the cell, was acutely aware of the prophecy and apparently felt that its fulfillment was near.

On this particular occasion Bahira looked out from his cell and noticed something highly unusual. As the caravan approached, he saw a very small cloud that moved with the caravan to provide shade for one or two of its members. When they stopped to take cool shelter under a tree, the cloud stopped with them. Moreover, the tree itself lowered its branches in order to shade them more effectively. Bahira, quite naturally, was intrigued. Thus, for the very first time that any of the veteran caravanners could recall, the monk invited them to partake of a meal with him, insisting that all should come, of whatever rank. When they arrived, Bahira inspected each one eagerly. But he could see nobody who corresponded to what his studies had led him to expect. Muhammad, in fact, as the youngest, had been chosen to stay behind to watch the caravan's goods and supplies. The monk insisted that they fetch him, and they did.[27]

As soon as the anchorite saw the boy, he knew that he was the one. Everything about Muhammad corresponded with what had been predicted in his mysterious book. Bahira plied him, quite politely but eagerly,

25. Peters, *Muhammad*, p. 71.

26. Peters, *Allah's Commonwealth*, p. 49, thinks Bahira's mysterious book was simply the Bible. This would accord with Muslim notions that — clearly in its original form, distortedly in the corrupt version available to us — the Bible predicts the advent of Muhammad.

27. The parallel to the story of the prophet Samuel, David, and the other sons of Jesse told in 1 Sam. 16:1-13 should be obvious.

with many questions, which the young boy answered truthfully. The monk even asked to see his back, and there was the confirmatory seal of prophethood, a slightly raised oval mark (like the impress of a cupping glass) between his shoulder blades. He asked Abu Talib what their relationship was, and the older man said the boy was his son. No, the monk responded, that was impossible. The boy's father was dead. Abu Talib admitted that this was so, and that Muhammad was in fact his nephew. The encounter ended with Bahira warning Abu Talib against the machinations of the Jews, who, he said, if they knew the role that the boy was destined to play, would seek to do him harm. (Traditional Muslim accounts report that the Jews, too, were expecting the arrival of a prophet in Arabia — but that they also expected him, naturally enough, to come through a Jewish lineage. The thought of a non-Jewish prophet would not have pleased them, nor even seemed plausible.)

During Muhammad's youth, the Quraysh became involved tangentially in what, since it began in one of the months when fighting was supposed to be banned, came to be known in the annals of Arabia as "the sacrilegious war." It is possible that this messy conflict may have heightened the sense of discontent that many felt with the situation in Arabia. Most of the Meccan elite had participated in trading caravans to Syro-Palestine and had seen the rule of (Roman) law as it was administered in those relatively civilized areas of the Byzantine Empire. In Arabia, however, order was maintained, to the extent it was, by the blood feud. Shortly thereafter another incident occurred, which seems to show that the people of Mecca were beginning to move in the direction of a real system of justice, beyond merely the often rather amoral demands of tribal and clan loyalty. When a visiting Yemeni merchant was the object of the fraud of an Arab of the Meccan region, who was quite aware that the Yemeni had no local kin and hence no support, the merchant appealed to the sense of justice of the Meccans. And in fact, they responded, and obliged the would-be con man to pay what he owed. An oath-bound league was founded to deal with the situation, in which the young Muhammad participated. This incident can be read as an illustration that some notion of justice, transcending blind loyalty to kin, was beginning perhaps to root itself in the Meccan mind.

As Muhammad grew older, he had frequent opportunities to participate in Meccan caravans and thus to learn more about the surrounding world and perhaps about surrounding religious faiths. Apparently, too, his participation gave others an opportunity to learn about him, and his reputation began to increase. Later Muslims say that, well before the advent of Islam, he had been given the sobriquet al-Amin, or "the trustworthy one." Eventually Muhammad was invited to manage the goods of a merchant whose circumstances did not allow him to go with the caravan. Muhammad evidently did well with his assignment, and so other, similar opportunities began to come his way. One of them was to prove vitally significant, not only for the personal life of Muhammad but very likely too for his role as an Arabian prophet.

Khadija, the daughter of Khuwaylid of the Asad clan, was a cousin of the Christian Waraqa and his sister, Qutayla, who had attempted to attract the attention of Muhammad's father, Abd Allah. Khadija was also quite wealthy. Twice widowed, she had been obliged to hire men to handle her caravan trading. Now she turned to Muhammad, whom tradition makes out to be fifteen years her junior. She offered him the chance to travel with some of her merchandise to Syria and promised him twice the remuneration that she had ever paid before. Further, she granted him the assistance of a young manservant of hers named Maysara. Not surprisingly, Muhammad accepted the generous offer.

During this trip the story of Bahira essentially repeated itself. When the caravan reached its usual stopping place near Bostra, in the southern part of Syria, Muhammad sought shelter from the hot Levantine sun under a tree. A monk by the name of Nestor came out of his cell and asked Maysara the identity of the man who was enjoying the shade of the tree.[28] (It is hard to imagine that this is not the same monastic cell and the same tree as in the earlier story of Bahira. Perhaps the previous monk had died and been replaced by Nestor. Or perhaps this story is simply an ahistorical doublet of the first. Syrian monks are invoked on several occasions in the traditional histories to point to the imminent coming or the arrival of an Arabian prophet.) Maysara replied that Muhammad was of the Quraysh, the tribe that controlled the Ka'ba. Nestor replied that, in fact, Muhammad was a prophet. (Maysara later reported seeing a pair of angels shielding his master from the heat of the day, rather like the earlier cloud and tree of Bahira's story.) At his return, Khadija was much impressed by Muhammad's handling of her affairs. And she must have been impressed, too, by Maysara's indications of her business manager's unusual status

28. The monk's name strongly suggests, if the story is historical at all, that he was a Nestorian Christian.

with God and men. (Tradition says her cousin Waraqa encouraged her reflections on the matter by telling her that he had long awaited an Arabian prophet, and that the signs indicated that he had arrived.) So she proposed marriage to him.

Khadija was apparently still beautiful, and she was wealthy and of good character. Muhammad's distinguished biographer Montgomery Watt offers an unromantically realistic view of the situation: "In this world of unscrupulous business men, how was a poor orphan, however gifted, to make his way? The one possibility was to find a rich woman to marry him, so that he could, as it were, enter into a business partnership with her."[29] Muhammad accepted Khadija's offer. On his wedding day he freed the faithful slave girl, Baraka, that he had inherited from his father. As if in exchange, though, as a wedding gift, Khadija gave him a fifteen-year-old slave boy named Zayd, who would figure importantly in subsequent Islamic history.[30]

Watt's antiromanticism may not be entirely apt in the case of Muhammad and Khadija. They seem to have dwelt together in great happiness and contentment. While she lived, he never took another wife. His marriage to Khadija was of immeasurable significance to Muhammad. She became not only his wife, and not only his friend and confidante, but, especially as later events would show, his moral support. Six children were born to the couple, including daughters named Zaynab, Ruqayya, Umm Kulthum, and Fatima, and a pair of sons.[31] But Muhammad was unlucky in the latter category, so very important to ancient Arabians. His eldest child was a son named Qasim, from which Muhammad gained the *kunya* name of Abu Qasim, or "father of Qasim," by which he is still sometimes called.[32] Unfortunately Qasim died before reaching his second birthday. And the sixth child of Muhammad and Khadija, also a son, died very young.

Muhammad's lack of male offspring — which would continue with his later wives as well — was to have serious implications for the future of

29. Watt, p. 10.

30. Watt, p. 35, thinks he was the first male convert to Islam.

31. The number of children she bore to him would seem to cast doubt on the traditional claim that Khadija was forty at the time of her marriage to Muhammad.

32. The *kunya* is an Arabic surname or agnomen received by a mother or father at the birth, usually, of a first son. (Sometimes, however, it is purely honorific.) It contains the name of the son, preceded either by *Abu* (father) or *Umm* (mother).

Islam. When controversy surged over the question of succession, there was no male heir to the Prophet. The Shi'ites, who were to claim that the succession belonged by right to the closest male relative, could do no better than to point to Muhammad's cousin Ali as their candidate — which did not carry the day for them. Had there been a son, things might have turned out rather differently. There is also reason to believe that Muhammad himself, though he doted on children and loved his daughters, felt keenly his lack of sons. As part of its polemic against Meccan belief in the three goddess daughters of Allah, the Qur'an repeatedly asks Muhammad's opponents why, when they crave sons so much, they believe that God himself has only daughters.[33]

Muhammad did gain another "son" by adoption. He grew very fond of the slave boy Zayd, whom Khadija had given him on their wedding day. And the devotion was mutual. In fact, when Zayd and his family, from whom he had been separated years before in a raid, were finally reunited, Zayd chose to stay with Muhammad. Muhammad, the young slave said, was like both father and mother to him. This remark, and his preference for his master, provoked an outcry from his relatives, who decried his lack of loyalty to his own flesh and blood. But Muhammad silenced the furor by taking the group to the Ka'ba and, while standing in the Hijr Ismail, a place particularly potent for the taking of oaths, announcing that Zayd was his son and heir. So the former slave became known as "Zayd, son of Muhammad." Under the customary law of pre-Islamic Arabia, adopted kinship was every bit as real as literal blood kinship. (This would change, and Muhammad's relationship with Zayd would, in after years, lead to a very important principle of Islamic law effectively banning adoptions.) Unfortunately Zayd, too, predeceased his "father," dying during one of the Muslim raids late in the Prophet's career.

Muhammad's growing reputation as a man of probity and competence, and his marriage to the rich widow Khadija, lifted him from the obscurity of herding sheep and goats and made him one of the rising stars of the new Meccan generation. There is little reason to doubt the traditional claim that the people of Hashim and its allies viewed him as a hopeful augury for the future.

One story that the traditional narratives tell about Muhammad says much about his increasing stature and his reputation for wisdom: When

---

33. Q 16:57; 37:149, 153; 52:39.

Muhammad was about thirty-five years old, the leaders of the Quraysh, flush with increasing wealth, decided to rebuild the Ka'ba. At the time, the walls of the structure were slightly more than the height of a man. Furthermore, the shrine lacked a roof, which meant that locking its door did not greatly increase its security, and in fact, some of the sanctuary's treasure had recently been stolen. Besides, with all the money flowing into Mecca, the city fathers felt they really ought to do something for the holy shrine that was the chief glory of their town. Fortunately for dwellers in a place so barren of vegetation, a great deal of wood had just arrived at their figurative doorstep in the form of a Greek-owned merchant ship that had run aground and split apart on the Red Sea coast near Jiddah. Moreover, a skilled Coptic carpenter was in town.

The Meccans approached their task with deep religious awe — the story, if true, does not accord well with the claim, mentioned above, that the pre-Islamic Arabians were flippantly irreligious — realizing that repair of the Ka'ba meant, in the first instance, doing it some damage. The traditional accounts make much of the hesitancy and even fear with which they attempted to figure out a way to demolish its walls so that they could be rebuilt, and many horrifying portents are said to have accompanied their first faltering efforts.

When they had finally begun excavating, they found a piece of writing in one of the corners of the shrine, written in Syriac. They could not read it, but they kept it until a Jew was able to read it to them. "I am God," the note said, "the Lord of Becca [Mecca]. I created her on the day when I created the heavens and the earth, the day I formed the sun and the moon, and I placed round about her seven inviolable angels. She shall stand so long as her two hills stand, blessed with milk and water for her people."

In addition to the stones they had taken from the earlier structure, the Meccans gathered yet more in order to increase the height of the sanctuary's walls. Each clan worked separately. But then a crisis arose. Who would put the sacred black meteoric stone into its new place in the wall of the shrine? Which of the clans would be accorded that honor? It was one thing for all the clans to work on the walls, but only one person, representing one of the factions of the Quraysh, would be privileged to reinstall the stone. The controversy lasted for days and was on the verge of becoming violent when the oldest participant proposed a solution that all could accept. They would wait and see who would be the first person to enter the sanctuary. That person would be the arbiter.

47

Needless to say, the first man to enter the sanctuary was Muhammad, the thirty-five-year-old son of Abd Allah. He had just returned to Mecca following an absence, and was unaware of the conflict at the Ka'ba. Instantly, as he walked in, those within the sacred area recognized that he was precisely the man for the task. Muhammad had the men bring him a cloak. When they had fetched it, he spread it out on the ground, then picked up the sacred stone and placed it in the middle of the cloak. He next instructed each clan represented among them to take hold of the edge of the cloak and to lift it up, all together. They did so. When the cloak had been raised to the right level, Muhammad himself took the stone and secured it in its place with his own two hands. Then the reconstruction of the Ka'ba continued, and was completed without further discord. Muhammad's future role as the uniter of the Arabs had been clearly foreshadowed.

The Calling of a Prophet

W. Montgomery Watt suggests that, while the fifteen years after Muhammad's marriage to Khadija were good ones for the future prophet, they may also have been frustrating. Though he was able to marry his daughters to Meccans of moderate importance, every one of these husbands was a relative either of himself or of his wife. His mercantile career prospered in a modest way, but he was, on the whole, excluded from the inner circle of politics and commerce in the town. Perhaps, Watt suggests, he felt that his abilities were not being recognized. From his subsequent career we know that he had capacities as a leader and organizer that were far superior to those of any other among his townsmen. If he himself was aware of these, it must have deepened his dissatisfaction and perhaps made more acute his awareness of the flaws and injustices of Mecca's stratified society.[1]

Muhammad appears eventually to have found himself among the *hunafa*. It seems most likely, however, although Muslim apologetics would strenuously deny it, that he originally shared the religious beliefs of his environment. The name of his son, Abd Manaf, is manifestly a pagan one, and it is extraordinarily unlikely that later Muslim sources would have invented so embarrassing a detail.[2] His uncle Abu Lahab was a vociferous defender of paganism, even to the point of becoming an enemy of Muham-

---

1. Watt, pp. 12-13.

2. See the discussion in A. Sprenger, *Das Leben und die Lehre des Mohammed*, 2nd ed. (Berlin: Nicolaische Verlagsbuchhandlung, 1869), 1:200; Leone Caetani, *Annali dell' Islām* (Milan: Ulrico Hoepli, 1905), 1:172-73.

mad and Islam as the story went on. His other uncle and ersatz father, Abu Talib, never accepted Islam, although he was friendly to Muhammad and lived some years after Muhammad's prophetic call. And the Muslim historian Ibn al-Kalbi reports that Muhammad once bought a sheep as a sacrifice to the goddess al-Uzza. (Once again, an item no later Muslim writer would voluntarily connect with the Prophet.) Thus, says the Qur'an to Muhammad, God "found you astray and guided [you]."[3] "And thus we have revealed to you a spirit, to you who did not know what book or belief was."[4] Even after his revelations began, traces of his pagan environment can arguably be identified in Muhammad's thinking. Western Orientalists have even pointed to the mysterious oaths of the Qur'an, and especially to its use of *saj'*, or rhymed prose — both of which were characteristic of the old Arab soothsayers of Muhammad's day and earlier.[5] At the most, however, these are side issues, and it is clear that, when he felt himself called by God, Muhammad's old ideas were driven out by the new revelation. Muhammad never saw himself as the continuation or fulfillment of old Arabian paganism; instead, and explicitly, he viewed himself as the continuation of Jewish and Christian revelation.[6]

Muhammad began the practice of withdrawing to a cave on Mount Hira, a few miles to the northeast of Mecca, where he apparently prayed and meditated, sometimes for several days and nights in a row.[7] It was a barren and monotonous place, perhaps therefore conducive to focused meditation. At some point in or near his fortieth year, Muhammad began to experience "true visions," which he said came to him while he was sleeping. They were, he said, "like the breaking of the light of dawn," and they made solitude become "dear" to him.

Serious Western scholars have long granted that something must

3. Q 93:7.

4. Q 42:52.

5. See Goldziher, *Abhandlungen zur arabischen Philologie,* 1:59ff.; al-Mas'udi, *Murūj al-dhahab wa-ma'adin al-jawhar* (Cairo: Al-maktaba al-tijariyya al-kubra, 1964-65), 3:381ff.

6. See, for example, Q 10:94.

7. Rodinson, p. 70, sees a parallel in earlier Christian practice. On the enigmatic word *tahannuth,* used in the sources to describe Muhammad's devotional activities in and near the cave, see Peters, *Muhammad,* pp. 128-30; M. J. Kister, "'Sha'bān Is My Month . . .': A Study of an Early Tradition," in *Studia Orientalia Memoriae D. H. Baneth Dedicata,* ed. J. Blau (Jerusalem: Magnes Press, 1979), pp. 34-37; reprinted as item XI in M. J. Kister, *Society and Religion from Jāhiliyya to Islam* (Aldershot: Variorum, 1990).

really have happened to Muhammad to begin his prophetic career, something sudden and out of the ordinary; few if any, for many decades, have been willing to call him insincere — at least in his earliest years as a prophet — and they have insisted that his prophetic self-consciousness could not have been the result, merely, of a process of gradual evolution.[8] Opinions have been divided, however, on the later, Medinan revelations. Skeptical Orientalists, especially those of an earlier generation, have suspected that the paroxysms recorded in connection with the battle of Badr and the slandering of the Prophet's young wife, A'isha, could have been artificially self-induced. Even A'isha herself is recorded as saying, on one occasion, "Your Lord seems to have been very quick in fulfilling your prayers."

One night, toward the end of the month of Ramadan (probably of the year 610) while he was in his cave on the mountain, an angel appeared to him, commanding him to "read" or "recite." (Our distinction between the two terms was not particularly clear in ancient times; ancient people virtually always read aloud.) To the angel's command Muhammad responded that he was not a reader, or a reciter, and the angel choked him until he thought he would pass out. The angel then repeated the command, and Muhammad reiterated his refusal or his denial of his competency. The angel choked him a second time, and reiterated the command. Muhammad responded as before, and was choked as before. The angel released him, and then spoke words that, now canonized in the Qur'an,[9] are traditionally regarded by Muslims as the first revelation of God to the Prophet of Islam: "Recite [*iqra*] in the name of thy Lord, who created, created the human being from a bloodclot! Recite! And thy Lord is most gra-

---

8. See Q 44:3ff.; 97:1; 2:185. Taking no stand on the ultimate source of Muhammad's revelations in this essay, I shall follow the rule enunciated by W. Montgomery Watt in his biographies of the Prophet. In citing the Qur'an, I shall neither write "God says" nor "Muhammad says," but "the Qur'an says." As evidence for Muhammad's early sincerity, Western scholars have pointed to such Qur'anic passages as 10:17, 21; 28:85ff.; 49:44; 75:16ff.; 7:203; 16:98; to the urgent imperatives of 79:2 and 96:1; and to the self-denunciation of 80:1ff. Biographers have noted Muhammad's unselfish dedication to what he must surely have believed to have been a divine cause, and to his patient endurance of hostility and humiliation.

9. The word *Qur'an*, which is unmistakably related to the Arabic verb *qara'a/yaqra'u* ("to read," "to recite"), was probably borrowed from the Syriac *qeryana* ("reading," "reader," "a lectionary" [*lectio*]). In the Syriac church the term referred to the scriptural lesson that was read in public worship, which has its obvious Islamic analogue in Muslim liturgical use of the Qur'an. Such use probably began very early. Within the Qur'an, the term *qur'an* frequently refers to individual passages of the revealed text.

cious, who taught by the pen, taught the human being that which he did not know."[10] When the angel had declared these words, he departed and Muhammad was left to ponder them. He was immediately concerned that he might have become *majnun* — a word that today means "crazy" but that, etymologically and originally, signified possession by jinn (the state of the inspired pre-Islamic Arabian poet). In shock and fear Muhammad fled the cave. Halfway down the slope toward Mecca, however, he heard a voice from above him, saying, "O Muhammad! You are the messenger of God, and I am Gabriel." Muhammad looked up and saw the angel again, filling the entire horizon in every direction.

This is the traditional story. But some commentators, both medieval Muslims and Westerners among them, regard another, different Qur'anic passage as the first of the revelations received by Muhammad:

> O you wrapped up in a cloak,
> Arise and warn!
> And magnify your Lord!
> And purify your garments!
> And flee impurity!
> And do not give in order to receive more!
> But be patient for your Lord![11]

According to the stories associated with this passage, Muhammad had already completed his meditation on the mountain and was descending toward his home when he heard a voice. Looking around, he could see nobody. Finally, though, he looked up into the sky, "and there he was, sitting upon the throne." It seems likely that this story tells of an anthropomorphic throne theophany — a vision of God in human form — that has been preserved by the scrupulous historians of the early Islamic tradition even though, given their own later, clearly antianthropomorphic theology, they find it rather awkward.[12] Such throne theophanies are commonplace in biblical and pseudepigraphical materials, and if this one is accepted as an accurate account (and there seems little motive for later Muslims to have invented so

10. Q 96:1-5.

11. Q 74:1-7.

12. Anthropomorphic depictions of God appear throughout the Qur'an itself, as Rodinson, p. 235, notes: "Throned in infinite majesty, his limbs, movements and gestures were nevertheless described in anthropomorphic terms."

embarrassing a tale in connection with their prophet), it locates Muhammad squarely within the prophetic tradition of the earlier Near East.[13]

While Muhammad's prophetic career appears to have commenced with a vision, and while visions occasionally came to him thereafter, the overwhelming majority of his revelations seem to have been auditory, or even heard internally.[14] The agent of the revelation is variously identified: God gave the Qur'an to Muhammad.[15] The "Spirit" gave it to him.[16] The angel gave it to him.[17] In a late passage the angel Gabriel is specifically identified as having delivered the Qur'an to Muhammad.[18] Frequently when revelation came to him, he would undergo violent trembling, seeming attacks of fever, and severe chills. He suffered great pain, sometimes feeling as if he had been struck with a severe blow; heard loud noises; and even on very cold days sweat profusely. The descriptions given in Qur'an 73:1 and 74:1 of his "wrapping up" in a mantle may refer to a preparation to receive divine revelation in the manner of the old Arabian *kahins*. His enemies repeatedly accused him of being "possessed" *(majnun)*, a "soothsayer" *(kahin)*, or a "magician" *(sahir)*. All were familiar figures on the Arabian scene, and he must indeed have resembled them in at least certain aspects if the accusations had, as they must have had, any force at all. In fact, the style of the Qur'an does resemble that of the pre-Islamic soothsayers.[19] Such descriptions of the mode of Muhammad's reception of revela-

13. For a fuller discussion of this alternate call narrative, with references, see Daniel C. Peterson and Stephen D. Ricks, "The Throne Theophany/Prophetic Call of Muḥammad," in *The Disciple as Scholar: Essays on Scripture and the Ancient World in Honor of Richard Lloyd Anderson*, ed. Stephen D. Ricks, Donald W. Parry, and Andrew H. Hedges (Provo, Utah: Foundation for Ancient Research and Mormon Studies, 2000), pp. 323-37. See also Peters, *Allah's Commonwealth*, p. 54; Watt, p. 15; Widengren, *Muḥammad*, p. 126 n. 3.

14. Visionary experiences are alluded to at Q 8:43; 48:27; 53:1-18; and 81:22-23. Indeed, if Q 53:1-25 is read as a whole, it seems to contrast the certainty of Muhammad's belief in God — certain because he had *seen* him — with the Meccans' misplaced faith in the goddesses al-Lat and al-Uzza (whom they had *not* seen). (Contrast especially Q 53:12 with Q 53:19.) Q 53:10 and 81:19 seem to point to the primacy of auditory revelation.

15. Q 75:16ff.

16. Q 26:192ff.; 16:102; 42:52.

17. Q 16:2; 15:8; cf. 53:5ff.; 81:23ff.

18. Q 2:97. Peters, *Muhammad*, pp. 142-43, 148-50, is almost certainly correct in identifying God as the object of the early visions and noting that Gabriel was identified as the vehicle of the revelation only comparatively late.

19. David Noel Freedman, "Between God and Man: Prophets in Ancient Israel," in *Prophecy and Prophets*, p. 57, notes that the biblical prophets, too, shared claims and status

tion must be admitted as authentic on the grounds, once again, that no later Muslim would have invented these potentially embarrassing details. It is from such stories that the notion soon arose that Muhammad was an epileptic.[20] Indeed, some Western scholars have also adopted the idea, particularly in the nineteenth century, despite the fact that, as W. Montgomery Watt has observed, "there are no real grounds for such a view. Epilepsy leads to physical and mental degeneration, and there are no signs of that in Muḥammad; on the contrary he was clearly in full possession of his faculties to the very end of his life."[21] Moreover, even if it were true, it is not clear how epilepsy would explain Muhammad's career: epileptic seizures have not commonly resulted in the foundation of major world religions. When the revelations arrived, tradition says, those around Muhammad wrote them down on potsherds, palm fronds, scraps of leather, camel bones, or whatever material lay ready to hand.[22] There is no indication that Muhammad wrote any of his own oracles down. As with Jesus, the earliest writing of the teachings of the Prophet of Islam came from his followers and disciples.

The earliest themes of Muhammad's revelations are easily summarized. They include the benevolence and omnipotence of God, especially as it is manifest in nature; the proper human response to God's goodness, which is gratitude, submissive worship, and generosity to the poor, the widow, and the orphan; the imminence of the last judgment, both personal and cosmic; the rewards of paradise; the terrors and agonies of hell; and the prophetic call of Muhammad himself.[23] The earth and the heavens will pass away. The sky will be torn, the mountains will be moved, the moon and the stars will be extinguished. The dead will be raised, gathered, judged, and sent to either paradise or the flames. "The basic conviction of

---

with various types of diviners in other cultures, who can be considered their counterparts. See the references listed there.

20. In, for instance, the Greek *Chronographia* of Theophanes the Confessor (d. 818 C.E.). See B. G. Niebuhr, ed., *Corpus Scriptorum Historiae Byzantinae* (Bonn: Weber, 1839), 1:512-13; or the English version of Harry Turtledove, trans., *The Chronicle of Theophanes* (Philadelphia: University of Pennsylvania Press, 1982), p. 35.

21. Watt, p. 19.

22. This may be an exaggeration designed to emphasize the simplicity of the early days of Islam.

23. Watt, pp. 23-34, offers a useful discussion of these themes and, particularly, of a plausible methodology for distinguishing earlier themes from subsequent ones.

Mohammed's preaching, and the heart of his prophetic message, is the certainty that he alone, in the midst of a light-headed and thoughtless generation, sees the fateful event which awaits all of those who are now jesting and laughing so carelessly."[24]

It is important to note that the Arabic word *kafir*, before it took on the technical meaning in Islam of "unbeliever" or "infidel," carried the sense of "ingratitude." The Qur'an launched a frontal assault on the pride and arrogance, the heedlessness, of the Meccan elite who, on the basis of their financial power, saw themselves not only as in control of the Arabian Peninsula but, in terms of their practical behavior at least, free from subservience to any higher power. In a striking phrase, Watt says they suffered from "the absence of a sense of creatureliness."[25] The very meaning of the term *Islam* is "submission [to the will of God]," and Muslim liturgical prayer, with its prostrations and its repeated touching of the forehead to the ground, is a striking physical representation of the creature's total surrender to the Creator, the monarch of the cosmos.

Perhaps surprisingly, the uniqueness of Allah and the utter nonexistence of other gods — the sine qua non of developed Islamic theology and, indeed, of Qur'anic doctrine itself — is apparently *not* a theme of the earliest revelations. Although the Qur'an eventually preaches a rigorous monotheism, it can be argued that, in their earliest phases, Muhammad and the Qur'an were only vaguely monotheistic, and that they were willing to recognize a number of other beings besides Allah as divine or at least archangelic.[26] But they were sharply subordinated to him and severely devalued:

> All that is upon the earth will perish,
> But the face of your Lord remains, majestic and noble.[27]

The diction of the revelations is elliptical and allusive rather than expository or explicit. The Qur'an often strikes non-Muslim readers as difficult because it refers to events and stories and peoples without explaining

24. Andrae, *Mohammed*, p. 53.
25. Watt, p. 29.
26. I am persuaded by Watt, pp. 25-26, 60-66, that this was the Prophet's earliest position, and that it continued until roughly 615 C.E. and the obscure incident of the so-called "satanic verses." See, too, Rodinson, pp. 48, 97, 106-7; Peters, *Muhammad*, pp. 152-53, 160-62.
27. Q 55:26-27.

them. It offers no continuous narrative, but addresses "occasions" for which the context must be furnished from the outside.[28] It presumes that its audience already knows the things to which it refers. Only God's voice is heard in the revelations. Using the "royal We," he addresses Muhammad or, indirectly, either the Muslims or the people in general. The Qur'an is almost always timeless and without context. Indeed, the revelations come very close to poetry, with all of the obscurity that poetic style sometimes exhibits but without the geographical and everyday details that, for many readers, make the Bible come to life.[29]

As the revelations continued to come, however, they took on a more historical character. God was present in the processes of history no less — and perhaps in fact more — than in those of nature. Max Weber wrote of "the distinctively and eminently historical character of the theorizing of the Hebrew prophets, which stands in sharp contrast to the speculations concerning nature characteristic of the priesthoods of India and Babylonia."[30] The same interest in history is one of the distinctions between the prophets and the philosophers of the Mediterranean. Both the Abrahamic prophetic tradition and the Hellenizing philosophic and scientific tradition dealt with comprehensive life-orientational problems; Socrates and Plato were religious figures every bit as much as Amos and Isaiah. However, where the philosophers (especially those of late antiquity) found their inspiration in the rational harmonies of nature — in subjects such as mathematics, astronomy, and medicine — the prophets found it in the moral judgments of history.[31] Where the Abrahamic prophets saw God in historical events — for example, in the exodus from Egypt, at Sinai, and in the judgments imposed on Israel by the Assyrians and Babylonians — the philosophers saw historical events in the realm of "change and decay" or "coming-to-be and ceasing-to-be" as contingent and less than fully real.[32] For the prophets God was an "experienced challenge"; for the philosophers God was a matter of

28. Peters, *Muhammad*, p. 2.

29. See Peters, *Muhammad*, p. 171, on the resemblance between the Qur'anic revelations and the poetry of ancient Arabia, and Muslim responses to it.

30. Weber, p. 22.

31. Clements, p. 103: "To a considerable extent, in the prophetic invective, the historical order was itself seen to be subject to moral judgement. In place of arbitrary and uncontrollable forces, history, with all its vicissitudes, was moralized."

32. Plato's doctrine of the Ideas or Forms makes this especially clear: triangularity is more real than any particular triangle in the physical world.

ontology — "a cosmic entity, as such not directly experienced, its very existence [needing] to be demonstrated."[33]

Max Weber defines a prophet as "a purely individual bearer of charisma, who by virtue of his mission proclaims a religious doctrine or divine commandment." The "decisive element distinguishing the prophet from the priest," Weber says, is his "personal call."[34] The notion of "charisma" is worth defining here. As Weber himself explained,

> The term "charisma" will be applied to a certain quality of an individual personality by virtue of which he is set apart from ordinary men and treated as endowed with supernatural, superhuman, or at least specifically exceptional powers or qualities. These are such as are not accessible to the ordinary person, but are regarded as of divine origin or as exemplary, and on the basis of them the individual concerned is treated as a leader. In primitive circumstances this peculiar deference is paid to prophets, to people with a reputation for therapeutic or legal wisdom, to leaders in the hunt, and heroes in war. . . . Charismatic authority is thus specifically outside the realm of every-day routine and the profane sphere.[35]

Clearly, under Max Weber's definition of prophethood, Muhammad is a textbook illustration of the class.[36] Weber goes on, however, to stress

---

33. Marshall G. S. Hodgson, *The Venture of Islam: Conscience and History in a World Civilization,* vol. 1 (Chicago: University of Chicago Press, 1974), p. 425. Hodgson's general discussion of the prophetic and philosophical worldviews in Islam, on pp. 410-43, is nothing less than brilliant. His distinction between the two seems to me far more fundamental and important than that suggested in Weber, p. 53.

34. Weber, p. 46; cf. 54. Van der Leeuw, pp. 251-54, distinguishes the prophet from the preacher and the teacher by the diminution of the immediate presence of "Power" *(das Verblassen des Machtelementes)* in the message brought by the latter, and by a change in tense: in preachers and teachers, as opposed to prophets, God is not speaking — God has spoken.

35. Weber, as cited by Clements, p. 93.

36. Plato distinguishes two distinct types of prophecy *(Phaedrus* 244). One is ecstatic prophecy *(mantikē entheos),* while the other is a species of technique, the systematic study and interpretation of divine signs. (Plato gives, as an example of the latter, augury based on the flight of birds. We might add to that Babylonian liver omens and Chinese *feng shui,* the science of water and wind.) Muhammad is obviously a prophet of the first kind.

the opposition of the priestly character to the prophetic, asserting that prophets rarely emerge from the ranks of priests, whether brahmins or Levites. While the priest, he says, claims authority because of his place in a tradition, the prophet's claim is based on his charisma and on the personal revelation that he claims.[37] Weber allows that there have been a few possible exceptions where prophets have emerged from priesthoods, such as Zoroaster and Ezekiel, but he is in fact scarcely willing to acknowledge the latter as a prophet at all.[38]

David Noel Freedman's characterization of the biblical prophets is entirely consistent with Weber's: "From beginning to end, the stress in prophetic utterance is on the ethical dimension of biblical religion and how it affects the well-being of the nation and its individual members. Over against the cultic domain of the priests, the prophets stress the moral demands of the deity and the ethical requirements of the covenant."[39]

However, while Muhammad was clearly a prophet under Weber's definition of the term, and while he was very much in the style of the biblical prophets as described by Freedman, he cannot be neatly divorced from his origin in an aristocratic Arabian religious family. Indeed, he seems another counterexample to Weber's strong opposition of the priestly to the prophetic. For the religious families of ancient Arabia, from among whose ranks Muhammad emerged, fit very well Weber's definition of priesthood: "The crucial feature of the priesthood," he says, is "the specialization of a particular group of persons in the continuous operation of a cultic enterprise, permanently associated with particular norms, places, and times, and related to specific social groups."[40] This describes precisely the role and status of the ancient Arabian sanctuary guardians from among whom Muhammad emerged.

37. This may reflect Weber's Protestant background. He also distinguishes between prophets and magicians. Both exert their power on the basis of personal experience, but the magician lacks the definite revelations, the doctrines and/or commandments, of the prophet. (See p. 47.)

38. Weber, pp. 46-47, 51. An analogous denial occurs in Eduard Meyer, *Ursprung und Geschichte der Mormonen: Mit Excursen über die Anfänge des Islams und des Christentums* (Halle an der Saale: Neimeyer, 1912). In both cases the effective denial of Ezekiel's prophethood seems to me arbitrary, tendentious, and ad hoc. Jeremiah, too, was a priest, although he and Ezekiel evidently came from different clans.

39. Freedman, "Between God and Man," p. 68.

40. Weber, p. 30. Furthermore, Joseph Smith (whom Weber instances on p. 54 as a notable illustration of the prophetic type), although he manifestly did not emerge from a sacerdotal class, is also unmistakably "priestly" in the Weberian sense.

Weber likewise distinguishes prophets and reformers. While the prophet's message may contain a strong element of reform, he differs from the reformer by claiming a substantively new revelation and speaking on the basis of a divine injunction unique to him.[41] "Fundamentally," says one scholar, "Weber's notion of charisma is to be understood in connection with the qualitative difference of a relatively few outstanding individuals who are capable of initiating major social change." Thus, according to Weber, prophets tend to come from socially marginal and economically weak social strata, from groups that are alienated from the central structures of the society and hence have something considerable to gain from overturning them.[42]

Here too, though, the distinction may be too starkly drawn. "The thesis that the major prophets of the Hebrew Bible were drawn from socially marginal groups appears largely to have arisen in order to fit such figures into a recognizable pattern, rather than on the basis of substantive evidence." Indeed, Isaiah and Ezekiel seem to have arisen rather from the inner circles of government and sacerdotal authority, and their intent seems to have been rather a conservative one, to renew and reassert the authority of Israel's established religious and political institutions.[43] For that matter, Moses and Muhammad both, whatever the circumstances of their birth and lineage, indisputably married into prestigious families or clans, and both were helped in their careers by their newly acquired relatives. The same may be true of the early Mesopotamian prophets at Mari, who apparently did not belong to marginalized social groups either. Indeed, again contrary to Weber's dichotomy, at least some of them seem to have held official status at Mari.[44]

Likewise, "Muḥammad did not so much create a new movement as revive and redirect currents that already existed among the Arabs of his time."[45] The ritual of Islam owes a great deal to the traditions not only of

---

41. Weber, p. 54. Thus he contrasts Shankara, Ramanuja, Luther, Zwingli, Calvin, and Wesley, on the one hand, with such figures as Montanus, Mani, Joseph Smith, and Muhammad.

42. Clements, p. 95.

43. Clements, p. 100.

44. See Herbert B. Huffmon, "The Expansion of Prophecy in the Mari Archives: New Texts, New Readings, New Interpretations," in *Prophecy and Prophets*, pp. 7-22, with its abundant references.

45. Lewis, p. 48. Yet Andrae, *Mohammed*, pp. 74-77, argues persuasively against a simplistic view of Muhammad as a secular-style reformer.

pre-Islamic Arabia but of the wider ancient Near East.[46] "It might be said that Muḥammad fitted into the system of law and custom into which he was born," and one well-informed scholar can speak plausibly of "the un-broken continuity of Arabian religion."[47] As we have seen, even the style of his revelations and the manner of his receiving them were reminiscent of the pre-Islamic Arabian *kahins,* or seers.[48] Muhammad did not claim orig-inality; indeed, he expressly disavowed it. "Heresy," in Arabic, is denoted by the word *bidʿa* (innovation) and opposes *sunna* ("customary action" or "wont").[49] "I am not an innovator [*bidʿ*] among the messengers," Muham-mad is commanded to tell his audience.[50] And the Qur'an repeatedly ex-horts believers to do good and to behave honorably, with the term used for "the good" or "the honorable" being *al-maʿruf* (the known).[51] Muham-mad saw himself as getting behind the divisions of Judaism and Christian-ity, back to the original *muslim* or "submitter," Abraham.[52] He was thus, in

46. Widengren, *Religionsphänomenologie,* pp. 564-65; F. E. Peters, *Children of Abra-ham: Judaism/Christianity/Islam* (Princeton: Princeton University Press, 1984), p. 128.

47. Serjeant, "Ḥaram and Ḥawṭah," pp. 51, 53; cf. 42. A willingness to recognize the *Arabian* character of Islam has modified the earlier desire to see it as derivative largely from early forms of Christianity and Judaism. As an example of that earlier view, see Andrae, *Mo-hammed,* pp. 11, 82, 87-92. Andrae sees heavy Syriac Christian influence giving way, in the lat-ter years of the Prophet's life, to Jewish ideas. Such influences were undeniably present. (See, for example, Watt, p. 27; Widengren, *Religionsphänomenologie,* pp. 447-48.) The descriptions of paradise in Nestorian writings and in the Qur'an are, in some regards, strikingly similar. For instance, the wonderful maidens of paradise, the so-called *houris* (whose mention in the Qur'an has been mocked by Westerners), appear also in the sermons of Ephraim the Syrian. Christ is distinct from other prophets in the view of the Qur'an, which not only affirms his virgin birth and his miracles, but even seems to teach a form of *logos* doctrine in connection with him (as at Q 3:39; 4:171). Peters, *Muhammad,* pp. 127-28, briefly discusses evidence that the pre-Islamic Arabs had some knowledge, albeit indirect, of biblical lore. On the other hand, and this is crucial, the Qur'an's rejection of the divine sonship of Jesus of Nazareth, which is already apparent in the Meccan period of Muhammad's ministry (as at Q 43:57ff.), and its denial of his death and resurrection, starkly contradict Nestorian Christology. Whether or not the parallels to Christian belief compromise the truth or uniqueness of Is-lam is a theological issue, not a historical one.

48. Rodinson, pp. 81-82.

49. For sunna, see Q 4:26; 15:13; 17:77; 33:38, 62; 35:43; 40:85; 48:23.

50. Q 46:9. Religions naturally tend to be conservative. See Andrae, *Mohammed,* pp. 138-39.

51. As at Q 2:178, 180, 228-29, 231-36, 240-41, 263; 3:104, 110, 114; 4:5, 8, 19, 25, 114; 7:157; 9:67, 71, 112; 22:41; 24:53; 31:15, 17; 33:6, 32; 47:21; 60:12; 65:2, 6.

52. Q 3:67. That is *muslim* with a lowercase *m.* Abraham's near sacrifice of his son

this and other senses, a conservative rather than a revolutionary. He was attempting to restore what had been before. He was getting back, as well, to the founder of the Ka'ba shrine in Mecca. It has, furthermore, been plausibly argued that Muhammad had, at least at the first, no thought of founding a new religion. He was to be a "warner" to the Arabs, since no previous prophet had been sent to the people of Arabia.[53]

None of this should be surprising. We should ever keep in mind the necessary, indeed unavoidable, dialectic between the prophet and the society and culture into which he was born.[54] "Every founding," says G. van der Leeuw, "must, to a certain extent, be a reformation. And that is actually the case. No 'man of God' builds his experience upon entirely new ground; all build further on the rubbish heap of earlier settlements. A reformer is also a kind of founder. . . . Just as the founder desires not to break up but to fulfill, so does the reformer wish to prove the new system that he is erecting to be the authentic ancient one, and to demonstrate the old, against which he struggles, to be falsely understood."[55] Muhammad was summoning his people back to their old worship of Allah, the one God of Abraham. His was, as he regarded it, the message of the former prophets, a restoration of the ancient, forgotten truth. His message was not a novelty; it was a new synthesis of ideas that had been present in Arabia for many decades at least.[56] Montgomery Watt offers useful insight into the stories of ancient prophets that appear throughout the pages of the Qur'an:

(who is not named in the Qur'an) often figures in Islamic thinking as an illustration of his willingness to submit to the will of God. For a discussion of Abraham's role in Islam, see Rodinson, pp. 185-88.

53. See Q 51:50; 74:2; 79:45; 80:11; 88:21ff. on Muhammad as "warner"; see Q 6:157; 28:46; 32:3; 34:44; 36:6 on the absence of earlier Arabian prophets. For reasons that remain unclear, the Qur'anic prophets Hud and Salih — specifically identified as Arabian — go unnoticed in the latter passages.

54. As Clements, pp. 92, 99, reminds us to do with reference to the biblical prophets.

55. Van der Leeuw, p. 755. In this light Weber's model prophetic types all seem rather less distinct from the reformers than his somewhat schematic statement might suggest: The Montanist movement can easily be viewed as an attempt to return to the spiritual gifts (particularly prophecy) of the primitive church. Mani regarded himself as the latest in a series of prophets that included Jesus and the Buddha. Joseph Smith sought to restore pristine Christianity following a universal apostasy, and Muhammad believed he had received the pure religion of Adam, Abraham, and the prophets.

56. Rodinson, pp. 96, 98.

The stories give encouragement to Muḥammad and his followers in their troubles. They must sometimes have felt they were deserting their ancestors, especially when they were asked difficult questions about the present or future state of deceased pagans. The stories of the Old Testament prophets and others helped them to realize that, as themselves followers of a prophet, they had a distinguished spiritual ancestry. They also were members of a community with its roots deep in the past and, like most Arab tribes, able to boast of the excellence of its stock and the great merits of the forerunners.[57]

When he reached his house, the new prophet was terrified and upset. He asked his wife to cover him. When he was able to stammer out something of what had happened to him, Khadija attempted to comfort him as best she could. She then went to tell her cousin Waraqa. He was instantly supportive. "By Him in whose hand is Waraqa's soul," the now aged Christian said, "there has come to Muhammad the greatest Namus, even the one who used to come to Moses. Truly, Muhammad is the prophet of this people. Let him be assured." (The word *Namus* evidently reflects the Greek *nomos,* or "law," which Waraqa seems to have taken in the sense of the Torah as referring to divinely inspired scripture, and even to have personified as the angelic agent of the revelation itself.) But Muhammad was not left merely to human reassurances. Soon after the first revelation came a second: "By the pen and what they write, by the grace of your Lord you are not possessed [*majnun*]. And there shall be for you a reward that shall not be diminished, and truly you are of a great character."[58] The reception of the Qur'an must have been an awesome, intimidating, even terrifying experience. As a later revelation said, "Had We sent this Qur'an down upon a mountain, you would have seen it humbled and split asunder for fear of God."[59]

But then, troublingly, there was a lengthy interval during which no revelations came to the new prophet, and he was left once again to ponder and even to doubt, or at least to wonder whether or not he had done something to anger or displease God. At long last the word of the Lord again came to him: "By the brightness of dawn and by the nighttime when all is

57. Watt, p. 72.
58. Q 68:1-4.
59. Q 59:21.

still, your Lord has not abandoned you nor does he hate you, and the last shall be better for you than the first, and your Lord will give to you so that you will be well pleased. Did he not find you an orphan and give you shelter, and find you astray and guide you, and find you poor and make you rich? Therefore, as for the orphan, do not treat him harshly, and as for the beggar, do not turn him away, but as for the grace of your Lord, proclaim it!"[60] Muhammad accordingly began to speak to his closest kin of his revelations and of his experience with the angelic messenger.

There was still very little content to the new religion, but tradition says the angel Gabriel appeared to the Prophet shortly thereafter and, meeting him on one of the slopes above the town, taught him the ritual washing and gestures and recitations that were to accompany liturgical prayer among those who accepted Muhammad's inspiration. So Muhammad descended from the hill and taught the new practice to his wife and then to others. Such prayer became part of the procedure by which one entered into the Islamic faith. One was required to wash oneself, from head to foot, in order to be ritually pure, and to purify one's garments as well. Then one was required to testify that "There is no god but God, and Muhammad is the Messenger of God."

The first to embrace the new faith, as yet largely undeveloped in doctrine and practice, were, besides Khadija, Ali and Zayd and Muhammad's good friend Abu Bakr. Ali was but a boy, perhaps ten years old, and Zayd had little or no influence in Mecca. But Abu Bakr was a man of excellent reputation, three years older than Muhammad, a calm and steady man, and he used his influence without hesitation to spread the messages that were now coming through the Prophet.

We are told of miraculous signs that came to other Arabs at about this time, alerting them to the calling of the new prophet. Uthman b. Affan, who would later become the third caliph of Islam, was returning from a trading journey to Syria when he heard a voice in the desert calling out "Sleepers, awake! For verily Ahmad has come forth in Mecca." Uthman did not know what this meant, but the message occupied his mind, and when he had returned to Mecca he encountered another man who had just been asked by a monk of Bostra whether Ahmad had appeared among the people of the Ka'ba shrine. When the man inquired "Who is Ahmad?" the monk replied that he was the son of Abd Allah and the grandson of Abd al-

60. Q 91.

63

Muttalib. "This is his month, in which he shall come forth," explained the monk, no doubt drawing on the same mysterious book that had told his fellow monks of Bostra so remarkably much about the coming of the messenger. "He is the last of the prophets." This was specific enough that both men were soon able to meet Muhammad — whose name comes from the same Semitic root *(hmd)*, connoting "praise," as does Ahmad — and to enter Islam. Muhammad himself claimed no miracles except the Qur'an, although Muslim tradition was quick to ascribe spectacular miracles to him.

Rejection at Mecca

Muhammad waited for some time, perhaps three years, before beginning his public ministry, before openly summoning his Meccan neighbors to accept the imperious call of Allah for the submission *(islam)* of their wills to his, as expressed through his earthly messenger. Even before the commencement of the public ministry, however (it probably occurred about 613), a nucleus of believers began to gather about Muhammad. By 614, according to one careful estimate, thirty-nine people acknowledged his prophethood.[1] Both men and women were among them, but most were relatively young and, with low social status, relatively powerless in Meccan society. Slaves and freedmen were willing to listen to him, as were the younger sons and daughters of even some of the prominent families — those who stood to benefit rather less from the increasing wealth of their parents and of Mecca in general. Most of the free members of the Quraysh who accepted Islam in the earliest period were affiliated, on the other hand, with families that had been relegated, as less significant and influential, to the outskirts of Mecca.

The wealthy and influential citizens of Mecca largely held back from the new religion.[2] The ruling elite were too comfortable, too satisfied with the status quo, to feel any strong spur to change. (It is a phenomenon well known to proselytizing religions even today, and is apparent in the rise of Christianity too, where the well-rooted dwellers on the heath, the heathen,

---

1. Watt, p. 57.

2. See Q 19:73; 34:31ff.; 38:62ff.; 73:11; 80:1ff.; cf. 7:75; 11:27; 17:16; 26:111. See, too, Watt, pp. 36-39.

and the villagers [*pagani*] were far less willing to accept the new faith than the uprooted urban proletariat of Rome and the other cities of the empire.) Those who possessed wealth and honor saw little reason to change when Muhammad arrived with his message. And those whose satisfaction consisted in the very earthly achievements and possessions that Muhammad condemned could scarcely be expected to warm up easily to his preachments on the vanity of temporal things and the brevity of mortal life. "What is the life of this world," asked one of the Qur'anic revelations, "but amusement and play? But truly the abode of the hereafter, that indeed is life — if they only knew."[3] They wanted things to continue as they were; their satisfaction, their status, their very sense of meaningfulness depended on the stability of the values with which they had been raised. If they were not to live on in the praise of their descendants and successors, if the things they valued were to be devalued, what then could be the purpose of life? "There is nothing except the life of this world," the Qur'an quotes the infidels as saying, "and we will not be resurrected."[4]

At first there seemed no cause for concern. Maxime Rodinson observes that "the Qurayshites regarded the new group, which was gradually shedding its cloak of secrecy and emerging into the open, with amused tolerance, very much as Londoners today might watch a Salvation Army meeting on a street corner. They were harmless visionaries and there was no need to take them seriously. At the most, there was a certain contempt for the low social status of those involved."[5] Occasionally, though, there were confrontations. One day an infidel brought a decaying bone to Muhammad and demanded to know if he really claimed that God was going to bring such things back to life. To make his point he crumbled the bone in his hand and blew the dust of it into the Prophet's face. Muhammad waited until the man was finished with his little display and then replied that, yes, that was indeed what he believed. Someday, the Prophet told the disdainful Meccan, God would raise not only that bone but the man who had crumbled it and blown it into his face — and would then thrust that arrogant skeptic into the flames of hell. "Truly, those who do not yearn to meet Us, and are satisfied with the life of this world and pleased with it,

3. Q 29:64.
4. Q 6:29.
5. Rodinson, p. 102. Others have noted that social contempt. See, for example, Andrae, *Mohammed*, pp. 122-23; Peters, *Muhammad*, pp. 167-69.

and those who pay no heed to Our signs, the inferno is their abode, according to what they have merited."[6] But Muhammad's predictions of the end of the world did not seem plausible to many in his Meccan audience. The years went by, and the eschaton did not seem to be arriving.

The oligarchy of the Quraysh could hardly accept Muhammad's claim to prophethood without surrendering their privileges. What is more, acceptance of Muhammad as the messenger of God virtually entailed recognition of his right to political supremacy. For, if God commanded, who could legitimately resist? Montgomery Watt points out that those who resisted Muhammad most strenuously tended to be people of his own generation rather than their elders, for the obvious reason that he was a direct competitor with them for the control of Mecca.[7] Moreover — and this seems to have been an inflammatory issue from the start — if he were right, his preaching seemed to entail that their venerable polytheistic ancestors, the founders of their polity and the establishers of their traditions, were, at that very moment, burning in the flames of hell. That the Quraysh could not grant.[8]

"Warn your nearest kinfolk," commanded an early revelation.[9] And Muhammad did so. Yet not a single one of Muhammad's four uncles accepted his message at the first. Abu Talib seems to have had no great interest in the subject, although he freely allowed his sons Jafar and Ali (the latter eventually to become the fourth and last of the "orthodox" caliphs, and the focus of veneration for the Shi'ite faction of Islam) to enter the new religion. Hamza would accept Islam a few years later, becoming a great warrior and ultimately a notable martyr for the faith. Abbas, in whose name the illustrious Abbasid dynasty of Baghdad would come to power somewhat more than a century later, seems to have been waiting to see which way the winds were blowing. As the likelihood of Muhammad's triumph became ever clearer with the passing years, Abbas's Islam became ever more open.[10] Abu Lahab, by contrast, remained an intractable enemy of the new faith, and openly said that his nephew was, if not a conscious

---

6. Q 10:7-8.

7. Watt, pp. 59, 74.

8. This issue is recognized by Peters, *Muhammad*, p. 169; Andrae, *Mohammed*, p. 116.

9. Q 26:214.

10. Peters, *Allah's Commonwealth*, p. 70 n. 34, is hardly alone in seeing Abbas's sympathetic role as a politically motivated retrojection. Watt, p. 200, thinks Abbas may actually have fought against Muhammad in his earlier days.

fraud, at the very best a madman. An old story (very likely of Shi'ite tinge) tells of a gathering in which Muhammad invited the menfolk of his family to accept his message, and only the thirteen-year-old Ali was willing to speak up. Whereupon Muhammad pronounced the boy his executor and successor.

Muhammad no doubt wished to attract some influential men to his cause. To do so would clearly give prestige to the new faith, and would afford a measure of protection to its followers. A story is told of his eager attempt to win over one of the leaders of the Quraysh. While they were conversing, a blind man, a recent convert, happened to pass by. Recognizing Muhammad's voice, he implored the Prophet to recite to him some passage of the Qur'an. Muhammad, however, anxious lest he lose this relatively rare opportunity to have the respectful ear of one of the Meccan leaders, grew impatient with the blind man when he insisted on hearing a recitation. In the end the conversation went nowhere; the Meccan leader was deaf to the appeal of the divine message. But a stinging rebuke came to Muhammad: "He frowned," said a revelation referring to Muhammad, speaking first in the third person and then in the second, "and turned away because the blind man came to him. And what would teach you? Perhaps he would cleanse himself, or remember, and the reminder might profit him. But the self-sufficient one, to him you pay attention even though there is no blame upon you if he does not cleanse himself. And as for him who came to you earnestly and fearfully, to him you paid no attention."[11]

Muhammad's perhaps overly developed sense of the importance of the Meccan elite was not unique to him. They shared it. Why, asked the lords of the Quraysh, did the revelation not come to us? Why, if God were truly to speak to someone in Arabia, would he have chosen someone from Muhammad's declining clan rather than from one of the powerful and prestigious clans that had come to the fore in the previous generation or two? "Why are the angels not sent down to us," the Qur'an reports the Meccan leaders as demanding, "and why do we not see our Lord?" As R. B. Serjeant writes,

> The Meccan Saiyids constituted much of the opposition to Muḥam-mad himself. Expressing amazement that Muḥammad should claim

11. Q 80:1-10. Such changes of person are not uncommon in Semitic poetry (e.g., in the Psalms).

revelation, al-Walīd ibn al-Mughīrah exclaims: "Is revelation given to Muḥammad while I am left, although I am the Ka'bīr of Quraish and their Saiyid, and Abū Mas'ūd 'Amr ibn 'Umar al-Thaqafi, the Saiyid of Thaqīf, is left [also], though we be the two great persons of the two cities [Mecca and Ṭā'if]?" The plain interpretation of al-Walīd's protest is that, as the spiritual head, the Saiyid, of Quraish, and the Ka'bīr or temporal ruler, he himself is the natural repository of that virtue of spiritual power and of revelation.[12]

"They are arrogant in their souls," comments the Qur'an of such men, "and they are immensely insolent."[13] One of the Meccan chiefs even saw Muhammad's prophethood as an ambitious, self-aggrandizing lie that attempted to regain his family's prestige by an unprecedented and underhanded shortcut. The proper way to vie for honor and status, in the chief's view, was through generosity and largesse, not by suddenly claiming to receive revelations from the one true God of heaven — a gambit with which, once the unique honor had been claimed, nobody else could really compete.

The leaders of the Quraysh wanted the verification of a miracle from Muhammad. Or so they claimed. (They were probably quite confident that he could not produce what they demanded.) They suggested that an angel come down in plain view to confirm the prophethood of their townsman. Or, they said, why did he not rise up to heaven? Such demands evidently made an impact on Muslim believers, who were eager to supply confirmatory miracles, even if Muhammad himself had not claimed them. Tradition attaches the stories of many miracles to Muhammad, such as the feeding of the family of Abd al-Muttalib with food that could not be diminished by their consumption of it. (It is impossible here not to detect echoes of the miracle of Elisha and the cruse of oil or, perhaps even more, of Jesus' feeding of the multitudes as recorded in the four Gospels.)[14] On one occasion several infidels are supposed to have approached the Prophet with the rather odd demand that he split the moon in half as a sign that he

12. Serjeant, "The Saiyids of Ḥaḍramawt," p. 5.

13. Q 25:21.

14. See Matt. 14:13-21; Mark 6:32-44; Luke 9:10-17; John 6:1-15. The only miracle of Jesus recorded in all four Gospels, this story may have been known to Muhammad as well. Some have suggested that it finds an echo in the Qur'an at 5:112-15, although others relate that passage to the Last Supper or even to Peter's vision in Acts 10:9-18.

was truly God's prophet. When he did so, though, in plain view of all, they dismissed it as mere magic and refused to accept Islam despite their earlier promise that such a sign would settle the question for them.

In the first days of the revelation, the Muslims often went forth from the city in order to perform the ritual prayers away from the prying eyes of their disbelieving townspeople. Yet their attempts at seclusion did not always work. One day a group of Meccan pagans came upon them during their prayers and began to mock them, interrupting their devotions. The situation finally grew so intolerable that one of the believers grabbed the jawbone of a camel and smote a pagan with it, thus shedding the first blood in the short history of Islam. At this stage, though, God and his prophet did not approve of such responses. "Be patient with what they say," admonished a revelation, "and separate yourself from them pleasantly [*ahjurhum hajran jamilan*]."[15] "Deal gently with the infidels," said another, "grant them gentle respite."[16] Such pacifism would not last forever, but the Muslim community at this point was so small that no other practical course was open to them.

At this early stage there was little call for violence on the part of the rulers of the Quraysh, who surely did not yet perceive any kind of threat from this tiny movement of what must have seemed to them harmless eccentrics. As the disciples of Islam multiplied, however, it became ever clearer that the message of the new revelation was fundamentally hostile to the gods of the Meccans, to their way of life, to the traditions handed down to them from their ancestors, and, so it seemed at first, to the sanctuary that was the chief glory of their town. Fairly soon thereafter a delegation of them went to the Prophet's unbelieving uncle, Abu Talib, insisting that he put an end to his nephew's nonsense. At first he did nothing, perhaps hoping simply that Muhammad would outgrow this phase. But Muhammad did not, and the leaders of the Quraysh began to bring more and more pressure to bear on Abu Talib. Finally he went to Muhammad and asked him, as a member of the family with whom he had always maintained warm and close relations, to cease these activities that exposed his kin to potential harm. Muhammad, no disloyal relative but a man consumed with the conviction that he had been called by God, said he could not

15. Q 73:10. There is, in the Arabic of this passage, a foreshadowing of the emigration of Muhammad and his community, the *hijra,* from Mecca to Medina.
16. Q 86:17.

cease. The refusal — a clear offense against traditional notions of filial piety — must have caused the Prophet some pain, for Muhammad rose to go with tears in his eyes. But his uncle called him back, saying, "O son of my brother, go and say whatever you will, for by God I will never forsake you for anything." Such was the strength of family loyalty.

And it was a strength with which the Prophet's opponents found it immensely difficult to contend. If Abu Talib granted protection to his nephew, the other clan chiefs would be very reluctant to attempt anything against Muhammad, for they did not want to open up a blood feud and were no doubt concerned that any violation of the rights of one chief would undercut the legitimacy and moral authority of them all. But they had to take action. Here, in the heart of Arabian paganism, a vocal and charismatic preacher was casting doubt on the very foundation of their religion — and he would not hesitate to do so, as well, among the pilgrims who came to Mecca from all over the peninsula. If he weakened their faith in the gods, would those pilgrims return? And if they did not, what would that mean for the economic future of the town? It was a situation rather like that of Paul in Ephesus, when he seemed to threaten the livelihood of that city's silversmiths by disparaging the goddess Artemis, for whose temple they manufactured profitable votive figurines.[17] At one point, seeing no other way short of violence to dissuade him from preaching further, the leaders of the Quraysh decided to offer Muhammad a lavish bribe as an inducement to silence. He refused it.

Still, if Muhammad himself was essentially untouchable, many of his followers were not. One prominent convert, a man of wealth named Arqam, had a large house in the center of Mecca, which he put at the disposal of the fledgling Muslim community. There the believers could meet to pray and recite the Qur'an and discuss the revelations without fear of being observed or molested by their hostile neighbors. But even those who could not be physically hurt could be mocked and harassed, or boycotted. Stories are told of unbelieving fathers torturing and attempting to starve their Muslim children into recanting their religion. No tribal rule protected an unfilial son or daughter against a father's authority.[18] Nor would

---

17. See Acts 19:21-41.

18. A similar situation has long been recognized in the law of the ancient classical world. See Henry Sumner Maine, *Ancient Law: Its Connection with the Early History of Society and Its Relation to Modern Ideas* [1861] (N.p.: Dorset Press, 1986).

any other tribe or clan intervene to spare someone who did not pertain to them. Accordingly, each kinship unit in Mecca dealt with its Muslims in whatever way it chose. There are many stories of imprisonment, beating, starvation, and thirst, and perhaps worst of all, of believers staked out on the ground under the scorching heat of the Arabian sun until they could be induced to repudiate their faith.

Slaves were particularly vulnerable, for they had no one to protect them against their masters. One of them, a black Abyssinian named Bilal, was pinned to the ground by his master, with a large rock on his chest, and told that he would remain there until he either died or recanted — whichever came first. He was spared only because Abu Bakr, passing by, was horrified at this maltreatment of a fellow believer and bought Bilal's freedom. (This was not the first time he had manumitted a slave, and Abu Bakr would eventually spend his entire fortune in the service of Islam and the Muslims.) Some, it is said, died under torture. And others did indeed renounce their faith. If they were asked, "Are al-Lat and al-Uzza not your gods, along with Allah?" they would answer yes in order to be delivered from their agony. But their pain was so intense, relates Ibn Ishaq, that they would have acknowledged the deity of a passing dung beetle if doing so would have delivered them.[19]

On at least one occasion, though, the remorse of a persecutor led to a very significant conversion. Umar, who would later succeed Abu Bakr to become the second caliph of Islam, began his experience with the new faith as one of its most ardent and fiery opponents. His sister, Fatima, had already accepted Muhammad's prophethood but was afraid to tell Umar of her faith because of his violent character. Umar was a serious man who seems to have been genuinely devout in the manner of Arabian paganism and appears to have been angered by the divisions introduced into the Quraysh by this innovator Muhammad — whose followers still numbered probably fewer than a hundred but were increasing.[20] One day, when Umar was about twenty-six, he suddenly formed the resolution to go and kill the man who was responsible for all the problems that he saw afflicting his town and people. He was met en route, however, by a man who told him that he should first go to the people of his own house, to set them to

19. Translated at Guillaume, p. 145. Is there an implicit reference here to the scarab beetle, sacred to the ancient Egyptians?

20. So much, again, for the supposed irreligiousness of pagan Arabia.

rights. Umar had been kept in the dark, and was bewildered by this re-mark. When he was told that his sister and her husband were Muslims, he was furious.

He went hurriedly to the place where Fatima and her husband, as fortune would have it, were listening to a recitation of the Qur'an. When they heard his angry voice, Fatima took the manuscript of the revelation and hid it under her robe.[21] But it was too late. Umar had heard the sound of the recitation, and demanded to know what they had been saying. They tried to convince him that he had heard nothing, but he insisted that he had indeed heard them reciting, and that he knew they were secret Mus-lims. He assaulted his brother-in-law and, when Fatima came to his de-fense, struck her so violently that it broke the skin.[22] Yes, they said, they were Muslims. He could do with them what he wanted.

This sobered him. When he saw the blood of his sister, he was in-stantly remorseful. He asked if he could read the revelation that they had been sharing with one another before his entry. Fatima responded, rather daringly, that he could not, since his idolatry rendered him too impure to touch the document. But Umar was now thoroughly chastened, and when he had washed himself, she gave him the page containing the revelation. As he began to read, he was moved and transformed by the beauty and nobil-ity of the words and immediately decided to embrace the religion of Islam. He went to the Prophet and made the formal profession of faith, and then went about openly summoning other Meccans to do as he had done. In-deed, true to his bold nature, he deliberately went to the most hostile among the Quraysh, proclaiming the truth of Muhammad's revelation.

Upon his conversion, Umar took to praying publicly at the Ka'ba, sometimes accompanied by Muhammad's redoubtable uncle Hamza and a company of other believers. The pagans of the Quraysh were not at all happy about this, but were reluctant to confront people of Umar and Hamza's forceful character. Since they could not simply stand by and ap-

---

21. Note that, in this story, at least a portion of the Qur'an had already been commit-ted to writing during the lifetime of the Prophet — indeed, while he was still in Mecca. An argument has long raged as to when the Qur'an began to be written down.

22. Though he was a man of undisputed integrity, Umar's temper was legendary. Af-ter his conversion, and during his tenure as caliph, he enforced Islamic law very sternly. Once when his own son was caught drinking wine, he punished him so severely that the young man cried out that he had killed him. "Then go," Umar is said to have replied, "and tell God how your father carries out his penalties!"

pear to ratify Muslim use of the Ka'ba sanctuary, they chose instead to stay away — which can be seen, in retrospect, as one of the earliest of what would become a long series of Qurayshi surrenders and accommodations to the upstart new religion.

But the leaders of the Quraysh were not merely passive in the face of the growing threat. They decided about this time to launch an economic embargo and general ban against the entire clan of Hashim, Muhammad's clan, which was protecting Muhammad against persecution out of family loyalty, if not from religious conviction. (Muhammad's uncle Abu Lahab was an exception. He and his wife were bitter enemies to the Prophet.) Roughly forty of the Meccan elite composed a document pledging no intermarriages with the Hashimites and no commercial trafficking. The demand was that the Hashimites either pronounce Muhammad an outlaw — thus depriving him of any defense against persecution or even assassination — or convince him to yield up his claim of prophethood. Tradition says the text of the agreement was placed within the Ka'ba.

The interdiction lasted at least two years but, as often happens, seems to have had little of the desired impact. Indeed, it may actually have drawn attention to the claims of Muhammad and to have elicited for him a degree of sympathy. Certainly there was sympathy for many of the ordinary people of Hashim, since they had kinsfolk among the surrounding clans who did not enjoy seeing them suffer. When, finally, it was decided to lift the ineffective ban, someone went into the Ka'ba to fetch the document in which it had been decreed. And when he emerged, it was discovered that worms had eaten virtually all of the vellum on which the ban had been written, leaving only the opening words, "In thy name, O God!"

Not long after the lifting of the interdiction, however, in 619, two events dulled the joy Muhammad must have felt over surviving a serious challenge from the Quraysh. Khadija, his wife for a quarter of a century, his adviser, his first convert and his patroness, died. And not long — perhaps, indeed, only a few days — after Khadija's passing, Muhammad's protector and uncle Abu Talib died also, still a pagan and an unbeliever.

Abu Talib was succeeded as chief of the Banu Hashim by none other than Abu Lahab, the sworn enemy, as tradition represents him, of the Prophet. Actually he may at first not have been as hostile to Muhammad as he is commonly depicted. Some sources represent him as having been moved by the troubles of his nephew, and as having promised him that he would take care of him as Abu Talib had done. But he soon changed his

mind. Some of Muhammad's enemies sought out Abu Lahab and reminded him that, in the view of the Prophet, both Abd al-Muttalib and
Abu Talib, despite their loyal protection, were even now suffering the flam-
ing torments of hell because they had died pagans. When Muhammad
confirmed to Abu Lahab that this was indeed so, his uncle was horrified
and deeply offended at the brazen lack of filial piety that such an attitude
disclosed.

Abu Lahab continued to do his family duty by Muhammad, but only
perfunctorily, and the Prophet now found himself subject to ill-treatment as
he had never before experienced it. Much of the persecution was petty and
mean-spirited. Someone threw a sheep's uterus at him. Another cast a piece
of offal into his cooking pot. Abu Lahab did nothing to deal with such acts.

The leaders of the Quraysh sought also to discredit Muhammad by
casting doubt on the validity of his claim to revelation. The early biographies tell of a delegation sent to Yathrib to consult the Jews resident there
about Muhammad, as they were surely greater experts on prophets and
how to deal with them than were the pagans of Mecca. The Jews, say the
accounts, supplied three diagnostic questions to put to Muhammad. If he
could answer the questions, they said, he was a genuine prophet of God. If
he could not, he was a fraud.

They were to ask him, first, about some young men who left their
people in ancient times. He should be able to tell them about these young
men and their wonderful story. Second, they were to ask Muhammad
about a traveler who had reached the ends of the earth, both to the east
and to the west. Third, they were to request that he tell them about the
Spirit, and exactly what it is.

After a lengthy and rather embarrassing silence, the Prophet was enabled by revelation to answer the questions: First, the Qur'an recounted a
fascinating but somewhat unclear tale about a group of men sleeping in a
cave.[23] This story is generally connected by scholars, both medieval and
modern, with the very old legend concerning the third century c.e. "seven
sleepers of Ephesus," although at least one scholar has suggested that it
rests on dim memories of the community at ancient Qumran, near the
Dead Sea.[24] The second story was that of Dhu al-Qarnayn, "he of the two

---

23. Q 18:9-25.

24. Hugh Nibley, "Qumran and the Companions of the Cave," *Revue de Qumran* 5,
no. 2 (April 1965): 177-98; reprinted as "Qumran and the Companions of the Cave: The

horns," who is often connected with the widely traveled hero of the old romance about Alexander the Great.[25] In answer to the third question, about the nature of the Spirit, the Qur'anic revelation said simply that the Spirit exceeds the understanding of humankind.[26] Still, although the Prophet had answered the questions well, neither the Jews who had formulated them nor the people of the Quraysh who actually posed them converted to Islam.

Eventually the stress in Mecca grew so severe that the Prophet began to cast about for some way of escape, some sanctuary or refuge where he and his followers could practice Islam without resistance or persecution. One promising place was Christian Abyssinia, with which the Arabs had long had relatively close contact.

Haunted Wilderness," in Hugh Nibley, *Old Testament and Related Studies* (Salt Lake City: Deseret Book and the Foundation for Ancient Research and Mormon Studies, 1986), pp. 253-84.

25. Q 18:93-99.
26. Q 17:85.

The *Hijra*

About eighty Muslims, not counting small children, had fled to the court of the Negus in Abyssinia, probably in or near 615. They did not go all at once but, fearing that the Meccan leadership would attempt to stop their emigration, left secretly in small groups. There they received a friendly reception from the Ethiopian Christians.

When the heads of the Quraysh noticed their departure, however, Mecca sent an embassy to the Abyssinian court to attempt to bring them back. The question naturally arises why the Meccan rulers would do such a thing, and why it would matter to them if some of those who were causing problems in their town were to leave. The answer probably has something to do with trade. Mecca and Abyssinia had commercial relations, and perhaps the Quraysh feared an attempt on the part of Muhammad to interfere with their livelihood and divert it toward his own followers. (Subsequent events show him doing precisely that, elsewhere.) It may be that Muhammad was attempting to open up an alternative trade route, beyond the reach of Meccan authority.

The Meccans brought with them gifts for the Negus and his retainers, to induce them to listen. The Negus, however, refused to send the Muslims back to Mecca without first granting them a hearing. This was precisely what the Meccans had sought to prevent, for they were aware that the religious views of the Muslims might well find a more sympathetic hearing among the Ethiopic Christians than would their own pagan and polytheistic objections to Islam. Although Mecca had good commercial relations with Abyssinia, there remained an ideological gulf between them

— the gap between a morally serious monotheism and, as it must have seemed to the Abyssinians, a rather lax heathenism.

When all were assembled, the Negus inquired about the new religious views that had caused this breach among the inhabitants of Mecca. A Muslim spokesman stepped forward and, confirming the worst fears of the Qurayshi leadership, told of how, before the revelation, they had been an ignorant, idol-worshiping people, among whom the rich and powerful oppressed the poor and the weak. But now, the Muslim speaker said, God had sent a messenger to them who had summoned them to recognize the one true God, to renounce idolatry and the shedding of blood, to speak the truth and fulfill promises. The speech could not have been better calculated to impress the Negus and his Christian entourage. And when the monarch asked if they could provide for him a sample of the revelation that their prophet had brought to them, they responded with a brilliantly chosen passage from the recently received chapter of "Mary":

> And mention in the book Mary, when she withdrew from her people in a place to the east and veiled herself from them. So we sent to her Our Spirit, which appeared to her in the likeness of a perfect man. She said, "I take refuge from you in the Merciful One, if you are God-fearing." He said, "I am none other than a messenger of your Lord, to give unto you a pure son." She said, "How shall I have a son, when no man has touched me and I have not been unchaste?" He said, "Thus it shall be. Your Lord has said, 'It is easy for Me, that We make him a sign to the people and a mercy from Us, and it is a matter decreed.'"[1]

The Negus was delighted when the interpreters had rendered the Arabic of the Qur'an into his language. This was, he said weeping, the very same doctrine that Jesus had brought, and he was certain that it came from the same source. No, he would not give the Muslims back to their pagan pursuers.

But the Meccans were themselves not without ability, and they soon thought of a way to sow strife between the Abyssinian Christians and the Arabian Muslims, who had won their favor by seeming to believe the same things about Jesus and Mary. For the Muslims denied the deity of Christ and regarded him merely as a servant of God — a great servant, to be sure, and a prophet, but not essentially different from any other mortal and still

1. Q 19:16-21.

divided from God by the unbridgeable gulf that separates divinity from humanity.

The next morning, when the Negus questioned them, at the prodding of the Quraysh, about the nature of Jesus, the Muslims were troubled at the potentially dangerous trap that had been set for them. Finally they elected to tell the Ethiopian monarch the truth, that they believed Jesus to have been a virgin-born prophet, but a human. Perhaps to their surprise, and certainly to the astonishment of the Meccan delegation, the Negus agreed with them and again promised them his protection. However, when the Abyssinian people heard of the apparent apostasy of their ruler from Christian orthodoxy, strife arose, and the Negus was obliged for the sake of domestic peace and the stability of his throne to disassociate himself from the Qur'anic position on the status of Jesus — though he privately remained a believing Muslim to the day of his death.

There are some things about this story that do not ring true. It is scarcely plausible, for instance, that the Negus of Abyssinia would publicly repudiate perhaps the central tenet of his Christian faith on the basis of so little as the traditional narratives recount. Moreover, something led him to distance himself from the Muslim position, and it may be that the second day of questioning did not go as well as the traditional accounts say. He might have seen in the Muslims a belief indisputably far closer to his own than the pagan polytheism of the Meccan elite but might still have found their Christology defective and unacceptable, so that he chose a middle course of dismissing the Meccan delegation and allowing the Muslims to remain.

Meanwhile, with the death of Abu Talib and the succession of the hostile Abu Lahab to the leadership of the Banu Hashim, Muhammad's situation in Mecca had materially worsened. Besides, the death of his beloved wife, Khadija, had perhaps weakened his emotional tie to the town. He began to cast around for a place to which he and his followers could go for refuge. He first looked at the mountain town of Ta'if, the stronghold of the people of Thaqif, the guardians of the shrine of the goddess al-Lat. But his visit to Ta'if proved to be humiliating and nearly disastrous, as he had to withdraw from the town under a hail of stones from the unwelcoming pagans.

It may also have been during this time — the years 617 and 619 are often suggested — that one of the most famous events of the Prophet's life occurred, at least according to the traditional accounts. This was his famous *mir'aj,* or "Night Journey." Among the principal objections raised by the people of Mecca against Muhammad was what Mircea Eliade has termed his "existential banality."[2] He was simply an ordinary person, and it seemed wildly implausible that the God of the universe had somehow singled him out for special attention. (This would very likely be a powerful objection to *any* prophet, in any time.) The Qur'an preserves some of their reasoning: "What's with this 'messenger'? He eats food and walks about in the marketplace. Why hasn't an angel been sent down to him, to be a warner with him? Or a treasure bestowed upon him? Or why does he not have a garden from which he can eat?"[3] "What the sceptical citizens here demand of the Prophet," observes Geo Widengren, "is nothing else than that he should be capable of bringing forth the Garden of Paradise."[4] The Meccans' somewhat enigmatic mention of the "garden" may also be connected with the idea of a *haram* or *hawta* sanctuary, which was often associated, in its turn, with a *hima*, a sacred grove or garden enclosure.[5] Possession of such an enclosure was expected of sacred families.

> We shall not believe in you until you cause a spring to
>   burst forth for us from the earth,
> Or until you have a garden of dates and grapes and cause rivers
>   to burst forth abundantly in their midst,
> Or until you cause the sky to fall upon us in pieces, as you
>   have pretended it will, or you bring God and the angels
>   before us,
> Or until you have a gilded house or you mount up into the sky.
>   And we will not believe in your mounting up until you cause
>   to come down upon us a book that we can read.[6]

Those who disbelieve say, "Why is the Qur'an not sent down to him all at once?" Thus, that your heart might be built up by it, and We recite it to you gradually.[7]

---

2. Eliade, *History of Religious Ideas*, 3:69.

3. Q 25:7-8.

4. Widengren, *Muḥammad*, p. 99.

5. See Andrae, *Mohammed*, pp. 14-15. The two concepts are not mutually exclusive. See Donald W. Parry, "Garden of Eden: Prototype Sanctuary," in *Temples of the Ancient World: Ritual and Symbolism*, ed. Donald W. Parry (Salt Lake City: Deseret Book and the Foundation for Ancient Research and Mormon Studies, 1994), pp. 126-51.

6. Q 17:90-93.

7. Q 25:32.

The Qur'an advises Muhammad to respond to such complaints with a simple declaration: "Say, 'Glory to my Lord, am I anything but a mortal human being and a messenger?'"[8] But Islamic tradition did not long remain content with this response.

Muhammad was being asked to confirm the authenticity of his prophethood by ascending to heaven and there receiving a holy book, in one instant of time. In this he was to conform to a model illustrated by many still-extant legends — at least some of which must have been known to his Meccan audience or they would not have made the demand — regarding Enoch, Moses, Daniel, Mani, and many other messengers who had risen to heaven, met God, and received from his right hand a book of scripture containing the revelation they were to proclaim.[9] Both rabbinic and apocalyptic Judaism knew the idea, as did the Samaritans and the Gnostics.[10] The Mandaeans believed in heavenly books existing before the creation of the earth, of which their savior figure brings transcripts to humankind.[11] It seems to go back at least to the legendary Mesopotamian king Emmenduraki, and to draw on a royal ideology in which the concepts of ruler and prophet were united (just as they would be again in the person of Muhammad).[12] Geo Widengren argues convincingly that Muhammad's

8. Q 17:93. Compare Q 6:35; 15:14-15.

9. Even David can perhaps be added here (1 Chron. 28:19), with Ezekiel (Ezek. 2:9–3:2). A classic treatment of the concept of the heavenly book is that of Johannes Pedersen, in his review of *Ursprung und Geschichte der Mormonen,* by Eduard Meyer, *Der Islam* 5 (1914): 113-15.

10. See Helmer Ringgren, *The Faith of Qumran: Theology of the Dead Sea Scrolls,* trans. Emilie T. Sander, expanded ed. (New York: Crossroad, 1995), pp. 54-55.

11. Widengren, *Religionsphänomenologie,* pp. 549-50.

12. Widengren, *Religionsphänomenologie,* pp. 483-500, 550, 553, 555 n. 36, 583-85, offers a good general discussion of the motif of celestial ascent, with many references. Also Widengren, *Ascension of the Apostle,* pp. 9, 9 n. 1, 10, 16-17, 20, 33 n. 3; Widengren, *Muḥammad,* pp. 52, 199, 202. Widengren has noted many parallels to the concept of the heavenly book in ancient Mesopotamian "Tablets of Destiny," by which, at the festival season of New Year, the gods determine the fate of the cosmos and all that is in it for the next year. "Few religious ideas in the Ancient Near East have played a more important role than the notion of the Heavenly Tablets, or the Heavenly Book . . . [and] the oft-recurring thought that the Heavenly Book is handed over at the ascension in an interview with a heavenly being, or several heavenly beings, mostly gods (a god)." See Widengren, *Ascension of the Apostle,* p. 7. Compare Widengren, *Religionsphänomenologie,* pp. 546-47; Widengren, *Muḥammad,* pp. 199, 204; Kister, "'Sha'bān Is My Month . . . ,'" pp. 15-37. Obvious similarities can be identified between Moses' ascent of Mount Sinai and the old Mesopotamian idea,

title of *rasul* ("messenger" or "sent one") is a time-honored designation, earlier belonging to royalty, given to those in the ancient Near East who were thought, following a celestial ascent, to have been "sent down" from heaven with a message.[13]

One night Muhammad was sleeping at the home of kinsfolk. But he awoke in the middle of the night and made his way down to the Ka'ba, where he seems to have enjoyed spending the midnight hours in meditation and reflection. Then he grew sleepy again, and eventually lay down to rest in the enclosure known as the Hijr. Sometime during the night, however, he was awakened by the angel Gabriel, who led him to the gate of the Ka'ba precinct, where a strange animal was waiting for him. It was Buraq, a white and winged beast, something of a cross between a mule and an ass in appearance, each of whose strides took him to the horizon. By means of this miraculous steed Muhammad made his way northward, accompanied by the angel Gabriel, past Yathrib to the holy city of Jerusalem. There, on the temple mount, he met a number of the ancient prophets, including Abraham, Moses, and Jesus, whom, as their imam, he led in prayer.

From the temple mount Muhammad then ascended through the seven heavens, each inhabited and supervised by a prophet from earlier times, and eventually entered into the presence of God himself.[14] It was directly from God — in this vision — that Muhammad received the commandment to lead the Muslims in five prayers daily. (The Qur'an it-

---

and the notion that persisted in Judaism in such texts as *1 Enoch, 2 Enoch,* and the *Testaments of the Twelve Patriarchs.* It existed among the Mandaeans and the Persians, and in Islamic sectarian movements even after the death of Muhammad. See Widengren, *Ascension of the Apostle,* pp. 10, 22-24, 26 n. 1, 27, 35, 42-43, 46, 58, 68, 72, 74-75, 84-85; Widengren, *Muḥammad,* pp. 29-30, 80-95. Dan. 10:21 may reflect a belief in the heavenly book.

13. Widengren, *Religionsphänomenologie,* pp. 505-6; Widengren, *Ascension of the Apostle,* pp. 19-21, 31-33, 47, 58, also adduces Moses and Ezekiel as parallels; Widengren, *Muḥammad,* cites a Syriac parallel to the title *rasul.* In some versions of the story, Muhammad (like Paul in 2 Cor. 12:1-5) is given secret knowledge, which later becomes important in the claims of the Shi'ite imams to esoteric wisdom. See Widengren, *Muḥammad,* pp. 106-7; Alan F. Segal, *Paul the Convert: The Apostolate and Apostasy of Saul the Pharisee* (New Haven: Yale University Press, 1990), pp. 34-71.

14. Peters, *Muhammad,* pp. 144-47, furnishes a good, brief discussion of the *mi'raj.* Widengren, *Muḥammad,* pp. 96-114, offers a much longer treatment, with comparative material. The anthropomorphism of the accounts is striking. See Widengren, *Ascension of the Apostle,* pp. 22 n. 1, 81, 108.

self knows only three — morning, noon, and night.) Actually, God first imposed on Muhammad a requirement of fifty daily prayers. But when Muhammad began his descent through the heavens to the surface of the earth, he encountered Moses once again. That great ancient prophet asked Muhammad how many prayers God had commanded. When the Arabian prophet replied "fifty," Moses told him to return to God and ask the burden to be lifted. Muhammad did so, and God removed ten prayers from the daily quota. But Moses remained unsatisfied, and continued to advise Muhammad to return until the number was reduced to five. Even that was too much, Moses declared, but Muhammad was embarrassed to bother God further and said he would petition for no more reductions.[15]

Soon after Gabriel and Muhammad had descended to Jerusalem, they returned to Mecca by the same route they had come, passing above several caravans that were returning to Mecca by the much slower means of earthly camels. The Prophet arrived back at his relatives' home before the dawn. But immediately prior to sunrise, he woke his kin and told them that, while he had prayed the evening prayer with them the night before and now stood in their midst in the valley of Mecca, during the night he had been to Jerusalem for prayer. One tradition says the journey was instantaneous: the jar that Muhammad had upset in his departure was still spilling its contents when he returned.

His relatives begged him to say nothing of this experience to the unbelieving Meccans, lest it give them unprecedentedly good reason to mock him. But Muhammad insisted. And the response was precisely as might have been expected. Still, when Muhammad was able to describe the caravans he had overflown in great detail and predict their time of arrival in the valley, some came to believe him. To the public he told only of his journey to the holy city of Jerusalem. To his inner circle, however, he spoke of his ascension through the heavens to the presence of God. The account may have been pivotal then, as it certainly has been in the centuries since, in establishing, in the minds of his disciples, Muhammad's "personal and private access" to God — the basis of his claim to authority, as it was for

15. Judaism, too, knew only three daily prayers, as did Nestorian Christianity (from which the Arabic *salat*, usually translated "prayer," may have been borrowed). It may be significant, though, that Magian or Zoroastrian prayers were to be said five times a day — at dawn, noon, midafternoon, sunset, and midnight. See Morony, p. 292; Peters, *Muhammad*, pp. 164-66; Watt, p. 100.

the prophets of the Bible.[16] "Glory be to Him," says the Qur'an, "who took His servant by night from the holy shrine [al-masjid al-haram][17] to the furthest shrine [al-masjid al-aqsa], the precincts of which We have blessed, in order to show him some of our signs. For He is hearing, seeing."[18] The Qur'anic evidence for Muhammad's ascension is ambiguous at best. While Qur'an 17:1 and perhaps 17:60 allude to a journey to "the furthest shrine" (al-masjid al-aqsa), scholars debate whether that phrase alludes to a location in Jerusalem (where the Al-Aqsa Mosque — in Arabic, al-masjid al-aqsa — stands today) or to a heavenly sanctuary. But the story attached itself to him early, and its roots in antiquity are very deep.

Muhammad clearly understood and accepted the notion of a heavenly book, and he always saw himself as producing a book on earth to represent the heavenly original.[19] In his view the revelations of the Qur'an, like the Torah (tawrat) and the Gospel (injil) before it, were "recitations" or "readings" from the very words of God, which were written in the "Mother of the Book" (umm al-kitab) and kept on a closely guarded tablet (lawh mahfuz) in the divine presence.[20] As noted, it was communicated orally to Muhammad, piece by piece, in an Arabic version.[21] Not all of the heavenly book was given to him, but only a portion.[22] Thus the Qur'an did not exhaust it. Other revelations to the "people of the book" (ahl al-kitab) — not, be it noted, the "people of the books" — were derived from it and were thus, at least originally, consistent with it and confirmed by it. (Unfortunately the Jews and the Christians had corrupted the revelations they had received.) Islamic tradition soon assimilated Muhammad to the ancient model of a single, complete reception of a heavenly book during an ascension into the presence of God. Somehow, it was felt, the Prophet had received the Qur'an all at once; it had been brought down to earth on the night of the first revelation. That night, probably the twenty-sixth of Ramadan, was later described as "the Night of Power" or "the Night of Destiny" (laylat al-qadr).

---

16. The phrase, originally intended to characterize the Hebrew prophets, is from Freedman, "Between God and Man," p. 57.

17. Presumably the precincts of the Ka'ba in Mecca.

18. Q 17:1.

19. See the discussion and references at Widengren, *Religionsphänomenologie*, pp. 568-69; Widengren, *Muhammad*, pp. 115-19.

20. Q 80:13ff.; 56:79; 85:21ff.; 93:3ff.

21. See Q 12:1; 13:37; 20:113; 26:192ff.; 41:3; 44:58; and esp. 91:44.

22. Q 90:78; 4:164.

We have indeed revealed it in the Night of Destiny.
And what will make you understand what the Night of Destiny is?
The Night of Destiny is better than a thousand months.
By God's leave, the angels and the Spirit come down in it on
    every kind of errand.
Peace it is, until the rising of the dawn.[23]

Meanwhile two hundred miles north, in Yathrib, there was also strife, but of a rather distinct kind. Yathrib was a very different place from Mecca. Situated on a high plain partially covered by lava, it was an agricultural oasis of perhaps more than twenty square miles, whereas Mecca was a commercial town. For several miles around it the land was intensively cultivated. The settlement was especially famous for its date palms. More importantly, Yathrib was far less urbanized than Mecca; its residents still lived in various fortified compounds scattered about the oasis. Its two main Arab tribes, Aws and Khazraj, could not get along. A bloody quarrel had broken out between a man of Aws and a man of Khazraj, and, as often happened, others of the tribes had become involved along with their allies from the three local Arab-Jewish tribes — Jewish in religion, deeply Arabian in culture — of Qurayza, Nadir, and Qaynuqa (who may actually have been the first inhabitants of the oasis). Four indecisive but deadly battles had served only to make the situation worse, and to give more reasons for the seeking of revenge. Moreover, although Aws and Khazraj maintained alliances with the various Jewish groupings in the settlement, even those relations were not always cordial, as the traditional accounts indicate and as subsequent events seem unmistakably to confirm. The Jews, though Arabized (if not natively Arabian), remained both monotheistic and, probably as a consequence, rather aloof from the pagans of Yathrib. They were conscious of being the chosen people of God through whom the prophets had come and through whom, presumably, any future divine message would also be delivered.

No real peace had arrived, even following the fourth battle, and the people of Yathrib lived together uneasily, in constant expectation of further violence. In fact, several unexplained murders had recently disturbed the residents. Without any central authority to enforce order,

---

23. Q 97. For another account of the "Night of Destiny," see Peters, *Muhammad*, pp. 203-7, 215-18.

even the slightest provocation could easily lead to civil war, and the ancient Arabian practice of the blood feud, which maintained a rough order in the vast spaces of the desert, posed a huge risk in a relatively densely settled oasis. In the midst of these century-old difficulties, the leaders of Aws had once determined even to send a delegation to Mecca to ask for Qurayshi help against Khazraj. To others, though, it was becoming apparent that Yathrib needed a ruler with a strong hand, someone who could stand above the endless tribal bickering and dispel the chaos that had plagued them for so long. In fact, there was a man in the oasis, one Abd Allah b. Ubayy, whose stature and reputation for fairness had already led many, including himself, to see him as a possible king of Yathrib. But opinion had not yet coalesced sufficiently to permit his assumption of such a role.

The people of Khazraj may have recalled that they were linked by ties of kinship to Muhammad. (Every Arab was acutely aware of genealogical links several generations back. One's lineage, in fact, was a substantial component of one's name.) The Prophet had spent time in Yathrib with his relatives. His mother was buried nearby, his father was buried there, and he had probably visited at least a few times in subsequent years as he participated in the caravans to Syria. In 620 six men of Khazraj accepted Islam upon meeting the Prophet while away from Yathrib. The next summer, in 621, five of them came to Mecca on the pilgrimage, accompanied by seven others, including two members of the rival tribe of Aws. At Aqaba, a place not far from Mecca, these twelve men — the number is perhaps significant, and perhaps suspicious — pledged their allegiance to Muhammad in what is often known as the First Pledge of Aqaba. Included in the pledge were promises to refrain from the worship of any being other than the one God, to forgo theft, infanticide, slander, and fornication. More relevant to the political scene at Yathrib, they promised obedience to Muhammad — a promise that would have ramifications that they could probably never have foreseen in their wildest imaginings.

In the next year twelve men, perhaps representing a larger group totaling seventy-five,[24] again made a pledge to Muhammad, known as the

---

24. David Noel Freedman reminds me in a personal communication that, just as the number twelve is biblical, the number seventy-five may derive from the story of those who went down to Egypt with Jacob. He observes that the round number is seventy (Gen. 46:24-27), but that the number seventy-two also appears and that seventy-five is found as well, especially in the Septuagint (also Gen. 46:24-27) and in the account given by Stephen at Acts 7:14.

Second Pledge of Aqaba. (A number of secret meetings seem to have occurred between the two pledges and continued thereafter, as the terms of Muhammad's emigration to Yathrib were settled. The Prophet did not want to repeat his mistake at Ta'if.) But this time, the sources say, the pledge of obedience included an obligation to fight on behalf of Islam. Henceforward, because it contained no mention of warfare, the First Pledge began to be known and continued to be used as "the pledge of the women." It is unlikely that those making the pledge envisioned an attack on Mecca, or even the necessity of defending their own city against Meccan attack; one is entitled to doubt that they would have entered into the pledge had they seen the immediate consequences it was to drag down on their heads. They probably intended merely to extend to Muhammad and his followers — who would, by forsaking homes and families in Mecca, be leaving their tribal ties behind — the protections typically afforded by a tribe to its members. The Meccan Muslims were, in a sense, being adopted.

At this point, in 622, the Prophet began to encourage his followers to emigrate to Yathrib — in small groups and without fanfare, as had earlier been done in the emigrations to Abyssinia. As before, the leaders of the Quraysh attempted to stop the emigrants, and stories are told of some being held prisoner in Mecca in order to prevent their going. As with the emigration to Abyssinia, the Meccan leaders may have sensed a threat to their trade supremacy. And they were right. But, over the months of July, August, and September, almost all the Muslims who wanted to leave Mecca managed to do so. One of those most eager to leave was Abu Bakr. But the Prophet asked him to wait, hinting that, once the others had gotten safely away, he himself would accompany Abu Bakr to Yathrib. Perhaps the Prophet wanted to remain behind in order to encourage waverers.

The increasingly desperate leaders of the Quraysh finally came up with a plan that, although dramatic, they must have felt would pose few risks to them and was almost certain to be successful. Each clan was asked to nominate a representative, and the men chosen were to come together and, at the very same instant, plunge a dagger into Muhammad. The theory was that, with each clan of the Quraysh guilty in the death of Muhammad, the Banu Hashim would realize that they were far too weak to enter into a blood feud with everybody else in Mecca, and would thus be unable to seek revenge and obliged to accept blood money. And the plan called for this to be generously offered. The cost would be relatively cheap for ridding the community of an obnoxious and persistent troublemaker.

Somehow forewarned — traditional sources say the angel Gabriel came to the Prophet and informed him of what was afoot — Muhammad told Abu Bakr that, at last, the time had arrived for them to emigrate together to Yathrib. And, since virtually all the other believers had already left, the time was indeed appropriate. However, Muhammad asked Ali to remain behind to settle outstanding economic obligations. But Ali also served another important function at this crucial moment of Muhammad's life. Giving him the cloak in which he often slept, the Prophet advised Ali to wrap himself in it and to sleep on Muhammad's bed, assuring him that he would not be hurt. Then the Prophet slipped away, eluding the conspirators, who had been keeping his house under guard to make sure he did not escape.

As time passed, the would-be assassins grew ill at ease, but one of them managed to catch a glimpse inside the Prophet's home and assured them that Muhammad was asleep on his bed. The extra time this bought for the Prophet and Abu Bakr was very useful for their successful escape. (Ali did, in fact, eventually arrive quite safely in Yathrib, only a few days after Muhammad and Abu Bakr. Although the Qurayshi assassins were undoubtedly quite angry at the way they had been tricked, their conspiratorial covenant covered only the killing of the Prophet.) Meanwhile, to throw their expected pursuers off the scent, Muhammad and his friend Abu Bakr headed south rather than northward toward Yathrib. They took refuge for several days in a mountain cave.

Incensed at Muhammad's escape, the leaders of the Quraysh offered the handsome reward of a hundred camels for whoever found him. All the routes northward were combed carefully for any sign of the fugitive. But as the hours went by and he was not found, some began to think that maybe he was hiding in one of the caves near Mecca, and they began to look in all directions around the city, not merely on the roads to the north. This was a real danger for the Prophet, for the bedouin trackers of the desert are legendarily effective. On the third day Muhammad and Abu Bakr heard birds cooing and fluttering at the entrance to their cavern hideout, and then, not long thereafter, they heard men's voices, faint at first but drawing ever nearer. Oddly, though, the men paused outside the cave, loudly discussing their options and concluding that there was no need to search it. Finally they left. What had prevented their entry into the cave, in which they would certainly have found the Prophet? When they were safely gone, Muhammad and Abu Bakr made their way to the mouth of the cave where, the traditional narratives say, they found an acacia tree taller than a man. Although it had not been there that morning, it now covered the entrance of the cave almost entirely. Moreover, a spider had spun its web between the tree and the cave wall, signaling to the Meccan searchers, quite falsely, that a great deal of time had elapsed since anybody had passed that way. And a pair of rock doves had built their nest at the entrance to the cave.

Having eluded the Meccans thus far, Abu Bakr and Muhammad now continued their journey to Yathrib with the help of a bedouin guide who knew all the least-traveled paths. First they went farther away from Mecca toward the west, and then somewhat to the south, reaching the shore of the Red Sea. From there they followed the coastal road to the northwest for several days. Finally they headed toward Yathrib. They arrived at an oasis outside the town proper on Monday, September 27, 622. There they stayed for a few days, until on Friday they actually went into the settlement.

Naturally, everybody in Yathrib wanted the honor of hosting the Prophet, this new dignitary. They cried out for him to sit his camel down here, or over there. But Muhammad wisely let his camel have free rein, and told them that her movements were under the control of God. Finally the camel turned into a large walled enclosure that was used for the drying of dates and, at one end, as a burial ground. There she settled to the earth, and Muhammad announced that this spot, the very place where she sat down, would be his dwelling place. The Prophet bought the site, and he soon decreed that the enclosure be transformed into a mosque, a place for Muslims to meet for worship and other purposes.[25] In the work of construction, the Prophet labored along with all the rest. The few palms that stood within the walls of the courtyard were hewn down, and their trunks were used as columns to support a roof of palm branches at the northern end. Most of the mosque was left open to the sky. Bricks were used for most of the construction, although stones were placed on either side of the prayer niche, or mihrab, that occupied the middle of the northern wall and marked the direction of Jerusalem.

25. Rodinson, pp. 149-50, explains the Syriac origin of the word (Arabic *masjid*), and describes the structure.

Now that Islam could manifest itself openly in Yathrib, believers routinely performed the five daily ritual prayers in the mosque as a congregation. People would judge the times of the day by checking the position of the sun in the sky and, when they felt it was the appropriate time for prayer, go to the mosque. In a relatively simple society like that of seventh-century Arabia, this was probably the customary mode of telling time. But it was too imprecise for managing congregational worship, and, rather like the need for a unified authority to settle disputes in Yathrib, Muslims soon realized that a single authority should determine the times of liturgical prayer in the mosque and announce the times to the worshipers dispersed throughout Yathrib and its environs. Some suggested using a horn, like the shofar of the Jews. The Prophet settled, for a time, on following the lead of certain eastern Christians: he had a wooden clapper made, a *naqus*. But this device was never used, for, shortly thereafter, a Khazrajite named Abd Allah b. Zayd, a man who had been present at the Second Pledge of Aqaba, related a dream to the Prophet in which he had been told that the best way to summon believers to prayer was by crying out "Allahu akbar" (God is most great). This was to be repeated four times, followed by a twofold repetition of each of the following phrases: "I testify that there is no god but God"; "I testify that Muhammad is the messenger of God"; "Come unto prayer"; "Come unto salvation"; "God is most great." The call to prayer was to be closed, then, with one final declaration that "There is no god but God."

Muhammad responded that this was indeed a true vision — it is noteworthy that he was not averse to recognizing divine inspiration in others — and he appointed the Abyssinian former slave Bilal, who had a strong voice, to be the first muezzin, or caller to prayer, in the history of Islam. Thereafter, at the appropriate times, Bilal would climb to the roof of the tallest house in the vicinity of the mosque and issue the call to prayer. From this rather humble beginning has come the romantic call of the minaret, one of the most characteristic and lovely aspects of daily life throughout the world of Islam.

Yathrib is not well known to most Westerners, despite its crucially important role in the life of the Prophet. Why? Because it soon lost its name. Instead of Yathrib, the oasis settlement began to be known as *madinat al-nabi*, "the city of the Prophet," or even simply as *al-madina*, "The City." And it is under this name, Medina, that it is universally known today.[26]

---

26. This is the standard account. However, Rodinson, p. 139, may be correct in contending that the name *Medina* antedates Muhammad's arrival.

The year of the *hijra,* rather than the birth year of Muhammad or the year of the commencement of his revelations, marks the beginning of the Muslim calendar.[27] This may seem strange, but it is really quite appropriate. For the move of Muhammad from Mecca to his new home placed Islam and its message, as well as the Prophet himself, on an entirely new plane. From being merely a messenger, a rather lonely voice crying in the wilderness, Muhammad became a prophet-statesman, the founder of a political order and eventually of an empire that would change the history of the world. And Islam took on a political dimension that it has never abandoned in all the centuries that have passed since then.

The people who had made the *hijra,* or emigration, with Muhammad to Yathrib came almost immediately to be known as the "Emigrants" or *muhajirun.* The natives of Medina who had converted to Islam were called the *ansar,* or "Helpers."[28] One of the first things Muhammad did upon establishing himself in Medina was to work out a covenant between the Helpers, the Emigrants, and the other monotheists of the town, the Jews, which has been known ever since — with a certain rough appropriateness — as the Constitution of Medina.[29] The notion was to link them together in a community, while allowing for the religious differences between the two faiths of Islam and Judaism and granting each a position of legal equality. They were to be allies against the polytheists, and promised that they would enter into no separate peace or alliance with pagans. (This provision would be important in subsequent events.) They were to defend each other against wrongs. In a

27. One cannot, however, determine a year in the Islamic calendar simply by subtracting 622 from the common era date. Islamic years are lunar, and hence are incongruent with the modified solar year of the Gregorian calendar. The year of the *hijra* was not actually selected as the starting point of the Muslim era until half a decade after the death of Muhammad, during the caliphate of Umar, in 637.

28. It may be significant that, as Serjeant, "Ḥaram and Ḥawṭah," p. 45, observes, the term *ansar* is used in modern-day Arabia for the tribes supporting a *hawta,* or sacred enclave.

29. Actually, as R. B. Serjeant has persuasively argued, the so-called Constitution is probably a composite document, composed on various occasions over time rather than at a single point. But the ramifications of this are beyond the scope of the present paper. See R. B. Serjeant, "The 'Constitution of Medina,'" *Islamic Quarterly* 8 (1964): 3-16; R. B. Serjeant, "The *Sunnah Jāmi'ah,* Pacts with the Yathrib Jews, and the *taḥrīm* of Yathrib: Analysis and Translation of the Documents Comprised in the So-called 'Constitution of Medina,'" *Bulletin of the School of Oriental and African Studies* 41 (1978): 1-42. Both articles are conveniently reprinted in Serjeant, *Studies in Arabian History and Civilisation.* For a good brief discussion of the document as we have it, see Peters, *Muhammad,* pp. 198-202.

marked departure from the tribal ethics of pre-Islamic Arabia, Muslims were to defend a Jew against injustice, even if that injustice had been committed by a fellow Muslim, and Jews were to take the part of an injured Muslim against a Jewish wrongdoer. Although the Jews were not required to recognize him as a prophet, Muhammad was to be the arbiter in disputed matters.

Muhammad was constructing a new Arabian community, an *umma*, in which the social bond was not blood but a shared faith, or at least a shared allegiance to him.[30] Political authority was a foreign concept to the pre-Islamic Arabs, but personal obligation and religious authority were not, and it was only on such a basis that any organization other than a kin group could be constructed in Arabia.[31] And in fact, it is very likely that "the ummah in the sense of a confederation round a religious nucleus was a pattern well established long before Muḥammad."[32] In any event, the Islamic *umma* became a kind of "supertribe," supplementing but not supplanting the social usages of its pagan, blood-based predecessors. It maintained pre-Islamic practices in such areas as property, marriage, and intratribal (i.e., intra-Muslim) relations, and it saw its relationships with non-Muslim Arabs, even with those related by blood, in much the way that members of one pre-Islamic kin group had seen their interactions with those of another: they were fair game for raiding and plundering.

A new Islamic community is precisely what Muhammad had set out to create in the first place; one of the recurring themes of the Qur'an is that revelation engenders communities. Additionally, the fact that Islam built a polity so early in its existence has had fundamental ramifications for its character to the present day. Where Christianity had three centuries in which to develop its own character before assuming political rule, Islam had existed for only a few years and was still in its initial stages of development. Accordingly, notions such as the separation of "church" and "state," which had a difficult enough time evolving within Christendom, have had virtually no soil from which to grow in Islam. For Christians who seek the ideal model there is Christ, who held no political office. Thus a Christian

---

30. See Watt, pp. 106-7.

31. Personal obligation, rather than political/institutional loyalties, continued to be an important element in the construction of Islamic polities for many centuries, as shown, for example, in Roy P. Mottahedeh's study of the Buyids in the tenth and eleventh centuries, *Loyalty and Leadership in an Early Islamic Society* (Princeton: Princeton University Press, 1980). It is still characteristic of the Near East in many ways.

32. Serjeant, "Ḥaram and Ḥawṭah," p. 49.

can follow Christ without attempting to implement Christianity via the state. The ideal Islamic paradigm, however, is Muhammad, who ruled a state for nearly half his prophetic ministry and received numerous revelations instructing him how to do it.

Given his new status as a ruler, Muhammad's role changed dramatically from what it had been in Mecca. From being a voice crying in the wilderness, he grew into a prophet and statesman. The change is clearly manifest in the revelations he received, and the distinction between Meccan and Medinan suras in the Qur'an is the fundamental chronological device for dating the revelations even today. Where the earlier, Meccan revelations tended to be short, composed of terse and powerfully poetic verses on apocalyptic themes, the later, Medinan revelations were much longer and dealt with legal, organizational, and sociopolitical issues as much as purely "religious" ones. Where the basic theology of Islam was in place by the time of the *hijra*, it was only in Medina that the details of Islamic cultic practice — in such matters as prayer, fasting, almsgiving, and pilgrimage — were revealed.

As part of the development of his new Islamic community in Medina, Muhammad appears to have established a *haram,* a sacred enclave, in his new residence to rival that of his hometown, Mecca.[33] Several years after his arrival there, he is said to have sent Ka'b b. Malik out to mark the points of the boundary of the *haram* about the settlement; some traditions relate that an area of twelve miles surrounding Medina was declared a *hima,* or inviolate pasture — perhaps this was a partial response to the Meccans' demand for a sacred and miraculous "garden" — and that, just as in Mecca, severe penalties were decreed for homicide committed within the *haram.* "Each prophet has a *haram,*" Muhammad is supposed to have said, "and Medina is my *haram.*" Or, according to another tradition, "Mecca was Abraham's *haram,* and Medina is my *haram.*" True to ancient Arabian tradition, Muhammad, scion of a holy family and now the lord of a sacred sanctuary in Medina, was the person, as the Constitution of Medina repeatedly stipulates, to whom disputes were to be referred for adjudication.[34] Like the bib-

---

33. Several decades later, having lost control (temporarily, as it turned out) of the sacred cities of Mecca and Medina, the Umayyad caliph Abd al-Malik did precisely the same thing: he established a *haram* — the word is still used for the area — around his new Dome of the Rock in Jerusalem, which is clearly designed for Meccan-style circumambulation centered on a sacred rock. On this, see Serjeant, "Ḥaram and Ḥawṭah," p. 56.

34. See the discussion of Serjeant, "Ḥaram and Ḥawṭah," pp. 50-51; compare Serjeant, "The Saiyids of Ḥaḍramawt," p. 15.

lical Samuel before him, he was seer, judge, and priest. He also established a market, something of a "free trade zone," which may have been connected with his sacred precinct, just as the two were connected in the commercial shrine town from which he had come.[35]

Muhammad's domestic routine in Medina was constrained by his obligations as the head of a community. A stone bench along one of the sides of the mosque was reserved for those who, newly arrived in Medina, had no place to live and no way to support themselves. Accordingly, they became known as "the people of the bench." The mosque was attached to the Prophet's house, and so he apparently felt himself responsible for these people, who had come to the town because they had heard reports of his prophethood and had accepted his message. He would often share his family's food with them, and apparently also called on those who lived in the immediate neighborhood of the mosque to do likewise. "The food of one person is enough for two," he used to say, "the food of two is enough for four, and the food of four is enough for eight." Yet his problems and challenges were far from over. The Qur'an speaks repeatedly of the various groups in Medina. Two of them were very much like the cast of characters in Mecca. There were the believers, who accepted the revelation of God, and the infidels, who rejected it.

> This is the book in which there is no doubt, a guidance
>   to the God-fearing,
> Who believe in the unseen, who pray, who expend from that
>   with which we have blessed them,
> And who believe in that which has been sent down upon you
>   and that which was sent before you, and who are certain
>   of the life to come.
> These are truly guided by their Lord, and these are they
>   who will prosper.
> As for the infidels, it is all the same to them whether you
>   warn them or you don't warn them: They will not believe.
> God has sealed their hearts and their hearing, and a veil covers
>   their sight, and a great punishment awaits them.[36]

35. The phrase is from Peters, *Muhammad*, pp. 197-98.
36. Q 2:2-7.

Besides the monotheistic Muslims and Jews, however, and the still-considerable number of people who simply had no interest and no faith in the new revelation, another group of Medinans confronted Muhammad with a challenge he had not been required to face in Mecca. These were the people the Qur'an labels with the unflattering title of "hypocrites" *(munafiqun)*.

> And among the people there are those who say, "We believe in God and in the Last Day," but they are not believers.
>
> They attempt to deceive God and those who believe, but they deceive only themselves and do not realize it.
>
> In their hearts is a disease, and God has increased their disease, and theirs is a painful punishment for the lies they tell.
>
> If it is said to them, "Do not spread corruption in the earth," they reply, "Why, we only want to do what is right!"
>
> But they are the spreaders of corruption, although they do not realize it.
>
> And if it is said to them, "Believe as the people believe!" they reply, "Shall we believe as the simpletons believe?" But they are the simpletons, though they don't know it.
>
> When they meet those who believe, they say, "We believe." But when they are alone with their satans, they say, "We are with you. We were only mocking."
>
> God will mock *them*. . . .
>
> These are they who have purchased error in exchange for guidance. But their commerce profits them nothing, and they will not be guided.[37]

In Mecca there had been no worldly inducement to feign acceptance of Islam. Conversion there brought disdain, ostracism, persecution, harassment, and occasionally torture and death. In the new climate of Medina, though, where the Prophet was the ruler of the community, insincere people could see outward profession of Islam as a route to social advancement, or at least as a means of preserving their earlier status or maintaining space in which to maneuver for advantage. Much as with Christianity in an earlier time, particularly following Constantine's legal establishment

---

37. Q 2:8-16.

of the church, the rapid expansion of Islam and its power now ensured that the Islamic community would never again be totally free — if it ever had been — of hypocrites with an eye open to worldly gain rather than the will of God.

The arch-hypocrite of the traditional sources is the Khazrajite named Abd Allah b. Ubayy, whom we have already met. He had valid reason to feel injured by the coming of Muhammad to Medina. As we have seen, amidst all the strife and bloodshed and the yearning for a strong central authority that eventually led to the summoning of Muhammad, Ibn Ubayy had been poised to become the ruler, if not the king, of the city. But Muhammad now filled the void into which Ibn Ubayy had been set to step. The Khazrajite seems to have decided from an early time to wait patiently, trying not to oppose the Prophet in any obvious way, even professing support for him, but endeavoring at the same moment to avoid giving any real support. Muhammad apparently understood this, and treated Ibn Ubayy, on the whole, with gentleness and sympathy throughout the man's life.

Attempting to unite the believers and to deal with the practical problem of how to sustain the Emigrants from Mecca, who had left their property and kinship networks behind to come to Medina, Muhammad created new relationships between them and the Helpers. Each Helper was assigned an Emigrant as a brother, for whom he was to have special, essentially kinlike responsibilities. Not wanting to create jealousies, the Prophet wisely exempted himself from this system, announcing rather that Ali — his cousin and son-in-law, and one of the earliest converts to Islam — was his brother. In the meantime he was entering into other important personal alliances as well. A'isha was the daughter of Muhammad's close friend and lieutenant Abu Bakr, and one of the first children to be born and raised a Muslim. Thus she knew only an Islamic home life, and she had grown up expecting the Prophet as a daily visitor to the home of her father. Gradually there grew in Muhammad the sense that A'isha was to be his wife, and he and Abu Bakr eventually signed a marriage contract making her so. A'isha herself was not present at the signing of the contract. She first learned about her marriage on a day when she was outside, playing with a few of her friends. Her mother came and took her by the hand, leading her inside. From now on, her mother told her, her friends must come to her house to play with her, since it was no longer appropriate for her, as a married woman, to be seen by everybody outside.

A'isha's betrothal to the Prophet took place when she was still living in Mecca and was only six years old, young even by the standards of ancient pagan Arabia. Her actual wedding to Muhammad occurred in Medina, in 623, when she was nine. She was too young, perhaps, to comprehend fully the significance of the event. In after years, at any rate, she recalled that, just before she and her family were supposed to leave their house for the ceremony, she had wandered off into the courtyard to play with a friend who had happened by. When the adults came to find her and prepare her for the wedding, she was playing on a seesaw with her hair flying in the breeze. And she was still a very young girl after her marriage to the Prophet. Her friends continued to visit her at her new home, where they would play with their dolls. But when the Prophet sometimes dropped in, the intimidated little girls would leave, and he had to go after them on occasion to bring them back for his wife to play with. Indeed, sometimes Muhammad himself joined in their play. A'isha would become, after Khadija, Muhammad's favorite wife, and in the years following the death of the Prophet, one of the major sources for information about his life, opinions, and practices. For, because of her youth when she married him, she outlived him for many years, and was one of the last intimate links to their prophet for the Muslims of the first generations after his passing. She always felt insecure, though, about her status in the affections of her husband, and required continual reassurance, especially when, as she apparently often did, she thought about his feelings for his departed first wife, Khadija, who had supported him during some of his greatest trials and disappointments.

As Muhammad's personal relationships changed, so too did the relationship of his religion to its Jewish precursor. Most ancient Semitic peoples prayed in a particular direction. Eastern Christians and others prayed to the east, in the direction of the rising sun. Jews and the earliest Muslims prayed toward Jerusalem.[38] Traditional sources say the first Muslim thought of praying toward Mecca rather than Jerusalem came to a chief of the Yathribi Khazraj by the name of Bara' even before the time of the *hijra*. He is said to have reasoned, as he and a number of his townspeople were making their way toward Mecca to meet the Prophet, that since Muhammad, the holy Ka'ba shrine, and the place of the revelation of the Qur'an were there, it was wrong that they turn their backs toward so holy a place in order to pray toward a city in far-off Palestine whose association with

---

38. See, for instance, 1 Kings 8:44 and Dan. 6:10.

prophets lay in the distant past. So he began for a brief period to pray to-ward Mecca, although his companions continued to follow what they cor-rectly believed to be, at the time, the practice of the Prophet. But God vin-dicated Bara'. In the month of Shaban in 624, Muhammad received a revelation whose importance can hardly be overstated, altering the direc-tion of prayer from facing Jerusalem to facing Mecca. He received it in a mosque belonging to the clan of Bara'. "The simpletons among the people will say, 'What has turned them from the prayer-orientation [*qibla*] that they were used to?' Say: 'To God belong both east and west.' He guides whomever He will to a straight path. . . . We see the turning of your face to the sky. Now we shall turn you to a *qibla* that will please you. Turn your face in the direction of the sacrosanct mosque. Wherever you are, turn your faces in that direction."[39] At the same time, a clan chief named Sa'd b. Mu'adh, a powerful rival of the "hypocrite" Ibn Ubayy — who had close ties to the local Jews — emerged as the leader of Muhammad's Medinan followers and a powerful ally to the Prophet. (Sa'd's harsh decision in the later case of the Banu Qurayza, a lethal one to be discussed below, may suggest ethnic or religious hostility.) Montgomery Watt sees practical po-litical considerations entering into the change, as well as revelation.[40] So the Muslims built a mihrab, a marker for the *qibla,* or direction of prayer, into the south wall of the mosque at Medina, facing Mecca and directly op-posite the former mihrab on the north wall, which had indicated the direc-tion of Jerusalem. At roughly the same time, the month-long Ramadan fast replaced the ten-day Jewish fast connected with the Day of Atonement, which the Muslims had observed as Ashura.[41] By these moves Islam made clear that it was not merely a strange sect of Judaism or Christianity. It was an independent, new, Arabian revelation.

39. Q 2:142, 144.
40. Watt, pp. 113-14.
41. Watt, pp. 99, 114.

Strife with Mecca

Not very long after his arrival in Medina, Muhammad received a revelation with fateful consequences for the subsequent history of Arabia and the world. "Permission is granted to those against whom war is being conducted, because they have been wronged. And truly God is able to grant them victory — those who have been unjustly expelled from their homes simply because they declare, 'Our Lord is God.'"[1] Muhammad had been facing a serious problem. His followers, who had fled Mecca with him, were now confronted with the necessity of earning a living in an agricultural settlement. But most of them had no agricultural experience at all (since Mecca was virtually without vegetation), and certainly no expertise in the cultivation of dates, and the arable land was in any event already divided up among the local population. Thus they had little choice but to hire themselves out to the Medinan Muslims and the Jews as day laborers. The work of drawing water from wells and tending date palms was demeaning and irregular. But the revelation offered a way out, consistent with the ethic of Arabia and with their own quite justifiable sense of having been wronged.[2]

In the fall and winter the caravans of Quraysh were generally directed to the south, particularly to the Yemen and, beyond that, to Abyssinia. But in the spring and early months of summer the caravans from Mecca went mostly northward, toward Syria, which meant they were po-

---

1. Q 22:39-40.
2. Watt, pp. 105-7, attempts to justify early Muslim raids within the ethical worldview of ancient Arabia.

tentially quite vulnerable to a hostile and highly motivated force operating out of Medina. The Muslims grasped this very quickly, and soon set about establishing alliances with the various bedouin tribes dwelling along the Red Sea coast where the trade routes ran. For their part the leaders of the Quraysh were not unaware of the threat they faced. But they must have been quite surprised when one of the first Muslim raids on their caravan traffic took place near Nakhla, a place between Mecca and Ta'if on the southern road to the Yemen. And their surprise was greatly magnified, beyond doubt, by the timing of the raid. Muhammad had sent one of his cousins along with eight other Muslims to spy on a caravan returning from the south, perhaps to find out how well guarded it would be. It was the month of Rajab, one of the four sacred months of the Arabian calendar in which fighting was prohibited.

The Prophet's instructions to the supposed reconnaissance party — sealed until the group was well away from Medina so as to avoid the intelligence leaks that seem to have spoiled earlier attempts — told them to proceed to Nakhla and attack the caravan. The letter did not mention the sacred months. When they found themselves, unobserved, looking over a small and vulnerable Meccan party bringing leather and raisins and other commodities from the Yemen, the temptation to attack the enemy was irresistible. But were the old Arabian taboos still in effect? By revelation God had authorized them, as aggrieved victims, to make war on those who had oppressed and robbed them, who were now profiting from and enjoying the property that the Emigrants had been forced to abandon. Could they wait for the attack? It was the last day of Rajab; in the morning the inviolable month would be past. But by that time the caravan would be within the sacred precinct surrounding Mecca. So they decided to attack, and their attack was quick and very successful. A fifth of the spoils were set aside for the Prophet, and the rest was divided among the members of the raiding party.[3] But their reception was at best cool when they returned to Medina. "I did not order you to fight in the sacred month," Muhammad told them, refusing to accept his designated portion of the booty. The Muslims and the Jews in Medina were unhappy with them for their violation of the taboo, and the Quraysh in

---

3. This may be significant, in regard to Muhammad's perceived status. In modern-day Arabia as well, the lord of a *hawta* or *haram* shrine enclave extracts from its people the *khums* tax — a "fifth," as its name indicates. See Serjeant, "Ḥaram and Ḥawṭah," p. 44. Arabian chieftains generally took a fourth, as Rodinson, p. 225, observes.

Mecca set about zealously to turn the episode into a public relations nightmare for the Prophet, who, they said, was guilty of sacrilege. But then came a revelation from God: "They ask you about fighting in the sacrosanct month. Say: 'Fighting therein is a serious offense. But barring men from the way of God and disbelief in him and in the sacrosanct mosque and driving his people from it are more serious with God. And persecution is more serious than killing.'"[4]

Muhammad said this revelation confirmed the customary ban on fighting in the sacred months — another indication of the truly Arabian character of the new religion — but also clearly justified an exception in the case of the Nakhla raid. He therefore accepted the fifth of the booty that the raiding party had allotted to him and, no doubt, greatly relieved the minds of the Muslim warriors, who feared that they had committed a sin and, perhaps worse, a blunder. Western students of Islam, however, have struggled with the morality of Muhammad's resort to offensive warfare. Tor Andrae, for example, calls it simple "banditry."[5] Maxime Rodinson labels it "brigandage."[6]

A much more serious battle took place in 624. A heavily laden Meccan caravan was returning from Syria, near the Red Sea shore. The sources say it included a thousand camels. Muhammad sent a party out to gather intelligence on the whereabouts, the numbers, and the armaments of the caravan. They apparently returned a glowing report, because Muhammad soon had a force of three hundred men eager to seize the caravan's wealth. Only a third of them were *muhajirun;* the rest were native Medinans.

The martial and martyr spirit that had taken root in Islam is illustrated poignantly by the story of a fifteen-year-old named Umayr, who stole along with the expeditionary force. When Muhammad assembled the warriors, he noticed Umayr, who, hoping perhaps to attain a martyr's death in conflict with the infidels, had been trying as hard as he could to look inconspicuous. Telling him that he was too young for warfare, Muhammad ordered Umayr to return home. But the boy wept so much that the Prophet relented and allowed him to come. "He was so young," the boy's cousin later recalled, "that I had to fasten the straps of his sword belt for him."

4. Q 2:217.
5. Andrae, *Mohammed,* p. 140.
6. Rodinson, p. 162.

The Prophet and his forces headed for Badr, a point on the coast route between Mecca and Syria. Muhammad sent a pair of observers ahead to discover what they could of the Meccan caravan's movements. But the caravan leader, Abu Sufyan, got word of the movements of the spies instead, and when he saw date stones in the dung left by their camels, he knew they were from Medina. Accordingly, he attempted to take evasive action and sent ahead to Mecca for reinforcements to guard the caravan. Eventually Abu Sufyan and the caravan did make their way safely home, evading the booty-seeking Medinans and leaving them to a battle over theology rather than spoils. Seeing now no threat to the caravan, the army that was still en route from Mecca desired to turn back. There seemed no purpose to any confrontation with Muhammad. But their leader, Abu Jahl, mocked them as cowards and urged them on.

The Muslim army hurried to reach the wells at Badr before the Meccans could get to them. At the first well they came to, Muhammad ordered his men to halt. But one of his fighters, a member of the Medinan tribe of Khazraj, came to him and asked, "O Messenger of God, this place that we are at now — Has God revealed it to you, so that we should neither move forward nor retreat from it, or is it a matter of opinion and military strategy?" Muhammad, who again showed here his willingness to learn from others and to adapt, replied that it was merely a matter of his own opinion. "This is not the place to stop," the Khazrajite then said. "Lead us further, O Messenger of God, until we come to the large well that is near the enemy. Let us then stop there and plug up the wells that are beyond it, and make a cistern for ourselves. Then we will fight the enemy, and all of the water will be ours to drink, and they will have none." The Prophet instantly agreed.[7] The Muslims stopped up the other wells, built a cistern, and filled their individual water containers. They now held a vastly important advantage over the Meccan army in the harsh desert environment. For the army's camels and men would be in desperate need of water, and the force from Medina controlled every available source.

On March 15, 624, the battle of Badr irretrievably altered the relations between the rising Islamic state in Medina and the pagan resistance headquartered at Mecca. When the forces of the Quraysh, needing the waters of Badr, began to advance toward the Muslims, they seemed few against the

7. For the incident and a slightly different alternate translation, see Guillaume, pp. 296-97.

vast background of the Arabian desert. But they outnumbered Muhammad and his men, and the Prophet withdrew to his tent to pray for divine help against them. When he emerged, he was able to tell Abu Bakr that no less a personage than Gabriel himself was on hand, armed for war and ready to assist the Muslims. A revelation received following the battle reminded Muhammad that "You implored your Lord for assistance, and he answered you: 'I will assist you with a thousand angels, rank upon rank.'"[8] The revelation even recounted the words of God to the angelic hosts: "I am with you. Fortify those who believe. I will cast terror into the hearts of the infidels, so you strike above their necks and strike off from them all their fingertips."[9] To his men the Prophet declared that the soul of any man killed that day while advancing against the enemy (retreating was another matter) would go immediately into the paradise of God. The early sources relate that young Umayr, when he heard of the Prophet's promise, was eating a handful of Medinan dates. "Wonder of wonders!" he cried out, tossing the dates to the ground and grabbing for his sword. "Is there nothing between me and my entry into paradise but that these men kill me?"

The battle commenced, as was the custom in ancient Arabia, with a series of single combats. The three chosen Muslim warriors, who included Muhammad's uncle Hamza and his cousin Ali, dispatched their three pagan opponents, but one of them, another relative of the Prophet named Ubayda, was himself fatally wounded. When he was carried back to the camp of the Muslims, his leg severed, he asked, "Am I not a martyr, O Messenger of God?" "Indeed, you are," the Prophet replied. A Khazrajite named Awf had actually been the first Muslim to accept the challenge of single combat, but Muhammad had restrained him. At this point, still standing beside the Prophet, he turned to Muhammad and asked, "O Messenger of God, what is it that causes the Lord to laugh with joy at his servant?" Muhammad responded that it was when such a servant plunged without armor into the midst of the enemy. At this, Awf removed the coat of mail that he was wearing. Meanwhile the Prophet reached down to the ground and brought up a handful of pebbles. Shouting "Defaced be those faces!" he flung them at the Quraysh and gave the order to charge.[10] "You

---

8. Q 8:9.

9. Q 8:12.

10. Widengren, *Ascension of the Apostle*, p. 28 n. 4, points to the analogous use of "battle magic" by Moses (Exod. 17:9-13) and Joshua (Josh. 8:18).

did not throw when you threw," a revelation to the Prophet commented after the battle, "rather it was God who threw."[11]

Awf was among the first to die. Later, veterans of the battle recalled that they had all felt the presence of angels during the fighting. Even the Meccans are supposed to have sensed something extraordinary, although they felt it not as joy but as terror. A few even claimed to have caught glimpses of the angelic host. A pair from a neighboring Arab tribe, not affiliated with either of the warring factions but watching, vulturelike, to see if any booty was to be had, stood at the top of a nearby hill to await the outcome. Suddenly a cloud rushed past them, filled with the loud neighing of stallions. One of the men instantly dropped dead of fright. A believer, in hot pursuit of one of the Meccans, was astonished to see the man's head severed from his body with nobody visibly near enough to have struck the blow. Yet others reported fleeting glimpses of angelic horses whose feet never touched the sand, ridden by supernatural beings in white turbans. (Only one, Gabriel, wore a yellow turban to indicate his archangelic status.)

When the fighting was over, between fifty and seventy of the Meccans were dead, including Abu Jahl. A number of prisoners were taken, and, true to form, Umar favored executing them all. Muhammad contented himself, though, with demanding ransoms for the prisoners. He ordered the execution of two men, both of whom knew something of Jewish and Persian lore and had mocked him with difficult questions. When one of them rather plaintively asked, "But who will take care of my sons, Muhammad?" the Prophet responded tersely, "Hell!" Only fourteen Muslims died at the battle of Badr. Among them was the fifteen-year-old Umayr, so young and so eager for martyrdom.

The bodies of the slain Meccans were thrown, at the Prophet's order, into a pit. Among them was the father of one of the Muslims. The son's face was sorrowful as his father's body was dragged toward the common grave. But when the Prophet noticed his sorrowing look and expressed compassion, the son quickly regained his composure. It was not, he said, that he questioned the Prophet's choice of a burial place for his infidel father. It was only that he had once known his father to be a man of wise counsel and virtue, and that he was sad to see his father die a pagan despite such qualities.

Muhammad's position was now immeasurably strengthened. His

11. Q 8:17.

unexpected defeat of a much larger force, sent from the great commercial power of Mecca, taught others to look on him with a new respect. In the minds of the Muslims, Badr was and is the great deliverance of God's people, comparable to the escape of the children of Israel from the armies of Pharaoh at the Red Sea. The ransoms paid into Muhammad's coffers for the release of prisoners gave him new leverage among his followers and with his rivals in Medina.

The momentum of the growth of Islam began to pick up substantially at around this time, and the success at Badr was certainly no hindrance to that. The story of Salman will serve to illustrate the appeal of Islam beyond its initial Arab audience. Salman was born a Zoroastrian in Persia, but he had converted to Christianity as a young man and gone to Syria and then to Iraq, associating himself always with Christian bishops and other wise Christian saints. As might have been predicted, Muslim tradition says that the last of these, speaking from his deathbed, told Salman that the time had come for a new prophet to appear and to restore in Arabia the true religion of ancient Abraham. Much like the monks of Bostra, he told Salman of the signs that would confirm the identity of the new prophet, including the seal of prophecy that would be found between his shoulders. The prophet, said the dying saint, would be forced to leave his home, but would make his way to a place of palm trees, situated between two lava flows. The place in question was none other than Yathrib, or Medina. Salman, the eager religious seeker, now determined to make his way to Arabia, to find this prophet of whom he had been told. He paid some Arabian caravan merchants to take him back with them to their native country, but they treacherously sold him into slavery. Eventually, though still a slave, he arrived in Yathrib and knew at once that this was the place he sought. Within a very short time of Muhammad's entry into the town, Salman had managed to meet him, and it took very little to convince the Persian slave that this was indeed the prophet for whom he had yearned.

On the other side, the death of many of the Meccan elite at Badr left Abu Sufyan the leading man of the Quraysh by default. And he was not inclined at this stage to compromise. In this he was supported by his wife Hind, who had lost several relatives at Badr, including her brother, her uncle, and her father — the latter two killed by Hamza, Muhammad's formidable uncle. Hind vowed that when the Quraysh finally defeated the Muslims, she would personally eat Hamza's liver raw from his body. In the meantime, despite the Muslim victory, the rich treasure of the caravan that had been the original Muslim target arrived safely at Mecca, and the leadership of the city unanimously resolved that all the profits from that caravan would be devoted to raising an invincible army to crush the upstarts in Medina. This time, too, following an ancient Arabian custom, the women would accompany the men of the army to urge them on and encourage them to acts of heroism. (And to provide tangible evidence, no doubt, of what another defeat would immediately cost them — their women.)

Muhammad decided that he needed to consolidate his position in Medina, and to eliminate potentially threatening weaknesses. He took action almost immediately against Asma bt. Marwan, a poetess whose verses had satirized and attacked him.[12] A Muslim member of her clan who had failed to join the fight at Badr demonstrated his loyalty to the Prophet by running her through with a sword at night, while she slept with her children. A month later another poet, the centenarian Abu Afak, met the same fate during his sleep for the same offense.

Muhammad was very concerned about the power of poets. The reason was not necessarily that he shared the ancient Arabian notion of poets as inspired by the jinn (*majnun*, which, as noted, has come to mean simple insanity in modern Arabic), although he very likely did. Rather he recognized the immense practical power that a poet possessed. For poets, in early Arabia, were very much like today's advertising executives or public relations consultants. To have one in one's tribe, praising the virtues and achievements of one's tribe in memorable lines that would be repeated, if they found audience appeal, from one end of Arabia to another, was a great blessing and asset. But to have a poet in a rival tribe satirizing one's tribe or clan in memorable and repeatable verses was a curse like no other, and was deemed an injury as serious as, if not more serious than, a defeat in literal battle. For a successful poet was not merely one enemy. As his verses began to be adopted and repeated by others, he became many foes.

The Quraysh knew the power of poets. The tale is told of the poet al-A'sha, who once set out to visit Muhammad at Medina in order to recite an ode that he had composed in the Prophet's honor. When the Quraysh heard of his intention, they were terrified, and they instantly set out to intercept him on his way. When he acknowledged that he was going to Medina to accept Islam, the Meccans pointed out that Muhammad's doctrine

12. The abbreviation "bt." represents the Arabic word *bint* (daughter [of]), the feminine equivalent of *ibn* (son [of]).

would prohibit certain things of which he was very fond. Al-Aʿsha asked for specifics. "Fornication," responded Abu Sufyan, the spokesman for the Qurayshi delegation. Al-Aʿsha replied that that would be no loss since, although he had not forsaken fornication, it had (presumably because of his advanced age) forsaken him. When mention of Islamic prohibitions against gambling, usury, and wine also failed to move him, Abu Sufyan offered the old poet a hundred camels if he would return to his home in Yamama and simply await the outcome of the struggle between the Quraysh and Muhammad. Al-Aʿsha accepted the offer, and Abu Sufyan turned to his associates. "O Quraysh!" he cried. "This is al-Aʿsha, and, by God, if he becomes a follower of Muhammad, he will inflame the Arabs against you with his poetry. So collect a hundred camels for him!"

Muhammad's own fear of the power of poets is apparent again in the story of Kaʿb b. al-Ashraf, a poet of the Jewish Banu al-Nadir, who composed verses satirizing the Prophet and his associates and summoning the Quraysh to take revenge for their defeat at Badr. It finally became intolerable for Muhammad, and he is said to have prayed, "O Lord, deliver me from the son of al-Ashraf however you choose, on account of the evil he declares and the poems he recites." Then, turning to those present, he said, "Who is for me against the son of al-Ashraf? For he has injured me greatly."[13] Five Muslims volunteered. But, as they thought about how they might gain access to Kaʿb and kill him, they began to realize that some form of deception would be necessary if they were to be successful and not become involved in a dangerous pitched battle with the entirety of the Banu Nadir, for Kaʿb had taken up his residence in their fortified stronghold and could not be easily reached.

They were troubled in conscience, for they wanted to carry out the Prophet's apparent desires, but they saw no way to do it except through a kind of treachery, and they knew that Muhammad hated treachery and lying. However, he assured them that they could do or say whatever they

---

13. The words are not unlike those attributed to Henry II ("Who will rid me of this turbulent priest?"), which led, whether by design or not, to the death of Saint Thomas à Becket. Note that Kaʿb's poetry was supposed to have done Muhammad real injury. The mentality here is a great distance from our common notion that "sticks and stones may break my bones, but words can never hurt me." Names, words, were thought to have their own intrinsic and potentially dangerous power. The modern case of the Anglo-Indian writer Salman Rushdie has its roots, in a certain sense, in the case of Kaʿb b. al-Ashraf and other poets who were targets of Muhammad's wrath.

needed to in order to accomplish their mission, for, he said, deception was legitimate as a stratagem of war, and since Ka'b's poetic attacks on him were acts of war, lying was legitimate here.[14] And indeed, in September 624, despite the warnings of the girl he had with him in bed, Ka'b was eventually lured from his fortress under false pretenses and killed. His triumphant assassins returned to the Prophet and laid Ka'b's head at his feet.

W. Montgomery Watt attempts to put the episode, a horrible act by modern standards, into perspective:

> In the gentler or (should we say?) less virile age in which we live men look askance at such conduct, particularly in a religious leader. But in Muḥammad's age and country it was quite normal. Men had no claims upon you on the basis of common humanity. Members of your tribe and of allied tribes, and those protected by your tribe, had very definite claims; but outside this circle no one had any claim at all. That is to say, in the case of a stranger or enemy there was no reason why you should not kill him if you felt inclined. . . . A man like Ka'b ibn-al-Ashraf was a clear enemy of the Islamic community, and so there was no obligation to consider him in any way. . . . So far were the Muslims who killed him from having any qualms about it that one of them, describing the return from the deed, wrote that they returned "five honourable men, steady and true, and God was the sixth with us."[15]

The Jews of the Banu Nadir were, naturally, both incensed and terrified at what had been done to one of them and at the seemingly underhanded way in which the act had been carried out. A delegation of their leaders went to the Prophet, complaining that one of them had been treacherously murdered — in their view, without cause. However, Muhammad did not apologize or acknowledge that they had a grievance. Rather he noted that Ka'b's execution — for so he viewed it — was entirely justified. "If he had remained as others of the same opinion are," the Prophet said, knowing full well that the opinion of him among the Nadir leaders was probably indistinguishable from that of their late poet, "he would not have been killed by stratagem. But he injured us and composed poetry against us, and none of you shall do this or he too shall be killed."

---

14. Again, the Arabian understanding of poetry as a real weapon is apparent.
15. Watt, pp. 128-29.

The Qur'an warned believers against the designs of those in Medina who appeared to be friends but were, in reality, enemies.

> Oh you who believe! Do not take outsiders as your close friends. They will not fail to corrupt you. They desire your ruin. Hatred has already appeared from their mouths; what their breasts conceal is still worse. . . . You are those who love them, but they do not love you although you believe in the entirety of the Book. When they meet you, they say "We believe." But when they are alone, they gnaw their fingers against you for rage. Say, "Die in your rage! God knows what is in your hearts." If any good thing touches you, it grieves them. But if some evil strikes you, they rejoice at it. Still, if you are patient and devout, their scheming will not harm you in the slightest. Truly, God encompasses what they do.[16]

Troubles between the Muslims and the Jews of the Banu Qaynuqa came to a head over a trivial incident that occurred in the marketplace of Medina. A Muslim woman who had come to do business there was grossly insulted by one of the Jewish goldsmiths. A Medinan convert who was nearby came to her assistance, and in the struggle that followed, the goldsmith was killed.[17] At that the surrounding Jews attacked and killed the Muslim man who had aided his sister in the faith. True to Arabian custom, his family then demanded vengeance, stirring up hostile feelings among the so-called Helpers against the Jews. Even at this tense moment, though, the situation could have been resolved under the provisions of the so-called Constitution of Medina, had the parties resorted to arbitration as that document specified. Instead the Qaynuqa withdrew into their strongholds, which were fortified and stocked with provisions, and appealed to Ibn Ubayy and others of their former allies, the Khazraj, to come to their defense.

In the end, it was no good. After more than two weeks of blockade, the Jews surrendered. Some sources record that Muhammad wanted to execute them all, but that Ibn Ubayy passionately confronted him and, in a scarcely veiled threat, warned him that human events go in cycles. The Qaynuqa were ultimately obliged to migrate toward Syria, leaving their property be-

---

16. Q 3:118-20.
17. Watt, p. 130, doubts the traditional story of the goldsmith's insult.

hind. The Meccan Emigrants now moved into their deserted houses and, abandoning their work as day laborers, resumed their more accustomed activity as merchants. The Qaynuqa had probably been the weakest of the Jewish tribes in Medina, but they had been supporters and allies of Ibn Ubayy, who still saw himself as Muhammad's rival for temporal power in the oasis, and their removal benefited Muhammad immensely.

Other things in Muhammad's life were also going well. When Fatima, the youngest of his daughters, was about twenty years old, the Prophet married her to his cousin Ali. This bound Ali even more closely to the Prophet, who was now his father-in-law. Earlier Uthman b. Affan, who was to precede Ali as the third successor to Muhammad, had married Fatima's older sister Ruqayya. During the fasting month of Ramadan, just before the first anniversary of the Muslim victory in the battle of Badr, Fatima gave birth to a son, the Prophet's grandson, who would receive the name of al-Hasan, "the beautiful."

At the end of the month, though, Muhammad received word that a force of three thousand men was marching forth from Mecca against him. The sources say that seven hundred of the men bore armor and two hundred rode on horseback. It was, by the standards of early Arabia, a formidable army. In the week of preparation left to them, the Medinans concentrated on bringing all the people and animals in from the outlying areas of the settlement. Then they could only wait to see what the precise intention or plan of the Meccans might be. It soon became evident. The army came up the western caravan route, near the Red Sea coast. Then they turned inland and passed within about five miles of Medina before continuing on to its northeast. There, in an area of cultivated land in the plain at the base of Mount Uhud, which looks down upon Medina from the north, they came to a halt. The Prophet's scouts were able to confirm the predicted numbers and strength of the Meccan army, which included allies from Thaqif and Kinana and other groups. Worse, they reported that the large number of men and animals were devouring the pasture and consuming the crops to the north of the city, which had not yet been harvested. In a region where cultivable land and pasture were rare and where alternative food sources were very distant, this was serious news indeed. Even without striking a blow, the Meccans represented a serious threat to Medina. Moreover, the scouts said, there were no signs that the Meccans were in any particular hurry. With an abundance of Medinan pastureland and food, they could remain where they were indefinitely.

Nonetheless, Muhammad was at first inclined simply to wait his enemies out. He held a council with the leaders of the town and asked their advice. Ibn Ubayy, too, counseled restraint. Medina, he said, was like a virgin that had never been violated. No enemy had ever entered her without suffering defeat and severe losses. On the other hand, he declared, the Medinans had never gone out from her against an enemy without themselves suffering severe casualties. Eventually, Ibn Ubayy predicted, the Meccans would return home in frustration, having accomplished nothing. Others, both Emigrants and Helpers, agreed with Ibn Ubayy and supported Muhammad in his initial decision. If they simply remained within their fortifications, the cavalry of the Quraysh would be useless.

But the younger men were not satisfied. Hotheaded, perhaps, they did not want the Meccans to feel that the armies of Islam were too weak, or that they feared them. What is more, the argument went, to leave the Meccans unpunished despite their theft of Medinan crops and pasturage would be to encourage them to repeat such actions in the future, and would embolden the Meccans' bedouin allies to further depredations. Better to act now than to face worse situations in the days to come. Had the Prophet forgotten the experience of Badr, where he had inflicted a terrible defeat upon Quraysh with an army only a fraction of theirs in size? Now he was stronger. Why fear the godless forces of the enemies of Islam? One of the older men in the assembly then arose and spoke more personally. During the previous night, he reported, his son, who had been among the few Muslims killed at Badr, had appeared to him in a dream, standing in immortal beauty among the gardens of paradise. His son had confirmed to him that everything they had been told of paradise and the life to come was true, and had invited him to join him and the other martyrs there. Finally Malik b. Sinan stood, pointing out that there were really only two outcomes that could follow a Muslim attack upon the Meccan army: If the Muslims triumphed, that would be good. But if the Muslims were defeated, their dead would enter instantly into paradise, and that too was good. So there was really nothing to be lost either way. It soon became apparent that a majority of the assembly desired to take military action. Muhammad decided to attack.

The attitude of the Muslim army is clearly illustrated by the stories of two men who sought Muhammad out at the close of the meeting. One told of a dream he had experienced, rather like the one just recounted. In it he had been promised martyrdom and paradise, and he was eager to go to war. Muhammad confirmed his interpretation of the dream, and the man, a widower with a son and seven daughters, immediately went home to make arrangements for the maintenance of his daughters after his anticipated death. His son, too, was eagerly preparing for battle, but the father forbade him, requiring him to stay home to look after the unmarried girls. Another man, named Hanzala, told the Prophet that he was eager to fight, but that he was set to be married that day and did not want to postpone the wedding. Muhammad advised him to go ahead with the wedding and to spend the night in Medina. He could join the Muslim forces on the following day; no military action was likely to occur before then anyway. (That night, following their wedding, Hanzala's wife would have a dream in which she saw him standing at the entrance to paradise. A door opened for him, and he passed through it, whereupon the door closed on him and he was lost to her view. The next morning, although she begged him to stay with her and not to go out to battle, and although they both understood perfectly well what her dream portended, Hanzala could not be dissuaded from joining the Muslim forces on the plain before Mount Uhud.) There were still those, perhaps a majority among the older and wiser Medinans, who felt that Muhammad's first inclination had been the correct one. And perhaps certain others who had voiced a desire for battle were now reconsidering what they had said in the enthusiasm of a mass assembly. Give the decision back to the Prophet, some said. You have forced him to go against his first judgment, and it is he who communicates with God. But when the Prophet emerged from his house clad in armor, he informed them that prophets do not remove their armor once they have put it on, before they have gone forth against their enemies. Muhammad could probably not afford to give further evidence of indecision. His course was now fixed. He mounted his horse, slung his bow over his shoulder, and took a spear in his hand. Nobody else among his force, which numbered approximately one thousand, was mounted.

The Prophet gathered with his warriors at a place called Shaykhayn, which was located approximately halfway between Medina and Uhud. There he surveyed the men at his disposal. Among his soldiers Muhammad noticed eight boys who were, he felt, too young to participate in combat, and he ordered them to go home. Two, however, claiming and demonstrating great prowess in archery and wrestling, convinced him that they should be allowed to stay.

In the predawn hours of the next morning, when the Prophet ordered the Muslim army to be prepared to continue on to Uhud, Ibn Ubayy, who had evidently spent the previous evening discussing the situation with some of those who, like himself, were not entirely convinced of Muhammad's inspiration, instead took three hundred men — roughly 30 percent of the already grossly outnumbered Muslim force — and returned to Medina. As he explained it, Muhammad had refused to take his advice, but had instead listened to young men, zealots without sound judgment, and he could see no reason why he and those who followed him should lose their lives in a quixotic and foolish effort such as this.

Though weakened, the army from Medina nonetheless moved toward the Meccan force under the cover of early-morning darkness. No doubt aided by their superior knowledge of the local geography, they were able to position themselves between Mount Uhud and the Meccans — which gave them the considerable advantage of being uphill from their enemies. There they performed the morning prayer, simultaneously facing Mecca and their Meccan foe.

Muhammad placed a company of his finest archers on an elevation somewhat to the left of the main body of his fighters, with orders that they were to maintain their position there whatever seemed to be happening on the battlefield. They were not to leave their assigned location even if the Muslims appeared to be losing the struggle, and they were certainly not to evacuate it for the sake of grabbing booty if the battle seemed to be won. Their vitally important task was to protect the Muslim army against the highly mobile cavalry of its Meccan opponents, for which the Prophet had no equivalent force, and especially to keep the cavalry from coming in and attacking the Medinans from the rear.

When the sun rose over the plain of Uhud, the Meccans were already drawn up in a battle line. The Medinans watched in fury as men and horses trampled their rich barley and corn crops underfoot. The holy family known as the Banu Abd al-Dar, the "sons of the slave of the House," bore the standard of the Ka'ba and the Meccan *haram*.[18] On the right wing Khalid b. al-Walid (who, ironically, would later become one of the greatest generals of the Arab conquests, "the sword of Islam") commanded a hundred men on horseback; on the left Ikrima b. Abi Jahl controlled an equivalent number. In the center Abu Sufyan bore overall command. It was he who gave the order to advance.

18. Serjeant, "Ḥaram and Ḥawṭah," p. 54.

After an exchange of speeches and verbal abuse, however, it was the Muslims who began the actual combat, sending a flight of arrows into Khalid's cavalry. There followed a series of single combats, in which the Muslims — notable among them Ali and the Prophet's uncle Hamza — were very successful. A major setback to the Muslim forces came early in the battle, however, when an Ethiopian slave, an expert javelin thrower who had been promised his freedom if he killed Hamza, succeeded in slaying that fearsome warrior with a single long-distance strike. The newlywed Hanzala, who fought heroically, also fell early on, fulfilling the portentous dream of his young wife.

On the whole, however, the Muslim forces continued to advance against their Meccan enemies, and when it became apparent that they were likely to lose, the pagans began to flee in disarray. The opening in their ranks left the Meccan camp undefended, and, true to the nature of ancient Arabian warfare, a rush to take plunder now began. Muslim discipline itself collapsed at the very moment of triumph. Most significantly, a sizable body of the archers Muhammad had placed on the hill overlooking the battle, commanding them not to leave their post, now abandoned their position in a headlong rush for booty. The battle, they felt, was over, and they did not intend to be left out of the spoils.

The Meccan general Khalid, giving a foretaste of the military talent he would later display in the great Arab conquests that followed the death of the Prophet, immediately sensed what had happened and grasped his opportunity. Gathering his cavalry, who until now had scarcely been a factor in the battle, he charged the hill where a very small group of archers had remained faithful to Muhammad's assignment. He and his men killed them, every one. Then he attacked the main Muslim forces from their unprotected rear. Ikrima, the other cavalry commander, brought his troops into the same position as well, and together the two units of horsemen did great damage to the largely defenseless Muslims. The momentum of the battle had changed swiftly and lethally. As the Muslims turned to face the Meccan cavalry, the demoralized pagans who had been retreating before them now wheeled about and, renewed in spirit, attacked again. The struggle began slowly to move up the slopes of Mount Uhud, toward the place where Muhammad himself had taken his position. Some of the Muslims now fled for their lives.

The great concern of the Muslims who remained more or less lucid during these terrible moments suddenly became the safety of the Messenger of God, toward whom the fighting was swiftly moving. He and those immediately around him were defending themselves with volleys of arrows, greatly advantaged by their location on the slope where the cavalry of the Quraysh were unable to reach them, but they could not hold the seemingly inexorable Meccan attack off forever. For one thing, their supply of arrows was finite. Moreover, as the fighting came ever closer, archery became almost useless. Nonetheless, the Prophet and his little band of defenders, which included two women, fought fiercely. In the struggle Muhammad himself was nearly killed when a sword blow glanced off the side of his helmet, drove a portion of it into the flesh of his cheek, and knocked him briefly unconscious. Several among his bodyguard died. The Prophet's standard-bearer was cut down only a few feet from where the Messenger of God stood. The rumor now began to spread throughout the two armies that Muhammad himself, the hope of the Muslims and the bane of the pagan Quraysh, was dead.

And once again the indiscipline that characterized much early Arabian warfare came into play. The pagans could see that the battle had gone their way. They had regained their honor after the humiliating defeat at Badr. Now, hearing that the Prophet was dead, they relaxed their effort. And for those in close proximity to Muhammad and his guard, there seemed no further purpose in risking one's life against people who fought like dragons.

Only about twenty-two of the Meccan force had lost their lives, compared to approximately sixty-five slain among the Muslims. The pagans could not fail to take satisfaction in the ratio. But, try though they might, they could not find the body of Muhammad, whom they were certain they had killed. Still, there was reason enough for celebration, and some of it was conducted in a way that showed with painful clarity how little distance separated some of the Meccan pagans from sheer barbarism. Hind, the wife of Abu Sufyan, had made a vow to eat raw the liver of Hamza, the Prophet's uncle, because of the damage he had inflicted on her family at the earlier battle of Badr. This she now did, at least in a token portion. Not content with that, however, she mutilated him, cutting off his nose and his ears and other pieces of his flesh and making them into ornaments, and leading the women of Quraysh in doing similar things to others among the Muslim dead. Indeed, some of the Meccan men joined in such behavior, until the disgust and outrage of their bedouin allies shamed them into stopping it. Afterward, furious at learning what had been done to Hamza and other Muslim casualties, Muhammad vowed that he would mutilate thirty Meccans at the next opportunity. But a revelation soon advised him against such action, and he never fulfilled his vow. Indeed, he subsequently forbade his followers to mutilate the bodies of the dead, and taught them to show particular respect to the human face, for it was created, he said, in the image of God himself.

Abu Sufyan, perhaps by now suspecting that Muhammad was not dead after all, was nevertheless determined to make plain what he regarded as the lesson of the day. He rode to a point on the slope of the mountain, near the spot where Muhammad had last been sighted, and cried out, "War goes by turns, and this is a day in exchange for a day. Exalt yourself, O Hubal!" he said, addressing one of the pagan deities. "Make your religion prevail!" But Muhammad would not concede the last word to his pagan adversary. Instead, he ordered Umar to stand at the edge of a cliff above Abu Sufyan and to call out, "God is Most High, supreme in his majesty. We are not equal: Our dead are in paradise; yours are in Hell." Abu Sufyan, who knew that Umar could be trusted, now took the opportunity to settle the question once and for all. Was Muhammad dead? Umar replied that he was not, and that he was even now listening to their conversation.

Finally the pagans withdrew from the field, and the Muslims were greatly relieved to see them returning to Mecca rather than following up their advantage against the severely damaged and rather demoralized believers by attacking Medina. The Meccans knew better, perhaps, than to launch a difficult siege against the Medinans in their fortified settlements, which could only serve to unite the Jews and the faction of Ibn Ubayy with the Muslims in shared resentment. Their cavalry would be of no use in such a siege, and their infantry, on which the burden of the campaign would fall, had not performed especially well during the battle just concluded.

In a show of strength and perhaps bravado, the Prophet instantly ordered a force of Muslims, under his own leadership (though he himself was suffering badly from a sword blow to his shoulder), to follow the Meccan force as it returned homeward. That a show was intended is demonstrated by the fact that Muhammad, far from pursuing his enemies in stealth, went to great lengths to have his army observed. Indeed, he sought to deceive the pagans into overestimating his strength. At their first encampment out of Medina, at the Prophet's direction, the Muslims scattered themselves out over a wide area and then, gathering large quantities of wood, lit a fire for each man in the pursuing force (who reportedly numbered more than five hundred). It was a militarily risky move but, as psychological warfare, it was extremely effective. If the Quraysh and their allies had entertained any thoughts of returning to Medina and finishing off the wounded Muslim state — and the sources suggest that such notions were indeed under consideration — the deliberately misleading impression that Muhammad's stratagem gave to them, that there were hundreds of eager Muslim warriors hot on their trail, strangled the idea in its infancy. They could not even be sure that they had won.

And in fact, it is not clear in retrospect that Uhud was a Meccan victory, though it is generally described as such. Obviously it was a serious psychological blow to the Muslims. If Badr had been a sign of God's miraculous intervention and of his care for the new community, how was Uhud to be interpreted? But the Meccans had sought to eliminate Muhammad, and they had failed. Where once they had controlled much of Arabia, they had now managed at best to even the score of dead against the upstart Prophet.

In the next couple of months the Prophet would find himself obliged to take further military action in order to stave off attacks from those who, following the apparent setback at Uhud, thought to take advantage of what they thought would be Muslim weakness. When the Banu Asad b. Khuzayma tribe, allies of the Quraysh based in Najd, began preparations for a raid on Medina, Muhammad dispatched a small but well-equipped force to raid them first. The resulting battle was militarily inconclusive but highly effective politically. The tribesmen scattered, and the Muslim warriors returned home with camels and other plunder. At about the same time, the Prophet decreed the assassination of a chief of the Banu Lihyan, who was also planning an attack on the oasis of Medina. Again the attack fulfilled its purpose; no Lihyanite raid occurred.

Muhammad's departure from Medina created more than merely military risks, however. Back in the city, Ibn Ubayy was speaking with anyone who would listen about the foolishness of Muhammad's going out against the Meccans to battle. The results of the fighting had simply confirmed, in Ibn Ubayy's view, that he had been right to take his fighters and return to the city. And he was not alone. The sources suggest that many of the Medinan Jews, chafing under the chieftainship of this parvenu non-Hebrew claimant to prophecy, saw evidence of Muhammad's merely human status in his military defeat at Uhud. The Qur'an responded to such talk in a verse that would prove important for the day, some years in the future, when Muhammad really would depart from the scene and his followers would be obliged to carry on without him. "Muhammad," the revelation declared, "is nothing but a messenger. Many messengers have passed away before him. So if he were to die or were killed, would you turn upon your heels? Whoever turns upon his heels does not hurt God a bit, and God will reward the thankful."[19]

The Muslims, too, responded to the insinuations of Ibn Ubayy, who found his status in the town further reduced rather than enhanced by his conduct. Where his importance in pre-Muslim Medinan society had once secured him a privileged place in the mosque, he was now barred from it.

More serious social dislocations were about to follow, however. Sometime after Uhud, Muhammad was invited to a dinner hosted by the Jewish tribe called the Banu Nadir in their fortified settlement somewhat to the south of the main part of the Medinan oasis. But while he was waiting to be ushered in to the meal, the angel Gabriel came to him and warned him that the Jews were in fact planning to kill him, and that he must return home immediately. Nobody else saw the angel, and Muhammad left his associates there with neither explanation nor word of any kind. When he did not return, his companions also left. Muhammad then sent to the Banu Nadir a messenger, who not only recounted to them in precise detail the character of their plot but announced to them the fateful decree of the Prophet: They had ten days to leave the vicinity of Medina. Any member of their tribe found in the area thereafter would be decapitated.

Ibn Ubayy, though weaker than ever — indeed, perhaps *because* he felt himself weaker than ever, and bound to grow weaker still if his fellow critics of Muhammad were exiled — sent word to the Banu Nadir to stay, while others convinced them that their allies among the bedouin, and their fellow Jews, the Banu Qurayza, would stand by them. So the Jews determined to stay, and announced their determination to the Prophet, who regarded it as a declaration of rebellion and war. In little time at all, he and his followers were besieging the Jews in their fortresses, with arrows and stones passing back and forth until sunset. To the dismay of the besieged Banu Nadir, however, their expected reinforcements did not arrive. Ibn Ubayy, to the further diminution of his credibility, was unable to deliver any support whatever. After ten days or so, the Jews saw that their position

19. Q 3:144.

was hopeless. After some negotiation, they finally agreed to leave their land in Medina, taking with them all that they could load on camelback except their weapons and their armor. A revelation preserved in the Qur'an commented on these events and predicted the outcome:

> Have you not observed the hypocrites, saying to their brothers among the people of the Book who disbelieve, "If you are exiled, we will go into exile with you, and we will not obey anyone in your affair. And if you are attacked, we will help you." But God bears witness that they are lying. If they are exiled, they will never go into exile with them, and if they are attacked, they will not help them. And if they do help them, they will [eventually] turn their backs, and then they will not be helped. Truly, you are stronger than they are, owing to the terror in their breasts from God. That is because they are a people who do not comprehend. They will not fight you, except in fortified villages or from behind walls. Their hostility among themselves is strong. You think them united, but their hearts are divided. That is because they are a people who do not think.[20]

It was disunity, both between the Jews and their pagan allies and among the Jews themselves, that made Muhammad's successful siege of them possible. Then the revelation made a very unflattering comparison of the Jews' purported allies to the devil, and predicted the ultimate end of both groups: "Like Satan, when he says to a human being 'Disbelieve!' And when he does disbelieve, he says 'I have nothing to do with you. I fear God, the lord of the worlds.' The final end of both of them will be the inferno, dwelling in it forever. That is the reward of those who do wrong."[21]

The proximate factor in the surrender of the Banu Nadir was Muhammad's order to begin felling the date palm trees that were their pride and the chief source of their wealth. It is possible that they still held out hope of someday returning to their position within Medina; certainly the Quraysh were still promising to eradicate Islam and the rule of Muhammad, hateful both to the Meccan pagans and many of the Medinan Jews, and the defeat at Uhud made it plausible that they might succeed. Thus they probably still expected to return after a shorter or longer period to the

20. Q 59:11-14.
21. Q 59:16-17.

119

enjoyment of their lands and their trees. But if those trees were felled, it would take many years to replace them even if their most optimistic anticipations came true.

So the Banu Nadir left Medina. They went out in a blaze of glory and wealth, dressed in their finest jewels and accompanied by the sound of timbrels and fifes. Some went all the way to Jericho in Palestine, or to the north in Syria, but many settled on lands they owned at the oasis of Khaybar. Meanwhile their land and their weapons and their armor and whatever else they had been obliged to leave behind as uncarryable by their camels fell to the Prophet Muhammad, who used it to supply the poor and the destitute among his followers — particularly the Emigrants, who had fled Mecca and whose economic situation in Medina continued to be precarious even at this point.

Not long after the beginning of 626, Muhammad's daughter Fatima, married to Ali, gave birth to a second son. The baby was given the name of al-Husayn, a diminutive form of the name al-Hasan, which had already been bestowed on his older brother.

Mecca: The Beginning (of the End)

The Jews of the Banu Nadir, who had been exiled from Medina and had mostly settled in the oasis of Khaybar, were not resigned to the loss of their lands and their date palms. Near the commencement of 627, some of their leaders are said to have gone secretly to Mecca to urge the Quraysh to settle the thorny problem of Muhammad once and for all. They entered into oaths together, within the sacred Ka'ba, swearing that they would be allies for the destruction of the Prophet and his new religion. The Jews agreed to stir up the bedouin nomads of the Najd region, many of whom had grievances, real or imagined, against the inhabitants of Medina (or, at least, were aggrieved by the relative wealth of the settlement when contrasted with their own lean and difficult lives). The assistance of others was to be secured by bribes, or by the promise of spoils. The Banu Ghatafan, for instance, were offered half the annual Khaybar date harvest if they assisted the conspirators. The warriors of the Quraysh and their allies marched along the western or coastal road toward Medina, the same route they had taken on their way to the triumph at Uhud. The Jews and their motley group of allies and mercenaries, on the other hand, would come in against Medina from the deserts to the east. All totaled, there were ten thousand men in this new force — more than three times the number of those in the victorious battle of Uhud. It was late March 627, and surely the end of Muhammad and Islam was at hand.

But the Prophet received advance warning of the attack from sympathetic sources in Mecca, which gave him a week — but only a week — to prepare for the onslaught. As he had prior to the battle of Uhud, Muhammad summoned a council to discuss a course of action. Many suggestions were offered, but the one of Salman the Persian gained acceptance. Drawing on his experiences in Persia, he suggested that a trench would be an effective barrier against cavalry attack. The trench did not have to encircle the settlement, for large rocky areas to the northwest would serve as barrier enough if they could be connected, and there were several areas of fortified settlements that could be similarly tied together. At one end of the trench lay a hill from which Muslim archers would have an effective vantage point to fire on the attackers. Supplied by the Jewish Banu Qurayza with digging implements and date baskets for carrying away the dirt, the Muslims began to excavate a ditch that would be sufficiently deep and sufficiently wide to stymie the cavalry of Quraysh. Each faction of the community was assigned a certain portion of the trench to construct. The Prophet himself worked with his disciples, amidst chanting and singing. Traditional narratives relate miracles from this time, when the workers on the trench were unable to do their usual work and the normal economic and domestic activities of the settlement were in abeyance. Many of the workers, including the Prophet himself, were frequently unable to get enough to eat, especially as they were exerting themselves in unaccustomed and urgent physical labor. So God multiplied their food in remarkable ways, feeding many workers from meager rations that would normally have sufficed for only a few.

When the Meccan force and its allies from Najd arrived in the vicinity of Medina, they were dismayed to discover that the settlement's crops had already been harvested, perhaps intentionally early. This meant that their camels would have only the scarce local bushes to eat, which would soon be depleted, and that their horses would have to survive on such fodder as they had brought with them. Such constraints were crucial, as they would limit the time the attackers would be able to maintain a siege. The two separate armies, which had first pitched separate camps, now joined together and launched their advance toward the Muslim capital.

They must have been quite encouraged when they first saw the Muslim camp, at the end of March 627, not barricaded up within the settlement but lying directly in front of them outside the town. With their vast numerical superiority, it would be quick work to take care of the upstart Muhammad and his followers. It was only as they drew nearer that they saw a trench in the ground, lined with Muslim archers on the far side. This was an innovation for which they had not reckoned. Furthermore, the slope was in the favor of the Muslims, for the edge of the trench on their side was higher than that on the side of the Meccans, giving the Muslim archers considerable advantage.

But the attackers, too, had their stratagems. The traditional accounts relate that a man named Huyay, a leader of the exiled Banu Nadir who had encouraged this latest Meccan attempt to extirpate Muhammad and his followers, went to the dignitaries of the Quraysh with a plan. He would approach his fellow Jews, the Banu Qurayza, who were still part of the Medinan community, in an attempt to persuade them to renege on their covenant obligations to Muhammad. Thus a new battlefront would be opened at the enemy's rear, much like the literal second front that Khalid's cavalry had been able to open up behind the Muslims in the Meccan victory at Uhud.

At first the Banu Qurayza rejected Huyay's blandishments. But as he sketched for them the overwhelming strength of the Meccan and allied forces, as he stressed the determination of the Quraysh (this time) to end the nuisance of Muhammad's movement forever — and Huyay's powers of persuasion were near legendary — their resistance weakened. After all, Muhammad had made their life much more difficult. He was a newcomer to the settlement, but he had supplanted the old leaders and turned their traditional arrangements upside down, besides challenging their religious beliefs. Finally they agreed to withdraw from their agreement with the Prophet.

As expected, this created new problems for Muhammad and his warriors, who were now required to dispatch men from the front line at the trench in order to maintain a defensive garrison back in the previously secure center of the settlement. Rumors began to circulate, in fact, that the Quraysh and their allies were planning to sneak a thousand men each night into the fortresses of the Banu Qurayza, in preparation for a massive assault on the very homes of the Muslims and to carry off their wives and children. Though such an attack never materialized, the rumors themselves were undoubtedly demoralizing. A revelation received subsequent to the battle of the trench spoke of the mood that prevailed, and more than hints at discord among the ranks of Medina's defenders:

> Behold, they came upon you from above you and from below you, and behold, eyes were dimmed and hearts leaped to throats and you had second thoughts about God.
>
> In that situation, the believers were tested and were terribly shaken.

And behold, the hypocrites, in whose hearts is a disease, say, "God and his messenger promised us nothing more than vain hopes!"

And behold, a faction among them said, "O people of Yathrib! You cannot stand. So retreat!" And a group of them sought leave from the Prophet, saying, "Our houses lie exposed." But they were not exposed. They simply wanted to flee.

And if they had been entered upon from the sides of [the city] and they had been incited to sedition, they would have done it, and they wouldn't have hesitated for a moment.

Yet they had already covenanted with God not to turn their backs, and a covenant with God is something that must be answered for.[1]

Since the guard at the trench still had to be maintained both day and night, but now with reduced manpower, the hours of watch were increased and, with them, the fatigue of the Muslim defenders. To make things worse, the weather was unusually cold. And Khalid and Ikrima — who, as before, were commanding the Meccan cavalry — were constantly searching for weakness or any signs of carelessness along the trench. Once, indeed, when there was a momentary lack of defenders at one point on the line, several Meccan horsemen had been able, briefly, though ultimately with the loss of two of them, to cross the trench, thus demonstrating the possibility of breaching the Muslim defenses if conditions were suitable.

So tense was the situation that, for the first time in the history of Islam, the canonical daily prayers were neglected by the Muslim community as a whole. When the time for the noon prayer came, the Muslims simply could not relax their vigilance in order to perform it. When some of them came to the Prophet in concern about the issue, he replied that he, too, had been unable to pray. Only after sunset, when the advent of darkness had forced the attackers to return to their camp, could the believers resume their regular worship. And Muhammad led his disciples in four sets of prayers, to compensate for those they had missed.

Faithful believers knew that such tests and trials were to be expected. They had always beset the path of those who sought to do the will of God. "Do you think that you will enter paradise without there coming to you the like of what happened to those who passed away before you? Misfortunes and adversities afflicted them, and they were shaken so much that

1. Q 33:10-15.

the messenger of God and those who believed with him said, 'When is the victory of God?' Ah, truly the victory of God is near."[2]

But if things were difficult for the Muslim defenders of Medina, they were probably not significantly better — and may have been much worse — for the pagans of the besieging army. They too felt the cold. If the Muslims were hungry, they certainly were as well. Feed for their animals was growing scarce. Some of their valued horses were dying, from hunger as well as from arrows. The mercenaries among them must have begun to wonder if even the promised booty would be adequate compensation for their wretchedness, and whether, indeed, it would ever materialize. At one point Muhammad worked out a secret deal whereby a powerful faction of the Meccans' bedouin allies agreed to withdraw from the standoff in exchange for a third of the Medinan date harvest, but the Prophet's lieutenants, after ascertaining that he was acting out of compassion for his people rather than from divine commandment, rejected the arrangement.

But the Meccan-led coalition was beginning to unravel of its own accord, without bribes. One of the bedouin leaders came to Muhammad by night and professed his belief in Islam, putting himself at the Prophet's disposal. Muhammad knew instantly how to use him. He told the man to return to his camp and to commence sowing discord among the factions, for, he said, "war is deception."

Before long the Quraysh and the Medinan Jewish Banu Qurayza were deeply distrustful of one another's resolve and virtually at one another's throats. It was at this time that a fierce storm from the east hit the area, first dropping a torrential rain on the two armies and then rising to the force of a hurricane. The weather had been cold before, but now it was worse. However, the invaders got the brunt of the storm. While the camp of the Muslims was at least partially sheltered, that of the pagans was exposed on the open plain; no warming fire could be maintained, nor could any sheltering tent stand before the blast. It was too much. Wet, cold, hungry, with their horses dying, concerned about apparent treachery on the part of their allies, frustrated at the lack of any momentum or any realistic chance of ending the battle — casualties for the encounter totaled five or six for the defenders and three among the invaders; most of the time was spent exchanging versified insults and shooting arrows at one another from a safe remove — the leaders of the Quraysh decided to abandon the

2. Q 2:214.

field. The battle was over. And finished, too, were any real hopes of a
Meccan victory. They had thrown as much power against Medina as they
were capable of fielding, and they had failed. Never again would the
Quraysh be able to mount a serious threat to Muhammad or the religion
of Islam. The Qur'an memorialized this triumph for all time to come,
within the Muslim community: "O you who believe! Remember the grace
of God upon you, when armies came upon you. So we sent against them a
wind and armies that you did not see. And God observes all that you do.
. . . And God repelled those who disbelieved, in their fury. They gained
nothing. And God is sufficient for the believers in battle. And God is powerful and mighty."[3]

The doubt and despondency that had, for a time, afflicted the Muslim
fighters was now gone, as the Qur'an recalled: "'This is what God and his
messenger promised us, and God and his messenger told the truth.' And it
only increased their faith and their submissiveness [to God and his messen-
ger]."[4] But Muhammad did not spend much time basking in his triumph.
Just after the noon prayer the angel Gabriel visited him, dressed elaborately
in gold and silver brocade. He was surprised to see that Muhammad had
laid down his weapons, and commanded the Prophet to take them up again
and go with him against the treacherous Banu Qurayza. The siege of the last
remaining tribe of Medinan Jews lasted nearly a month. Finally the Banu
Qurayza sent to Muhammad, asking if he would permit one of their old
tribal allies, now a Muslim, to come out to their fortified dwellings to consult with them. The man, Abu Lubaba, went, and soon found his feelings
softened, against his will, by the obvious distress of his former friends.
When the men asked him if he felt they should submit to the Prophet, he
instantly replied that they should, but then indicated by pointing to his
throat that such submission would mean certain death. As soon as he had
done so, he felt guilty for having possibly prolonged their resistance, and he
spent many days thereafter in penance for his double-mindedness.

But the Banu Qurayza failed to heed his warning. On the following
day the Jews opened the gates of their fortresses and submitted to Muhammad. The Muslims immediately separated the men from the women and
children, leading the men out of the tribe's dwellings with their hands
bound behind their backs. Their armor and weapons were gathered to-

3. Q 33:9, 25.
4. Q 33:22.

gether with their garments and all their other possessions. Their grape and date wine was poured out onto the ground. The Banu Qurayza had, in the past, been allies of the clans of Aws. These now sent a deputation to the Prophet, requesting that he treat their former allies with the same degree of clemency with which he had earlier treated the Banu Qaynuqa, the former allies of their rivals, the Khazraj. On the face of it, it seemed a reasonable request. Muhammad responded by asking whether Aws would be content if it were one of their own who pronounced sentence on the treacherous Banu Qurayza. They responded that they would. So the Prophet had one of their chiefs, a man named Saʿd b. Muadh, brought out to perform the office. As he came, his fellow clansmen reminded him to treat the Jews well. After all, they informed him, the whole purpose for which judgment had been granted to Aws was to see that the Banu Qurayza were treated leniently.

Saʿd had been wounded during the battle of the trench, and though he was still alive, his wound was not mending. (It ultimately proved fatal.) Perhaps he was in ill temper. Certainly he had never been inclined toward leniency. With the rather fiery Umar, for instance, he had opposed sparing the prisoners at Badr. And those freed prisoners had lived on to kill Muslims again at Uhud, and yet again at the trench. Moreover, it might have been noted, this most recent threat to the Muslims and their leader had come about largely through the machinations of the exiled Banu Nadir. If the Muslims did not intend to face threat after threat from the same unrepentant enemies, perhaps it was time to make the repetition of their threat impossible while they were, as these enemies were now, wholly in Muslim power. Severe punishment would further serve to deter future treachery.

After receiving promises from all the Muslims present that they would indeed abide by his judgment, Saʿd decreed the execution of the men of Banu Qurayza, the enslaving of their women and children, and the division of their property among the Muslims.[5] "You have judged," said the Prophet, "with the judgment of God from above the seven heavens."[6]

---

5. Some of the women and children were later ransomed by their fellow Jews, the exiled Banu Nadir in Khaybar. They perhaps felt some responsibility for the catastrophe that had come upon Banu Qurayza, for it was one of their chieftains who had lured the Banu Qurayza to their fatal decision to go against their covenant with Muhammad.

6. Perhaps with some apologetic intent, the late English scholar Martin Lings notes, correctly, that Saʿd's judgment accords with that of the law of Moses as recorded in Deut. 20:10-14. See Lings, p. 232 n. 1.

The women and children were then removed from the area of their own dwellings and taken into the main part of Medina. The men remained in the camp, where the narratives recount that they recited from the Torah and exhorted one another to be of good courage and to endure their fates with patience and resignation. The next morning Muhammad ordered several large trenches dug in the marketplace. The mature men and youth of the Banu Qurayza were then taken to these trenches in small groups, and made to sit down beside them until Ali and Zubayr and some of the more vigorous Muslims were able to behead them with a sword stroke and push their bodies into the waiting mass graves. The bloody process continued into the evening, and had to be concluded by the light of torches. Traditional estimates place the number executed at between six hundred and nine hundred.

The Qur'an later recalled this episode as an example of God's grace toward the faithful: "And he brought down from their castles those among the people of the book [*ahl al-kitab*] who assisted them, and he cast terror into their hearts. Some of them you killed, and some you imprisoned. And he caused you to inherit their lands, their dwellings, and their goods, and a land you had not trod. Truly, God is all powerful."[7]

A rather touching story is told of an aged Jew named Zabir, who had once spared the life of a Khazrajite named Thabit b. Qays. Thabit now sought to return the favor, and interceded with Muhammad on Zabir's behalf. The Prophet granted the request, but Zabir, when presented with the gift of life, responded that he could see little point in survival without his wife and children. At Thabit's request, the Prophet now granted Zabir the freedom of his family. But, Zabir said, they could scarcely be expected to survive without their possessions. So, once again at the behest of Thabit, Muhammad allowed Zabir to regain his possessions, excepting his weapons and his armor. Even so, though, Zabir could see no purpose or sweetness in continuing to live when his people were either dead or enslaved, and he begged Thabit, for the sake of the favor that he had once done him, to allow him to join the rest of his people quickly. When Thabit realized that Zabir was fully serious, he escorted him to the side of one of the trenches, where Zabir's head was cut off by one of the Muslim executioners. Thabit did insist, however, on the freeing of Zabir's widow and her children, and on the restoration of their property to them.

7. Q 33:26-27.

128

Despite the horror of the destruction of the Banu Qurayza, the French Jewish Orientalist Maxime Rodinson is probably correct in his judgment that Muhammad's actions were not driven by any particular prejudice against Jews.[8] Contrary to repeated claims, for example, he did not attempt altogether to cleanse the region of its Jewish population. The Qur'an's criticisms of the Jews are no harsher, really, than those of the New Testament: they had received the law and the words of the prophets, but they had not obeyed. "The likeness of those upon whom the Torah was imposed and then did not obey it is as the likeness of a donkey bearing books."[9] Still, it is clear that Muhammad did not hesitate to act against the Jews with remarkable harshness, and that he did not regret his actions afterward. Not very long after the destruction of the Banu Qurayza, Saʿd b. Muadh, who had decreed their fate, lay on his deathbed. The Prophet came to him, held his head gently, and prayed: "O Lord, truly Saʿd has striven in the path, full of faith in your messenger and leaving nothing undone that he was supposed to do. Therefore, take unto yourself his spirit in the very best way that you take the spirits of your creatures." Within a couple of hours, Saʿd was dead. (His death, we are told, shook the very throne of God.) When the mourners were carrying him to his grave, they marveled at how light he was, particularly since he had been well known to be a very large man. Muhammad explained that angels had borne him, along with the earthly pallbearers.

Muhammad had, indeed, largely ended the civil strife that had plagued Yathrib, or Medina, for so many years, and that had occasioned his own invitation to the settlement as an arbitrator. Where once there had been division, now there were unity and strength, built solidly on an ideology shared by perhaps the large majority of the residents of the oasis. Where once Yathrib had been vulnerable to intrigue and even to outside attack because of its disunity, Medina could now project its strength far across the Arabian desert. But Muhammad had ended the city's disputes in a way that its leaders and original inhabitants probably did not envision and that some of them clearly did not approve of. He had thoroughly displaced them. Indeed, he had expelled two of the town's once powerful and wealthy Jewish tribes, and had essentially exterminated the third. He had drawn down upon the city the hostility of much of the central Arabian

8. Rodinson, p. 158.
9. Q 62:5.

Peninsula, where, not so long ago, nobody had given Yathrib a moment's thought.

Ibn Ubayy, in particular, was still willing to voice these objections. He had sought the leadership of Yathrib earlier, and Muhammad's arrival in the settlement had thwarted his ambitions. He had hoped to become something like a king — a role without precedent in the oasis, but which Muhammad was now filling to perfection. He would have attempted to unify the town, but probably without the foreign ambitions and complications in which the Prophet and his new religion had embroiled it. Muhammad was aware of Ibn Ubayy's scarcely concealed sentiments. Umar suggested that the man be decapitated as a traitor, but the Prophet refused the suggestion, declining to let it be said that Muhammad killed his own companions. But as Ibn Ubayy's murmuring continued, his son, Abd Allah, a very zealous Muslim, grew concerned that the Prophet would eventually find such behavior intolerable and would suspend his scruples and order him killed. So Abd Allah went to Muhammad with an interesting, and to our sensibilities quite unexpected, proposal. If, he said, the Prophet intended to kill Ibn Ubayy, his father, he hoped the assignment would be given to him. For he was, he continued, filled with an unusually strong feeling of duty toward his father, and he feared that, if the order to kill Ibn Ubayy were given to anyone else, he would feel himself irresistibly obliged to avenge the death of his father. Thus he would eventually have to kill the assassin and, having murdered a believer for the sake of an infidel, would go to hell. Therefore, in order to save his own soul, he sought the assignment of murdering his father. Muhammad declined his offer, saying rather that Ibn Ubayy should be treated with gentleness and his companionship enjoyed.

One night in March 628, Muhammad had a dream in which he saw himself, his head shaved like that of a pilgrim, entering the Ka'ba in Mecca, holding its key in his hand. The next day, having related the dream to some of his associates, he invited them to perform the *umra*, or "lesser pilgrimage," with him. Without hesitation they assented, and it was not long before they were under way with seventy camels to be sacrificed and then distributed to the poor in Mecca. Muhammad went bareheaded, wearing the traditional pilgrim's two-piece garb of unstitched cloth, one portion over his shoulders and the other about his waist.

The Prophet's decision to perform the pilgrimage was a dramatic indication of the truly Arabian character of Islam, and was perhaps intended as a signal to the Meccans that their interests would not really be harmed by the new religion. He was no longer campaigning against them, but was seeking to convert them. Still, the Quraysh were naturally alarmed when they heard of the departure of over a thousand Muslims from Medina in the direction of Mecca. As the hereditary guardians of the Ka'ba, they could scarcely block pilgrims from entering the sanctuary, for the shrine had traditionally been open to all. If they were to act in such a manner, they would, in the eyes of many Arabs, not merely Muslims, call into serious question their right to custodianship of the sacred quarter. On the other hand, to allow their archenemy to enter their city and to worship at their shrine without opposition was virtually unthinkable. Additionally, Muslim veneration of the ancient site would obviously mean that the Ka'ba, venerated by Arabs throughout the peninsula, would play a role in Islam. Heretofore that had been, at the least, unclear. But now it would perhaps tend to lessen the resistance of other Arabs to accepting the prophethood of Muhammad and the religion he taught. Meeting in assembly, the leaders of the Quraysh decided that he and his followers could not be permitted to enter the city. But how to keep him out without damaging their own status?

In the meantime Muhammad and the Muslims were drawing ever nearer. When they reached a place known as Hudaybiyya, near the edge of the sacred precincts of Mecca, the Prophet's camel suddenly stopped, knelt, and refused to advance any farther. For Muhammad this was a divine sign. (He had not forgotten the miraculous behavior of the elephant many years before, during Abraha's siege of Mecca.) There was little or no drinkable water at the site, but the traditional accounts tell of a miracle by which fresh water gushed forth in huge amounts for men and animals. Emissaries from the Quraysh now came out from Mecca to ascertain the precise numbers and intentions of the Muslims. Entering the Muslim camp, one of them informed the Prophet that the leaders of the city were determined that he would not enter, and had vowed to fight to the death to prevent it. Muhammad gave a conciliatory reply, offering the people of Mecca time to prepare and to clear the way for his approach, saying that the Muslims had come with no intention of fighting, although they would indeed fight those who stood in their way. Muhammad decided to send his own emissary into Mecca, and he chose Uthman b. Affan, a pious believer whose extensive kinship ties within the city would surely protect him from harm.

While Uthman was in Mecca, a kind of revelation descended on the Prophet — different from those that typically constituted the Qur'an, though, in that he remained conscious and alert to his surroundings while receiving it. The revelation directed Muhammad to have his followers pledge their allegiance to him, one by one. So he seated himself at the foot of an acacia tree while all but one of those present — the exception being one of the "hypocrites," who tried to hide himself — came forward and pledged themselves ready to obey whatever the Prophet had in mind. (He had given them no specific idea as to what was to claim their obedience.) Having thus secured the absolute obedience of his followers (of which, in any event, he could not have entertained much doubt, so frequently had it been illustrated), and with the significant refusal of his camel to advance well in mind, Muhammad was disposed to accept any reasonable offer the leaders of Mecca might proffer.

It was at this point, in fact, that they sent a trio of representatives out to him, in hopes of concluding some sort of treaty. The negotiations went well, for, as is shown in what happened at the conclusion of the discussions, Muhammad proved easy to please. When they had finally reached a mutually acceptable agreement, Muhammad asked Ali, who was serving as scribe, to record the terms of the treaty. He was to begin with the typical Muslim invocation, "In the name of God, the Merciful [al-rahman], the Compassionate." But the Quraysh spokesman objected, saying he did not know who or what al-rahman was. Rather, he insisted, Ali should write the traditional invocation, "In thy name, O God." This was met with a chorus of animated protests from the Muslims in attendance. But Muhammad directed Ali to accept the Meccan suggestion. Almost immediately thereafter, the Meccans again objected to the language Muhammad wanted to use. When he dictated to Ali "These are the terms of the treaty between Muhammad, the messenger of God, and Suhayl b. Amr," Suhayl erupted. If, he said, the Meccans knew Muhammad to be what he claimed — namely, the messenger of God — they would hardly bar him from the Ka'ba, nor would they have warred against him. Ali should write "Muhammad b. Abd Allah," and nothing more. But Ali had already written "Muhammad, the messenger of God," and when Muhammad asked him to cross the words out, he said he could not in conscience do it. So Muhammad had him point to the words with his finger — there is an unmistakable trace here of the traditional Muslim emphasis on Muhammad's illiteracy as a means of heightening the miracle of the Qur'an — and the Prophet himself crossed them out. Ali then willingly wrote in their place what Suhayl had demanded.

The agreement called for both the Muslims and the Meccans to refrain from fighting for the space of a decade. The Prophet undertook to return to the Quraysh any person who fled to him for refuge or as a convert without having obtained leave from parent, guardian, or master, but anyone fleeing from Medina back to Mecca would be allowed to stay there. Muhammad and his followers would not be permitted to perform the pilgrimage that year, but the Quraysh promised to vacate the city during the coming year for three days, during which Muhammad and the other Muslims would be permitted to come and worship in the sanctuary. Muhammad's followers — very loud among them the impulsive Umar — were horrified at the terms of the agreement. They had come to perform the pilgrimage, and were now obliged to return home to Medina having, in their view, accomplished nothing. What is more, the requirement that Muhammad return runaways while the Quraysh were under no such obligation was manifestly one-sided. (It probably reflected the Prophet's serene confidence in the superior appeal of Islam.) And, to make matters worse, while they yet sat there disappointed at Hudaybiyya, a young Muslim — the son of Suhayl himself, whom Suhayl had imprisoned because of his conversion — had, at this very time, just escaped from Mecca. He entered the Muslim camp to the great joy of his elder brother, who had come from Medina with the Prophet. But, true to the terms of the just-concluded agreement, Muhammad ordered him returned to Mecca.

When the Meccan envoys left the camp, the Prophet ordered his followers to sacrifice their camels as if they had actually completed the pilgrimage, and to shave their heads in pilgrim fashion. During the return journey a revelation descended on Muhammad, giving the view of the truce of Hudaybiyya that has, ever since, been that of believing Muslims around the world. It is recorded, now, in a chapter of the Qur'an known as *Surat al-fath,* "The Chapter of the Victory":

> Truly, we have granted unto you a manifest victory. . . .
>
> He it was who sent peace [*al-sakina*] down upon you in the hearts of the believers, that they might increase in faith upon their faith, for to God belong the armies of the heavens and the earth, and God is knowing, wise.
>
> That he might admit the believers, men and women, to gardens be-

neath which rivers flow, to dwell in them forever, that he might expiate their sins. And that, with God, is a great victory. . . .

Truly, those who pledge their allegiance to you pledge their allegiance to God. The hand of God is over their hands [as they make their pledge], so that anyone who violates his covenant violates it against himself and anyone who fulfills what he has sworn to God, God will grant him great reward. . . .

God was pleased with the believers when they pledged their allegiance to you beneath the tree. He knew what was in their hearts, and he sent peace [al-sakina] down upon them, and he rewarded them with imminent victory.[10]

It was, the revelation said, because of believers living quietly and perhaps unknown in Mecca who might have been harmed by battle that God had held the Muslims back from asserting by force their right to perform the pilgrimage. But ultimate triumph would be theirs: "God truly fulfilled the vision for his messenger. You will enter the inviolable mosque, if God wills, safely, with your heads shaved or your hair cut short, fearing nothing. For he knows what you do not know and, besides that, has granted you imminent victory."[11]

Even with such revelatory assurance, however, many of the Muslims must have wondered precisely wherein the victory of Hudaybiyya consisted. Perhaps it was related to the fact that, for the first time, the leadership of the Quraysh had been obliged to negotiate with Muhammad as at least an equal, and as, in effect, a head of state. But there is another plausible angle from which to regard this question. Under the truce agreement it was now possible for people from Mecca and Medina to meet and to speak with one another. This meant that Islam's missionary message could now be conveyed far more freely, even into the heart of hostile Meccan paganism. And there is reason to believe that this had its predictable effect. The early accounts suggest that the number of Muslims doubled over the next two years.

During this period, say the traditional sources, the Prophet dictated

10. Q 48:1, 4-5, 10, 18. The relationship between the *sakina* and the Jewish concept of the *Shekinah* demands further investigation. A good place to begin is Ignaz Goldziher, "La notion de la sakīna chez les Mohamétans," in Ignaz Goldziher, *Gesammelte Schriften*, ed. Joseph DeSomogyi (Hildesheim: Georg Olms Verlagsbuchhandlung, 1969), 3:296-308.

11. Q 48:27.

letters to the Chosroes, the shah of Persia, the Byzantine emperor Heraclius, the Ethiopian Negus, and the governors of Syria and Egypt, summoning them to accept the religion of Islam. Modern historians have doubted, however, that Muhammad's ambitions for Islam extended beyond the boundaries of the Arabian world, and they have universally dismissed the letters as figments of the imaginations of traditional historians, born of a desire to make of the Prophet a world-historical figure who was recognized as such and was already playing that role during his lifetime. According to the old stories, the shah, when he had read Muhammad's epistle, tore it to pieces. "Even so, Lord," said the Prophet, when the Persian king's reaction was related to him, "tear his kingdom from him." Also at this time, not long after the return of the would-be pilgrims from Hudaybiyya, early narratives say a Jewish sorcerer attempted to assassinate Muhammad by means of a magical spell involving knots tied in some clippings from the Prophet's hair, which were attached to a sprig from a palm tree and thrown into a well. The Prophet soon began to feel weak, as well as to sense that his memory was playing disorienting tricks on him. The curse was overcome by the recitation of two brief, recently revealed Qur'anic suras over the well in question. These two passages now form the last chapters of the Qur'an in its standard edition.

The peace with his enemies in Mecca now enabled Muhammad to turn his focus from the south to the north. Initially he concentrated on the oasis of Khaybar, where many of the exiled Banu Nadir had settled. It can scarcely have surprised him that they were deeply hostile to him, seething over their expulsion from Medina, and their hostility had expressed itself in concrete and threatening ways. It is quite probable, for instance, that the attempt by the Jewish sorcerer on the life of the Prophet, just alluded to, was sponsored by those in the oasis. And Khaybari encouragement had goaded the Quraysh into the abortive siege of Medina that had foundered on the edge of Salman's trench. Thus there was good reason for paying attention to the embittered exiles in Khaybar. Moreover, an attack on Khaybar promised rich reward in the form of spoils. Nobody in Medina could forget the Banu Nadir's splashy show of wealth as they marched out of the settlement into exile. And Khaybar itself was famed for its palm groves and its corn.

Unfortunately though, Khaybar also possessed a well-justified reputation for impregnability. And Muhammad was obliged to set off against the oasis with a relatively small force, because the Qur'an forbade him to take with him the desert bedouin who had failed to accompany him during his attempt to make the lesser pilgrimage.[12] The divine revelation consistently called into question the depth of conversion even of those bedouin who professed to have accepted Islam: "The Arabs [i.e., the bedouin] say, 'We believe.' Say, 'You do not believe, but say, "We have submitted [or accepted Islam, *aslamna*]," for belief has not entered your hearts. But if you obey God and his messenger, God will not belittle any of your deeds. Truly, God is forgiving and compassionate.'"[13] Since that earlier expedition had promised no booty, the bedouin had shown no interest in it — thus making their motives clear for all to see. As punishment, they were to have no share in the potential spoils of wealthy Khaybar.

When the two forces were finally mustered for engagement, the warriors of Khaybar and their allies numbered fourteen thousand — against which the attacking army from Medina could claim only sixteen hundred, or just over a tenth as many. But the smallness of the Muslim force did make it easier to conceal preparations for the expedition, which were aided by the widespread perception that the canny Muhammad could not really be contemplating an attack against such overwhelming odds. When Muhammad and his army were very close to Khaybar, he obtained the services of a guide and marched his troops — during the night, in complete silence — into the position he desired. It was very dark; the moon had already set. Reports indicate that no birds stirred, no animals sounded the alarm, and nothing moved in Khaybar, so stealthy was the approach of the Medinan force. Even when the sun rose and the time had come for the dawn prayer, it was conducted in virtual silence. Only when the agricultural workers of the oasis came out in the morning with their tools did they notice the Muslim army that had managed to interpose itself between Khaybar and its bedouin allies of the tribe of Ghatafan. In terror, they hastily retreated into their fortified dwellings.

Despite the threat, though, the leadership of the oasis was still confident of its ability to resist. Their numbers were far greater than those of the enemy. More importantly, they felt that their seven fortified strongholds

12. Q 48:15-16.

13. Q 49:14. Such comments, and the fact that Islam was actually born in the mercantile environment of an Arabian town — the Qur'an consistently uses commercial metaphors — exposes as essentially nonsense the frequently heard claim that Islam is a religion of the open deserts, a rigorous bedouin monotheism born of the simplicity of sand, endless sky, and a solitary, overwhelming, omnipresent sun.

here were more impressive than those they had been obliged to abandon in Medina. Thus, although some warned against it, the council of Khaybar chose not to form a unified battlefront, but rather to rely on the individual strength of its fortresses. In practice this meant that, when the Muslims attacked a fortress, its garrison was on its own. Its Khaybari allies did not come forth to break the siege, which might have changed the outcome of the struggle dramatically, but stayed behind their own walls, complacently attending to their own defenses. Muhammad was thus able to follow a policy of dividing and conquering his opponents, one fortress at a time, and their great numerical advantage was largely neutralized by their own strategic incompetence. Although the strategy of taking the fortified Jews on, one stronghold at a time, undoubtedly tested the patience and endurance of the Muslim forces, the army from Medina had the great advantage of ideologically based unity. "Truly," the Qur'an had declared, "God loves those who fight in his path in order of battle as if they were a firmly compacted building."[14]

The various campaigns to overcome the fortresses of Khaybar were taxing. The defenders of the strongholds showered arrows down on the Muslims who were besieging them, wounding many. At first the Medinans seemed to make little headway. But then, during the sixth night of their siege, they caught a spy in their camp who, upon promises that cooperation would save his life, agreed to help them out with information. He was able to tell them which of the fortresses were richest, and which housed caches of valuable weapons. Very importantly, he told them of siege engines that had been used during local civil discords in the past. (Once again, disunity would prove the undoing of the Banu Nadir.) The next day the Muslims took their first fortress. It yielded an engine for casting stones and two devices that would allow men to approach the walls beneath a roof that protected them against arrows. Thereafter the fortresses began to fall one after another. Meanwhile the bedouin allies of Khaybar, the Ghatafan, who had not only promised to come to the aid of the Jews of the oasis but had actually set forth, rather mysteriously returned home to their own families. The Muslim accounts say that this occurred because of a supernatural voice that came to them during the night. In any event, the expected reinforcements from the outside, which could have come in behind the Muslims and caught them from the rear, never arrived.

14. Q 61:4.

Meanwhile the siege continued, with the Prophet's son-in-law, Ali, distinguishing himself in the fighting and as the Muslim standard-bearer. The strongest of the Khaybari fortresses was the citadel of Zubayr, which sat high up on a rocky eminence with sheer cliff walls on three sides and a very steep approach to its gate on the fourth. Three days of siege had accomplished nothing, when a Jew from one of the other fortresses came to the Muslims with an offer. If they would spare him, his family, and his property, he would tell them the secret of the citadel of Zubayr. Muhammad, who well knew that war involved stratagem as well as heroism, quickly agreed. The man informed them of a subterranean stream that fed the citadel. The people within had cut steps down to it, protected from the outside, so that they could get water. And, since water was by far the most pressing need for any settlement under siege, they could, having taken care of that need, withstand attack indefinitely. But the Jewish informant showed the Muslims how they could dam the stream and cut off the flow of water to the defenders of the citadel. Since they had been supremely sure of their water supply, the defenders had never troubled themselves to keep a reserve. The effect was not long in coming. Forced by thirst to emerge from behind their walls, the warriors of the citadel of Zubayr were defeated in fierce fighting.

The last of the fortresses to put up real resistance was known as Qamus. Although it held out for two weeks, it too eventually fell, the Prophet granting the promise to its leaders that, if they left Khaybar and abandoned all their wealth, their lives would be spared. However, he reserved the right to annul that agreement if it were found that they had attempted to conceal any of their possessions. Unfortunately the leaders attempted to do just that. But the Muslims were not taken in. This was one of the richest of the Jewish clans, and one that had flaunted its wealth when it had withdrawn from Medina some years before. Nobody, therefore, was willing to accept its protestations that it had turned over all of its considerable possessions when in fact there was remarkably little brought forward. It took little time to find the hidden treasure, and the leader of the clan and one of his relatives paid with their lives for this attempt to deceive the Muslims and their prophet. The two fortresses that had remained defiant with Qamus now surrendered on the same terms that it had been granted. But they and their surviving fellow Jews now begged the Prophet to allow them to remain in the oasis. They were, they noted, experts in the agricultural work that was the settlement's chief source of wealth; who else would take care of the palm trees and the other crops? Muhammad saw the logic of their appeal and agreed to let them stay, demanding that they pay him an annual rent amounting to half the produce of the town and reserving the right to expel them in the future should he deem it wise to do so or regard them as rebellious.

Hearing what had happened, the Jews of the adjacent oasis of Fadak — smaller than Khaybar but still quite wealthy — hastened to submit to the Prophet on the same conditions, fearing that they would eventually be compelled anyway to submit to such terms or worse, and at the cost of many of their lives. Since it had not been won as booty in fighting, Fadak became the personal property of Muhammad (which, it should be noted, he generally used to help his poorer followers). The Prophet's triumph was marred somewhat by an attempt to assassinate him not long after the surrender terms had been settled, via a poisoned lamb that was served to him by one of the Jewish women. She had lost her father, her uncle, and her husband in the fighting, and was understandably bitter. Although the Prophet, it is said, instantly discerned the poison via supernatural gifts and spat it from his mouth, one of the other Muslims died from the lamb. Nonetheless, after questioning the woman, Muhammad pardoned her.

Mecca Submits

Finally the time drew near when, according to the terms of the truce at Hudaybiyya, Muhammad and his followers were to be allowed to enter Mecca to perform the rituals of the lesser pilgrimage. When the two thousand Muslims reached the edge of the sacred precincts of Mecca in March 629, the Quraysh withdrew, as they had promised, to the tops of the hills that surrounded the town, leaving the hollow of the valley where Mecca and its shrine lay open to the Prophet and those accompanying him. Muhammad came mounted on his favorite camel, while the others either rode or walked. They came with heads bare and dressed in white robes, in the traditional manner of Meccan pilgrims. Not hesitating anywhere else in the town, the Muslims went directly to the sacred enclosure of the Ka'ba. Muhammad, who had been absent from his native town for seven years, rode to the building's southeastern corner and there touched the black stone with the staff that he carried. Having done so, he circled the Ka'ba seven times and then traveled seven times back and forth between the hill known as Safa and another hill called Marwa. Closing that part of the ritual at the latter hill, he sacrificed a camel and had his head shaved.

Thus far Muhammad had complied with the traditional requirements of the lesser pilgrimage. Now he wished to enter the Ka'ba. But the leaders of the Quraysh, aware that such entry was not part of the traditional observances, had kept the key with them and informed a Muslim emissary sent to fetch it that yielding up the key was not among their treaty obligations. Muhammad was obliged, therefore, to forgo entering the shrine that year. But he did direct Bilal to climb onto the roof of the Ka'ba and intone the noon call to prayer. For the very first time the Muslim profession of faith, "I testify that there is no god but God; I testify that Muhammad is the messenger of God," rang out openly, loudly, and defiantly through the streets and the valley of Mecca. Hudaybiyya, it must now have been clear, had indeed been a victory.

Upon his return from the pilgrimage, Muhammad again turned his attention northward. He sent a delegation up to the Syrian border, summoning one of the Arab tribes there to accept Islam. The delegation was assaulted, and only one of them returned alive. The Prophet then sent a messenger to Bostra, the Byzantine headquarters. But the messenger was intercepted and murdered by a chief of the Byzantines' Christian Arab allies, the Ghassanids. Determined to punish the Ghassanids, Muhammad organized an army of roughly three thousand men and dispatched them under the leadership of his adoptive son, Zayd. The Prophet told the troops that if Zayd were killed, a man named Ja'far was to assume his place. And if Ja'far, in his turn, were slain, one Abd Allah b. Rawaha was to take charge of the expedition. Finally, if all three were killed or incapacitated, the troops were to choose themselves a leader.

According to the ancient accounts, Abd Allah was determined to find martyrdom for himself during this expedition, and his desire would prove to have consequences for more than just himself. When the Muslim force reached the borders of Syria, intelligence came to them of a much larger enemy army than they were prepared to meet. (Some said there were as many as a hundred thousand troops in the Byzantine-Arab force — which was doubtless a wild exaggeration. Still, there were more in the opposing army than the Muslims had envisioned.) Zayd decided to stop and hold a council. Many of those who expressed themselves counseled that, in the light of rather dramatically changed circumstances, they should send to the Prophet for further guidance. He might choose to call them back to Medina. Otherwise he would surely send them reinforcements. But Abd Allah was against either option. They should attack, he insisted. For either way, they would win. If they were victorious, it would be a magnificent triumph for the army of God. If, however, they were killed, they would go directly to paradise as martyrs and enjoy the delights of the heavenly garden. There was simply no bad option.

Abd Allah's opinion prevailed. So the Muslim army continued marching to the north, up to the region near the south end of the Dead Sea in Palestine. There they caught their first glimpse of the Byzantine forces and their Arab allies, who not only outnumbered them but represented a

far more sophisticated fighting force than anything Muslims had yet confronted. Zayd gave the order to withdraw to the south, toward a place
called Mu'ta that he deemed advantageous. The enemy pursued. Then,
suddenly, Zayd ordered his men to stop their retreat and to attack. Zayd
himself carried the white battle standard of his army against the foe. In the
ensuing struggle, first Zayd was killed, then Ja'far took up the standard until he died, and finally Abd Allah took it and led a charge in which he was
granted his dream of martyrdom. In the end Khalid b. al-Walid, the same
Khalid who had led important Qurayshi cavalry units at Uhud and the
battle of the trench but had now become a Muslim, took command of the
beleaguered Muslim force. Amidst the chaos of battle, he was able to re-
group his army and to drive the Byzantines and their allies back at least
sufficiently to allow a safe Muslim retreat. It was Khalid's first commanding role as a Muslim, but it would not be his last. He would go on to win
glory and fame in the Arab conquests after the death of the Prophet. And,
although Mu'ta was an undeniable defeat for Muhammad's warriors,
Khalid's role in saving the Muslim army from even greater disaster was
memorialized thereafter by his bearing the title "the sword of Islam." The
early Arabic sources say that only five other Muslims lost their lives that
day, besides the three appointed leaders of the expedition.[1]

The loss of his much-loved "son" Zayd was difficult for Muhammad,
and the traditional narratives, which claim that he saw the whole battle in
vision as it unfolded, represent him as weeping uncontrollably at the
death. Had he lived, Zayd might have succeeded Muhammad as the leader
of the Islamic community.[2] The Prophet was comforted that very night,
however, by a vision of Zayd and the other martyrs of Mu'ta in the gardens
of paradise. But Muhammad's personal loss was not the only concern that
arose from the defeat. Emboldened by the events at Mu'ta, some of the
northern Arabs decided to challenge the nascent Islamic state to their
south, whose obviously growing ambitions were undoubtedly and quite
understandably beginning to worry them. Many were finding the
Prophet's movement very alluring. The momentum was on his side, and
Muhammad had consistently demonstrated that he was a highly effective
enemy. (The Quraysh, powerful though they were, had been thwarted by

1. The casualty figures are a bit suspicious. Why, in so large a battle, would all of the
Muslim commanders perish while the losses among the ordinary soldiers were so low?
2. This is the suggestion of Watt, p. 157.

him at every turn.) At the same time, though, he had shown himself to be a generous and reliable ally, as well as an increasingly powerful one. For those who could tell which way the wind was blowing, Islam was clearly the party of the future. Thus purely secular motives — political and, in a sense, economic — made alliances with the Muslim state or even professions of Islamic faith increasingly attractive. Many of the tribes around Medina now hastened to line up with its ruler. But of course, the religious appeal of Islam was also a major factor. The doctrines of Muhammad offered meaning and purpose, and consolation in times of trial and loss, and they lacked both the ethnic exclusivism of Judaism, at least as the Arabs knew it, and the complex doctrines (trinitarian, christological, and others) of Christianity. But it would probably be folly, in any given case, to attempt to separate secular from spiritual appeal with absolute finality. In the Arabia of the seventh century, as indeed at any other time and place, human motives were inextricably mixed. Those who did not yet feel the allure of Islam, however, found Muhammad's increasing power a menace. Only a month after the death of Zayd, word reached the Prophet that Arab tribesmen were gathering on the Syrian border for a march to the south. In response Muhammad sent first one military unit and then another as a reinforcement toward Syria. The quick military response seems to have intimidated the tribesmen, and they dispersed with little fighting.

In the south, meanwhile, an event took place that was to have fatal and final consequences for the rule of the pagan Quraysh in Mecca. Not long after the successful expedition to Syria, fighting broke out in and around the sacred precincts of the city between allies of the Quraysh and allies of Medina. The Quraysh are said to have supplied weapons to their allies, and one or two of them even joined in the fighting. (They did so during the night, hoping that the darkness would protect their identity — which indicates that they very likely knew the political risk to which their actions were exposing them.) The tribe affiliated with Muhammad lost no time in sending a delegation to the Prophet, informing him of the wrongs they had suffered and calling on him to come to their aid. He declared that he would indeed. The Prophet was very angry at what had happened, and he regarded the fighting, and most particularly the surreptitious participation of the Quraysh in it, as a breach of the truce of Hudaybiyya. But there can be little doubt, too, that he recognized this as an opportunity. He was stronger than ever before, and he perhaps saw it as time to put an end to pagan rule in Mecca once and for all. When the Meccan leadership, suddenly aware of the potentially disastrous consequences of the incident, dispatched Abu Sufyan to Medina to attempt to ward off a breach of the truce, Muhammad treated him with deliberate coolness.

In fact, it is difficult not to feel some pity for the once proud lord of the Quraysh, even at the remove of centuries, as he tried to find some sympathetic or even listening ear among the Muslims. Rebuffed by the Prophet, Abu Sufyan went to visit his daughter, Umm Habiba, who, by now widowed of her first husband, had become one of Muhammad's wives. They had not seen each other for fifteen years, but he naturally hoped the ties of father to daughter would still incline her to listen to him and perhaps intervene on his behalf with the Prophet. But her reaction, too, was disdainful. As Abu Sufyan was about to sit down, she hastily (and quite literally) pulled the rug out from under him and folded it up. Addressing her in affectionate terms, the unsuspecting father asked if she had done so because it was too good for him, or because he was too good for such a rug. "It is the Prophet's rug," she explained. Her father, an impure idolater, was unworthy to sit on it. How, she demanded, could he, a lord of the Quraysh, bring himself to worship stones, mere idols that have power neither to see nor to hear? Why had he not accepted Islam? Shocked by her lack of daughterly respect, perhaps, Abu Sufyan was also astonished at her demand that he abandon the religion of his ancestors. "Am I," he asked, "to abandon that which my ancestors worshiped in order to follow the religion of Muhammad?"[3] But that is precisely what his daughter demanded of him. And, sensing that no help was to be gained from her, Abu Sufyan moved on. He went to Abu Bakr, but to no avail. He spoke with others he had once known in Mecca. They could offer him nothing. Finally he went to Ali, who was unmoved. In desperation the Meccan chief turned to Ali's wife, Fatima, the daughter of the Prophet, and to her son Hasan, who was sitting on the floor at her feet, and begged them to intervene. They would not. He repeated his imploring of Ali, made one last appeal to Muhammad himself, and then returned home to Mecca, having accomplished nothing and filled with foreboding about the future.

Muhammad immediately began to signal to those closest to him that he intended to march on Mecca, because the Quraysh had broken their agreement. But preparations were to be kept secret, and the leadership of the enemy were to be kept as much as possible in the dark about his inten-

---

3. Once again we see an indication of a rather passionate pagan religiosity.

tions. Indeed, even after the expedition had set forth, only a very few of the warriors had any certain idea against whom they were marching. At one point, when rumors were flying and the men were agonizing with curiosity, Ka'b b. Malik got up the nerve to approach the Prophet and attempt to get an answer to the question everybody was asking. Hesitant to pose the question directly, he instead recited a poem he had just composed, according to which the men were now reduced to drawing their swords and asking them if they knew against which enemy they would be used. The Prophet smiled, but answered nothing. When the army was finally assembled, it is said to have numbered something on the order of ten thousand. No Muslim who was capable of fighting was left behind. There were seven hundred "Emigrants," including three hundred on horseback. Four thousand of the Yathribi "Helpers" formed another portion of the army, including five hundred cavalry. The rest were the tribal allies of Medina, including many who joined the army as it passed by. Nine hundred mounted warriors from the Banu Sulaym added greatly to the strength of the Muslim expedition.

Arriving at Mecca, Muhammad used a trick he had employed before, when following the Quraysh after the battle of Uhud. He ordered his men to spread out and to light, each one, an individual campfire. Thus, when the Quraysh's spies surveyed the Muslim army that night, they saw ten thousand fires burning, and their hearts sank. Again Abu Sufyan was dispatched to see if talking could accomplish anything. When he was ushered into the Prophet's tent, Abu Sufyan began to rebuke him, faulting Muhammad for coming against his native city, his relatives, with such an assortment of men, some of them kin of the residents of Mecca and some of them unrelated and unknown. But Muhammad would have none of it. The conflict was not his responsibility, he said. It was the Quraysh who had broken the truce of Hudaybiyya and polluted the sacred enclosure by aiding and even participating in the violence against his allies, the Banu Ka'b. Abu Sufyan responded, not unreasonably, by suggesting that Muhammad's enmity ought to be concentrated instead on the primary perpetrators of the violence. After all, he pointed out, the Hawazin were the guilty party, and besides, they were even fiercer enemies of the Prophet than the Quraysh and not his relatives. In words that must have chilled the Meccan leader, Muhammad responded that he hoped, indeed, to punish the Hawazin — by conquering Mecca, establishing Islam as the religion of the city, and then going after them from a position of strength in the headquarters of their old ally. He thereupon turned to Abu Sufyan and his two fellow emissaries and ordered them to bear testimony of the unity of God and his own prophethood. Abu Sufyan's two companions immediately professed their faith in Islam by bearing the desired testimony. By contrast, the Qurayshi chief declared only that there was no god but God — in itself, a not insignificant concession for a pagan Arab — but could not bring himself to declare that Muhammad was the messenger of God. When he was told to make the second profession of faith, he asked for a temporary reprieve and was allowed to spend the night in the Muslim camp. He was awakened very early the next morning by the call to dawn prayer. Demanding to know what it meant, he was told that it was the first of five daily prayers, which struck him as excessive. But he was impressed that Muhammad had been able to persuade his people to perform frequent rituals. And he was even more impressed when he witnessed how deferential the normally rather anarchic Arabs were to their prophet-leader. Finally, pressed by his hosts, he asked to be taken to Muhammad, where he bore record of his conviction, not only that there was no god but God, but that Muhammad was God's messenger. In a very real sense, now that its leader had accepted Islam, Meccan paganism was dead. Muhammad's uncle Abbas, feeling compassion for his friend, kinsman, and former leader, now drew the Prophet aside and asked him to grant to Abu Sufyan some gesture that would help him preserve his honor and status after his surrender to Islam. Muhammad, who showed repeatedly throughout his life that he could be magnanimous in triumph, agreed without hesitation. He told the Qurayshi delegation to return to Mecca and tell the people there that, during the Muslim entry into the city, whoever had entered the dwelling of Abu Sufyan would be safe, as well as those who locked themselves within their own doors and those who sought sanctuary in the inner precincts of the Ka'ba.

The Medinan force prepared for its entry into the city. Muhammad divided the army into four parts. The central column of the expedition, in which Muhammad himself rode, was divided in two, while Zubayr led the column on the left and Khalid b. al-Walid — who, just two years before, had blocked the Muslims from approaching Mecca — commanded the column on the right. The four units now divided, with Khalid to enter the city from below and the three other groups coming down to the city from three passes in the hills surrounding. There was little resistance. Three of the Qurayshi chieftains, including Khalid's old cavalry colleague Ikrima, had gathered together a force of Meccans and bedouin allies, and when they saw Khalid's division approaching the city, they came down from the hills to attack it. It was an uneven battle, however, and the Muslims repulsed them — killing about thirty while losing only two — and continued into the city. Ikrima and one of his fellow leaders fled to the coast on horseback; the third leader, a man named Suhayl, escaped to his house and, now complying with the terms Muhammad had laid down to Abu Sufyan, locked himself behind his door.

When the Prophet entered the city, he went directly to the southeastern corner of the Ka'ba, where the black stone is mounted in the wall of the structure, and, as he had done the previous year during the lesser pilgrimage, touched the stone with his staff. As he did so, he exclaimed, "Allahu akbar! Allahu akbar!" meaning "God is most great!" repeated twice. Those standing nearest him repeated it, and then all of those in the shrine picked it up until Muhammad motioned with his hand and bade them be silent. Then he circumambulated the Ka'ba seven times, mounted. Following his circumambulation, he turned his attention to the idols that stood in a circle around the shrine. Tradition has it that there were 360 of them, which, if true, would seem to suggest an astronomical or calendrical association. He recited a verse from the Qur'an: "Truth has come," he declared, "and falsehood has vanished away. Indeed, falsehood vanishes by nature."[4] Then he destroyed each of the surrounding idols. (The traditional accounts say he simply pointed his staff at each of them, one after another, and they fell over.) He decreed that the idols be burned, and that Hubal, the largest of them, be smashed into pieces. Additionally, every home possessing a domestic idol or figurine was to see that it was destroyed. He prayed at the so-called "station of Abraham" and then proceeded to the well of Zamzam, where he took a drink. Following this, Muhammad entered the Ka'ba itself. Inside, all the walls of the building had been adorned with paintings of pagan deities. These he ordered Uthman to destroy, with the exception of a painting of an old man who was said to be Abraham and that of a painting of the Virgin Mary and the infant Jesus, an icon, over which he placed his hand in a gesture of protection.

By this time many of the Meccans who had taken refuge in the Ka'ba and in their homes were gathered near the shrine, waiting to see what their new lord would do and say. Muhammad turned to them and spoke to

4. Q 17:81.

them the words attributed by the Qur'an to the patriarch Joseph when, in forgiveness, he addressed his treacherous brothers, who had come to him in Egypt in hopes of temporal salvation and had belatedly recognized him for who he really was. "Truly," he declared, "I say as my brother Joseph said: 'There shall be no blame upon you today. God, the most merciful of those who show mercy, will forgive you.'"[5] The *harams* of Mecca and Medina were now coalesced under one lord, Muhammad.[6]

And he was indeed clement — quite contrary to the image by which he has been stigmatized in the West, of bloodthirstiness and cruelty. Perhaps only four people were executed as part of the Muslim seizure of Mecca, and these were, characteristically, poets and people who had satirized the Prophet. The actual leaders of the Quraysh were not only spared, but were treated with extreme generosity. When he was done in the city, Muhammad withdrew to the hill of Safa, very near to Mecca, and received the submission *(islam)* of hundreds of Meccans who came to profess their acceptance of his God and his prophetic authority. Among these was Hind, Abu Sufyan's wife, who had tasted of the liver of the Prophet's uncle Hamza at the battle of Uhud, and whose hatred of Islam and the Prophet had been implacable. Fearing for her life, she came before him wearing a veil and professed her submission before she identified herself. Muhammad welcomed her. He also pardoned Ikrima in absentia, at the behest of that warrior's wife.

The conquest of Mecca, though it dealt a crippling blow to Arabian paganism, had not yet eliminated it completely. No sooner was the situation in Mecca under control, in January 630, than Muhammad sent Khalid with a small detachment to Nakhla, where the principal shrine of the important pre-Islamic goddess al-Uzza was located. The guardian of the temple, say the Muslim accounts, learning of the approach of the victorious Muslims under their intimidating commander, girded the statue of the goddess with his sword and bade her defend herself. She did not, and Khalid demolished her shrine. But the Hawazin, the former allies of the Quraysh who had been centrally involved in the difficulties that led to Muhammad's attack on Mecca, were a far more dangerous enemy, and they remained. Indeed, Abu Sufyan's claim seems to have been accurate, that they

5. Q 12:92.

6. Serjeant, "Ḥaram and Ḥawṭah," pp. 55-56. Even today, Mecca and Medina are referred to as *al-Haramayn*, "the two sanctuaries."

were even more hostile to Muhammad than the Quraysh. Probably they saw the weakness and then the defeat of their old rival, Mecca, as an opportunity to seize control of its dominance in trade and to claim its religious prestige for themselves.

About two weeks after the occupation of Mecca by its new Muslim overlords, word came to Muhammad that Hawazin, mobilizing to the north of Ta'if, a town less than a hundred kilometers to the east-southeast of Mecca, had managed to put together an army of approximately twenty thousand warriors bent on attacking him in his new possession. Ta'if was the stronghold of the Thaqif tribe and was centered on a *haram* dedicated to the goddess al-Lat, which rivaled the sanctuary in Mecca.[7] The Prophet decided not to wait for them, but to go out on the offensive. He took with him the entire army with which he had come against Mecca, but which was now augmented with an additional two thousand men from the Quraysh of the city. Most of them were newly converted Muslims, but even a few of those who had not yet accepted Islam came out to fight in defense of their hometown and families.

When the two armies joined in battle, it was in a valley called Hunayn. The Hawazin launched a furious attack and, at the first, seemed to sweep the Muslim forces away. Indeed, many turned and fled. Muhammad, however, made a stand with a few of his closest associates and called for the others to cease their flight and to turn and stand with him. In the chaos and the noise, his voice could scarcely be heard. Gradually though, the tide of battle turned, and the warriors of Hawazin were themselves forced to flee, some to the oasis of Nakhla and some to the walled city of Ta'if. Muslim casualties had been heavy at the first, but in the rout with which the battle culminated they had inflicted heavy losses on their enemy while taking relatively few of their own. They captured many Hawazin women and children, for these had been just behind the enemy lines, and they took large numbers of livestock as well as four thousand ounces of silver that they found among the spoils.

The Prophet pursued the enemy all the way to Ta'if, where he besieged them behind their fortifications. But Ta'if was admirably equipped to withstand such a siege, and it had a year's supply of provisions within its walls. Moreover, the men of the city demonstrated that their reputation as expert bowmen was well deserved, and they made the besieging army pay

---

7. Serjeant, "Ḥaram and Ḥawṭah," p. 52.

dearly whenever it let down its guard. After nearly a month, Muhammad concluded that little was to be gained by prolonging the siege, and he lifted it. As the Muslim army was pulling away, some of his followers appealed to him to pronounce a curse upon the city and its recalcitrant residents. He made no other response than to lift his hands in the attitude of prayer and to ask God to guide the people of Ta'if and to lead them to him and the acceptance of Islam.

The battle at Hunayn was yet another great and remarkable victory for Muhammad and Islam, and a revelation commemorated it not long thereafter:

> Truly, God has helped you on many battlefields, and on the day of Hunayn, when you were so pleased with your numbers but they availed you nothing, and the earth, for all its spaciousness, constrained you and you turned to flee.
>
> But God caused his serenity [*sakinatuhu*] to descend upon his messenger and upon the believers, and he caused armies that you could not see to descend, and he punished those who disbelieve — that being the reward of the unbelievers.[8]

With the battle now behind them, members of Muhammad's army were eager, in the typical fashion of ancient Arabia, to divide up the booty. Muhammad stalled on the division of the spoils, however, for, as had been made clear by his raising of the siege against Ta'if, he had decided to treat his opponents there with leniency and to see if he could thereby win their hearts to Islam without further fighting. But the one-fifth portion of the spoils that came to him under Islamic practice was another thing altogether. The same Qur'anic revelation that had commented on the battle of Hunayn had also given him guidance on what to do with the alms that came his way — and these spoils were, he considered, to be used in precisely the same manner. "Alms are for the poor," the revelation explained, "and for the needy, and for those who collect them, and for those whose hearts are to be reconciled, for those in bondage and those in debt, and in the path of God, and for the wayfarer — an obligation from God, God being knowing and wise."[9]

8. Q 9:25-26.
9. Q 9:60.

Among "those whose hearts are to be reconciled," the Prophet clearly considered his recent allies of the Quraysh. So he treated them with remarkable generosity. To Abu Sufyan he gave a hundred camels. And when Abu Sufyan asked if his two sons, Yazid and the future caliph and founder of the Umayyad dynasty Muawiya, could not expect something as well, Muhammad gave to each of them a further one hundred camels.

The sources depict Muhammad returning to his adopted home in Medina from his victory at Hunayn and his conquest of Mecca in a reflective mood, as well he might have been. He told some of his followers that they were returning now from the lesser jihad to the greater jihad. Puzzled as to how he could be talking about any greater "holy war" than the one they had just concluded by their triumph over the capital city of Arabian paganism, they asked him what he meant. The greater jihad, the Prophet replied, alluding to the primary meaning of the word, which is not literally "war" but "struggle," is the struggle with one's own soul.

Arabia under Muhammad

The momentum continued to run in favor of Muhammad and his religion, as is shown in the conversion to Islam of Ka'b b. al-Zuhayr, one of the leading poets of the day. He had spent most of his life among the desert Arabs of Ghatafan, the allies of the Jews of Khaybar, and had therefore not entered Islam previously. Indeed, he had mocked the revelations of Muhammad and satirized the Prophet himself. But the conquest of Mecca helped him change his mind, and one day he appeared in the mosque at Medina, approached the Prophet, and took him by the hand. "O messenger of God," he said, "if Ka'b b. al-Zuhayr were to come to you, repentant, a Muslim, asking you to grant him immunity, would you receive him if I were to bring him to you?" Muhammad answered, quite in character, that he would. At that, Ka'b identified himself. One of the nearby Muslims instantly stood up and offered to decapitate the poet, but the Prophet forbade him. Ka'b, he pointed out, had repented, and was no longer an enemy of Islam but instead a brother Muslim.

Muhammad once again turned his attention to the north, toward Syria, and began to gather a huge army for a campaign against the Byzantines. His decision seems to have been precipitated by rumors — essentially baseless, as it turned out — of plans for a massive Byzantine offensive against the rising Muslim threat in Medina. But he may also have felt the need to channel the energies of his followers into outward aggression, since the time-honored Arab practice of raiding one another was no longer permitted among Muslims. Certainly the weakness of the Byzantines, who had just concluded their long war with the Persians, invited such attack, although the Prophet's primary goal was probably more to influence the Christian Arabs of northern Arabia and Syria than to confront the Byzantine Empire directly.

Muhammad made no attempt at covert activity this time; the summons for troops was sent out to Mecca and the tribal allies of the Muslims throughout Arabia. Not everybody was enthusiastic about the opportunity. It was one thing to fight desert bedouins, but quite another (as Mu'ta had clearly illustrated) to confront the professional soldiers of Constantinople, the successor state to imperial Rome. Additionally, the weather in the fall of 630 was unusually hot. Arabia, always dry, was in the grip of a drought. And it was harvest season. Still, an army of thirty thousand men, a third of them mounted, gathered to obey the command of the Prophet of God.

When they were ready, Muhammad came out to their encampment to take personal command. According to the traditional sources, he had asked his son-in-law, Ali, to stay behind and care for his wives and family. Some of the dissidents — the "hypocrites," who were still present in Medina even after the Prophet's long string of triumphs — began to spread disruptive tales that Ali had been left behind because Muhammad didn't like him and couldn't endure his presence. Ali, a legendarily heroic warrior who was probably already distressed at being left out of a great and important expedition, was now thoroughly upset. He donned his armor, grabbed his weapons, and set out in pursuit of Muhammad. When he caught up with him, he told him the kinds of rumors and murmuring he was being subjected to, and implored the Prophet to let him join the army. Muhammad denied the motives the "hypocrites" were imputing to him, but he also denied Ali's request. "Return," he ordered him, "and represent me among my family and yours. Aren't you satisfied, Ali, that you should be to me as Aaron was to Moses (except that, after me, there is to be no prophet)?" The story is, frankly, a bit suspicious. It seems too clearly to be constructing a basis for the succession of Ali as caliph after the death of Muhammad — the position of the Shi'ites — particularly in its careful formulation of an authoritative role for Ali that nonetheless closes the door on future claims of revelation or prophethood.

The Muslim army eventually reached a spring called Tabuk, located roughly midway between Medina and Jerusalem, and remained there for nearly three weeks. By the end of this period, it had become clear that the rumors of a Byzantine offensive against the Muslims were untrue, and perhaps the heat and drought had also become simply too oppressive. Whatever the precise motive, the Prophet took the main body of the Muslim force back to Medina, having engaged in no military action. But he did not return without results. During his stay at Tabuk, Muhammad entered into a truce agreement with some of the Jews and Christians who lived at the head of the Gulf of Aqaba (also known today, on some maps, as the Gulf of Eilat) and down its eastern coast. The Islamic state guaranteed them protection in exchange for an annual tribute, and thus greatly expanded the effective range of its rule. He also sent Khalid and a cavalry force of 420 to seize control of a stronghold called Dumat al-Jandal, located northeast of Tabuk along the road between Medina and Iraq and Syria.

When the Prophet had arrived back in Medina, he was visited by a delegation from the besieged city of Ta'if, offering to accept Islam and seeking a guarantee of safety for their families, their animals, and their lands. Although the Muslim forces outside their fortified town had made no progress on gaining entry into Ta'if, they had managed to make life very difficult indeed for its residents. Ironically, the leader of the forces opposing Muhammad at the nearly disastrous battle of Hunayn, a very effective fighter named Malik b. Awf, had since converted to Islam, and now made the life of the Banu Thaqif quite unpleasant. By the time of their delegation to the Prophet, they were surrounded not only by the besieging armies of the Muslims but by numerous communities that had accepted the religion of Islam and saw it as their duty to intercept any caravans bound for or leaving Ta'if and to seize any livestock sent out to graze on the city's pasturelands. Malik's men had furthermore promised to execute any Thaqifi they captured, unless he foreswore polytheism and entered Islam.

Muhammad readily accepted his erstwhile enemies into the Islamic community and, by that very act, granted them and their lands and goods protected status under the authority of the Medinan state. That did not, however, exhaust their requests. Could they retain their idol of the goddess al-Lat for three years? No, the Prophet replied, they could not. And he likewise refused their requests for a respite of two years, or just one year, or even one month. But he did grant that they would not be required to destroy their venerable idol with their own hands, and he sent one of his disciples, accompanied by Abu Sufyan, to take care of that duty. When they asked to be excused from the requirement of five daily prayers, he refused that, too, commenting that a religion that required no regular daily prayers was without value.

The residents of Ta'if were not alone in sensing that the tide had turned irrevocably against the old paganism, and that Muhammad and his Medinan state were the future of Arabia. The ninth year of the *hijra* is frequently labeled "the year of delegations" in the traditional sources. Emissaries came from various quarters of the Arabian Peninsula, pledging fealty to the Prophet and often renouncing polytheism and accepting Islam. In exchange Muhammad pledged the treaty protection of his new government, on condition that they receive his representatives well and remit their taxes to Medina. Needless to say, there was some reason to question whether all these conversions were entirely sincere or totally motivated by spiritual conviction, but Muhammad was happy to accept pledges of support and loyalty no matter their motivation, if they were kept.

Christians and Jews were also to receive the Prophet's protection, and would not be forced to convert to the new religion. On the other hand they were asked to pay a slightly higher tax. Adherents of Judaism and Christianity received protected status alongside those of Islam itself, all of them being considered "peoples of the Book." When a delegation from the Christians of Najran, to the south, came to Medina with hopes of a treaty covenant with Muhammad, the Prophet permitted them to pray in the mosque there, although their prayer was directed not to Mecca, which lay almost due south of Medina, but toward the east, the direction of sunrise. They spent considerable time in theological discussion with Muhammad, disputing with him the nature of Jesus, whether he was the Son of God or merely, much like every other human being, one of God's creatures. In the end they agreed to disagree, and the Prophet granted them his protection and that of his Islamic community for their churches and all that they owned.

Muhammad's tolerance of these Christians was fully consistent with the revelations he had received, in which God spoke to him and said:

> Truly we revealed the Torah, in which was guidance and light and by which the prophets and the rabbis and the learned scholars judged....
>
> And we sent Jesus, the son of Mary, in their footsteps, confirming the Torah that had come before him, and we gave him the Gospel, in which was guidance and light, confirming the Torah that had come before him — a guidance and an admonition to the God-fearing.
>
> Let the people of the Gospel judge according to that which God has revealed in it. And whoever does not judge according to what God has revealed, they are transgressors.

And we revealed the Book to you in truth, confirming the book that came before it. . . . To each one of you we have given a law and a path, and, had God willed it, he would have made you one people. But in order to test you according to what he has given you [he has not done so]. So compete with one another in good works. The return of all of you is unto God. Then he will inform you about that in which you have disagreed.[1]

The same tolerance did not, however, apply to paganism, which was not accepted as a religion of "the Book" or of revelation, but rather as an evil instance of rebellion and apostasy against God. When the time of the greater pilgrimage next approached, Muhammad let it be known that pagans would be permitted to participate in the ancient rites only one more season, and would then be banned from the precincts of the Ka'ba. Furthermore, nobody would be allowed to circumambulate the Ka'ba naked after that year, as some pagans occasionally did. Pagans would be given a grace period of four months to repent, but after that there was no guarantee of protection. Indeed, a war was effectively declared against any idolaters holding out beyond that period, and they were promised that, when the four months had expired, unless they could point to some special pre-existing treaty with the Prophet, they would be taken captive or killed wherever they were found.[2]

Muhammad had now reached a respectably advanced age, by Arabian standards. If he was not precisely old, he was nonetheless clearly no longer young. Yet he had not been fortunate in his posterity. Among all of his wives, only Khadija had thus far borne children to the Prophet. And when another child did come, it arrived via his beloved Coptic Christian concubine, Mariya. Having received a vision of the angel Gabriel during the night of the baby's birth, in which Gabriel addressed the Prophet as "father of Ibrahim," Muhammad gave to his new son the Arabic form of the name of the great biblical patriarch, the father of the monotheistic tra-

1. Q 5:44, 46-48.
2. It may well be significant that (as is noted in Lings, p. 323 n. 1) this revelation, which appears in the Qur'an as the *Surat al-tawba*, "the chapter of repentance," is the only one of the 114 chapters in the sacred book of the Muslims that does not begin with the words *Bismi Allah al-rahman al-rahim* (typically rendered "In the name of God, the Merciful, the Compassionate"). The absence of that formula certainly serves to heighten the sternness of the warning declared in the chapter.

dition. Muhammad loved the boy dearly, visiting him almost daily and often taking his midday rest with the baby.

Unfortunately the little boy was not destined to live. Muhammad was with the child as he died and, when the struggle was over, took Ibrahim in his arms and wept deeply. Earlier he had forbidden Muslims to engage in overly dramatic displays of grief or affliction, and some now questioned him about what they thought must be a double standard. But Muhammad responded that it was not sorrow that he forbade, nor the expression of sorrow, but exaggerated shows and even counterfeits of such emotion. Then he addressed his dead son: "O Ibrahim, if it were not that the promise of reunion is certain, and that this is a path that all must walk, and that the last of us shall catch up with the first, truly we would grieve for you with a greater sorrow still." Yet later, after the little boy had been buried, the Prophet sprinkled some water on the grave and tenderly smoothed the surface of the earth that covered his son's body. "It does no harm," he said, "and it does no good, but it does give some relief to the soul of an afflicted person."

Abu Bakr was delegated to direct the hajj in 631, but the Prophet announced that he would personally lead the next great Meccan pilgrimage. Multitudes came to Medina from all over Arabia, including many of the desert bedouin, eager to participate in the venerable rituals of the hajj under the personal tutelage of the Lord's messenger himself. Probably few if any suspected that it would be their only opportunity to do so. This would be the first year (at least since the ancient days of Abraham and his first descendants) when all the participants in the rites would be monotheists. When Muhammad left Medina, he not only took all of his wives with him but, so the accounts say, thirty thousand Muslim pilgrims.

What the Prophet did and said during this, the only full pilgrimage that he led, has become the pattern for all the world's Muslims during every hajj of every year throughout the nearly fourteen centuries that have elapsed since. In the course of it he delivered a great sermon that has been treasured ever since. "Hear me, O people," he cried out, "for I do not know whether I shall meet with you in this place after this year." He advised the Muslims to treat one another with justice and kindness, and instructed them on some of the commandments and prohibitions of the religion into which very many of them had only recently entered. "I have left among you something which, if you adhere closely to it, will keep you from all error — a clear guide, the book of God and the word of his prophet." Then he recited to them the last revelation that he would ever receive: "Today, those who disbelieve have despaired of prevailing against your religion, so don't fear them but fear me. Today I have perfected for you your religion and have completed my grace upon you, and have chosen Islam [submission] for you as your religion."[3] The Prophet ended his sermon with the question, "O people, have I faithfully delivered my message to you?" When the people answered yes, he raised his index finger and prayed, "O God, bear witness!"[4]

The journey back to Medina was slightly marred by some discord and murmuring concerning the Prophet's son-in-law, Ali. Muhammad was much distressed by it. "Am I not," he exclaimed to one of the complainers, "nearer to the faithful than their own souls?" When the man acknowledged that, yes, he was, Muhammad informed him that whoever was close to him would be close to Ali. Somewhat later in the journey, when the returning pilgrims had stopped to rest at a place called Ghadir al-Khumm, he assembled them and repeated what he had said to the man. Then he took Ali's hand in his and prayed, "O God, be the friend of whoever is his friend, and be the enemy of anyone who is his enemy!" The murmuring stopped, but the echoes of that declaration and prayer at Ghadir al-Khumm have resounded through the centuries. Shi'ite Muslims are convinced that Muhammad intended Ali to succeed him, and that the Prophet explicitly announced it there at Ghadir al-Khumm.

But the dispute between Sunnis and Shi'ites over the authority to lead the community as the successor of the Messenger properly belongs to the period after the Prophet's death. In the meantime there were rivals to Muhammad's own authority. If paganism was no longer a serious threat, perhaps the very success of Muhammad's prophethood was now inspiring yet another challenge. The Banu Tamim now claimed a prophetess, one Sajah, while the Banu Asad had a prophet by the name of Tulayha and the Yemen could boast of a prophet named Aswad b. Ka'b. None of these threats proved to be major. The Yemeni, for example, was soon assassinated by his disaffected followers, and Tulayha, defeated by Khalid, would accept Islam and yield up any pretense of prophethood. Not long after he returned from

3. Q 5:3.

4. Muhammad's question is reminiscent of the concern expressed by the apostle Paul in Acts 20:17-38, when, in Miletus, he took solemn leave of the elders of the church at Ephesus. Compare Ezek. 33:1-9; also Samuel's farewell speeches in 1 Sam. 8 and 12.

the Meccan pilgrimage, Muhammad received a letter from a man of the territory of Yamama addressed to "Muhammad the messenger of God" from "Musaylima the messenger of God." This Musaylima — his name was actually Maslama, but has come down to modern times transformed by Muslim hostility into an Arabic diminutive — claimed to be a prophet of his people, the Banu Hanifa, just as Muhammad was a prophet of and to the Quraysh, and he offered to share authority with Muhammad and to divide the land with him. Musaylima too was the lord of a *haram*.[5] He preached in the name of a deity he called Rahman — a name that also appears frequently in the Qur'an after a certain point (with the meaning, applied to Allah, of "Merciful" or "Compassionate") and that seems to have perplexed its Meccan audience.[6] He evidently possessed a written revelation in rhymed prose, rather like the Qur'an, and if Geo Widengren is correct, his claim of the title of "Messenger," or *rasul,* may indicate that he, too, claimed an ascension into heaven and a reading of the heavenly book.[7] Some have suggested that he actually proclaimed himself a prophet before Muhammad's own call. Muhammad responded with a note "from Muhammad the messenger of God to Musaylima the liar." Musaylima would eventually perish by a javelin thrown by the same man who had killed Hamza at the battle of Uhud.

Muhammad seems not to have lost much sleep over any of these rival claimants. His sights were set elsewhere. At the end of May 632 he announced a campaign against the Arab tribes of Syria, the Byzantine clients or mercenaries who had fought alongside the imperial army at the tragic battle of Mu'ta. He appointed as commander of an army numbering three thousand a young man named Usama, the son of his adoptive son, Zayd, who had died at Mu'ta.

But Muhammad would not live to see his army avenge that earlier defeat. He began to experience serious headaches and, the sources say, to express presentiments of his approaching death. Soon he was weak and feverish, unable to lead the prayers in the mosque except from a seated position. Seeing how ill he was, and knowing that he wished to be cared for in the dwelling of his beloved A'isha, the other wives waived their rights to his

---

5. Serjeant, "Ḥaram and Ḥawṭah," pp. 48, 52; Serjeant, "The Saiyids of Ḥaḍramawt," p. 15.

6. See Peters, *Muḥammad,* pp. 48-49, 156-59.

7. Widengren, *Muḥammad,* pp. 15-17, 135.

companionship and ceded him to her. But he was unable to walk to her home without the aid of his uncle Abbas and his son-in-law Ali. Eventually he was too weak to lead the prayers even sitting, so he designated Abu Bakr to lead the prayers in his absence. (Adherents of Sunni Islam cite this as evidence that Muhammad wanted his dear old friend and loyal supporter to succeed him, instead of Ali.) Lying on A'isha's lap, Muhammad suffered great pain.

But then, early in the morning of June 8, 632, his fever broke. He decided to attend the dawn prayer at the mosque, and the people were overjoyed to see him. Abu Bakr, who had been poised to commence the prayer, moved to withdraw in favor of Muhammad, but the Prophet, who was still feeling very weak, directed him to proceed as imam, or prayer leader, while he himself offered the prayer sitting at Abu Bakr's right. It was a false recovery. Muhammad returned to A'isha's and went downhill rapidly. She held his head while he lost consciousness. Just before he died, he spoke softly, and the report has circulated ever since that he told of being shown his place in paradise, and of being offered the choice of entering the garden or remaining on the earth.[8] His choice was clear. When A'isha realized that he was dead, she placed his head gently on a pillow and, with the other wives who had gathered when they realized that his passing was near, began her lament for her dead husband, the messenger of God.

Usama's army, although ordered to Syria, had waited just outside the city for news of the Prophet's health, and they had been greatly encouraged when they had heard of his apparent recovery. Now, with the dreadful news of his death, they returned home. Umar, who had been with the army, went to the mosque, where he assured the assembled and bewildered Muslims that Muhammad was not really dead, but that his spirit had simply left his body — as it had during his ascent into heaven — and that it would return and the Prophet would revive. While he was speaking, Abu Bakr, who had also been out of town, likewise returned. He went directly to the home of his daughter, A'isha, to see the situation for himself. Tenderly he uncovered Muhammad's face, looked at him, and then bent over to kiss him. "Dearer than my father and my mother," he murmured, "you have tasted that death which God decreed for you. Never again shall death befall you." Then, covering the Prophet's face again, he made his way to the

---

8. I think it worth noting that this choice is a common motif in modern accounts of so-called "near death experiences," or NDEs.

front of the mosque, where Umar, almost hysterically attempting to suppress his own doubts and anxieties as well as those of his audience, was still holding forth. "Gently, Umar!" he said. Still the younger man continued to shout his reassurances, but the people turned to hear what Abu Bakr had to say. First, he praised God in the traditional Muslim manner. Then he said, "O people, whoever worships Muhammad — truly, Muhammad is dead. And whoever worships God — truly, God lives and does not die." Thereupon he reminded them of the Qur'anic verse that had been revealed immediately following the battle of Uhud, in which the Prophet had been wounded and could easily have been killed: "Muhammad is nothing but a messenger. Messengers have passed away before him. If he were to die or was killed, would you turn back upon your heels? Whoever turns back upon his heels will not harm God in the least, and God will reward the grateful."[9] This brought Umar to his senses, and he afterward recalled that it was only then that he realized that the Prophet was really dead. He fell to the ground, and his legs were too weak to support him. Muhammad was buried beneath the floor of A'isha's house, in the very spot where he died.

9. Q 3:144.

Reflections

When the Prophet died, he left a political vacuum in Arabia. Out of the chaos that followed over the next few days, his loyal lieutenant Abu Bakr emerged as the caliph or vicar of the Messenger of God. But the selection of the older man left Muhammad's kinsman Ali feeling that he had been slighted, and his legitimate right to rule usurped. He withdrew for several years from active participation in the affairs of the Muslim community, while there coalesced around him a group of sympathizers who came to be known as the "faction of Ali," the *shi'at Ali*, or, as the West knows them, the Shi'ites. When Abu Bakr died after only two years, he named Umar to succeed him, and when Umar was assassinated, he was, in his turn, succeeded by Uthman b. Affan. Uthman too met a violent end, which left the caliphate open, at last, to Ali. But Ali never really had time to savor his vindication; he himself eventually fell to an assassin and, in what surely must rank as one of the supreme ironies of history, left the rising empire to the descendants of the Prophet's old enemies, the Quraysh. Less than three decades after Muhammad's death, the Ummayads, the descendants of Abu Sufyan, ruled the empire from Damascus. The strongest leader of that house was Mu'awiya, the son of Abu Sufyan and of Hind, who had torn out and eaten the liver of Muhammad's uncle Hamza following the battle of Uhud. And when they were overthrown a century later, it was by another faction of the Quraysh, the posterity of Muhammad's ever prudent uncle Abbas, who continued to rule from their new capital of Baghdad until the Mongols destroyed them in the middle of the thirteenth century.

It was a vast empire. The Qur'an had elevated the status of the Arabs and impelled them to the remarkable conquests of the seventh and subsequent few centuries that took them into Spain and over to India. "A century after an obscure camel-driver named Muḥammad had begun collecting a few poor Meccans round him in his house, his successors were ruling from the banks of the Loire to beyond the Indus, from Poitiers to Samarkand."[1] And once there, the appealing simplicity of Islam, aided by its power as a tool of social advancement and the prestige of its association with the rulers, slowly transformed the region from Morocco to India into the Islamic world that we know today.

As Muhammad's revelations arrived, at least some of them had been written down and all of them had been committed to memory by various of the faithful Muslims.[2] (In a culture centered on the memorization and recitation of vast quantities of poetry, this was no serious challenge.) Now that Muhammad was no longer on the scene to receive new guidance through divine directive and to interpret what had already been received, and especially now that Muslim rule of a huge territory confronted them daily with unprecedented questions and demanded the instruction of new converts, it became vitally important to establish a reliable and complete text of the revelations so that the community could look to them with confidence. The final gathering of the Qur'an probably occurred under Uthman just after 650, or roughly two decades following the Prophet's death.

The creation of a canon commences when revelation is thought to have come to a halt, and in turn the concept of a canon reinforces the notion that revelation has ceased.[3] And the writing down of a revelation, and eventually its establishment as "canon," inevitably and by definition indicates and strengthens a conservative tendency in a developing religious tradition.[4] As Max Weber noted, "a religious community arises in connec-

1. Rodinson, p. 295.
2. Widengren, *Religionsphänomenologie*, pp. 567-71, sees evidence for a very early commitment of the Qur'an to writing, and argues that this grew out of a general Near Eastern equation of God's word with written scripture.
3. See the discussion of Widengren, *Religionsphänomenologie*, pp. 591-93.
4. See Widengren, *Religionsphänomenologie*, pp. 571-72. Widengren points to the often observed preference of religious groups for archaic or archaizing language — which, in the Catholic Church, led for many centuries to a privileging of Latin and the Vulgate Bible, corresponding to ancient Egyptian cultivation of hieroglyphs long after they had ceased to be generally used. Modern-day Muslims everywhere read the Qur'an in its original Arabic,

tion with a prophetic movement as a result of routinization *(Veralltäg-lichung)*, i.e., as a result of the process whereby either the prophet himself or his disciples secure the permanence of his preaching and the congregation's distribution of grace, hence ensuring the economic existence of the enterprise and those who man it, and thereby monopolizing as well the privileges reserved for those charged with religious functions."[5] On the basis of his study of the biblical prophets in the light of Weber's sociological insights, Ronald E. Clements says that "charismatic authority tended to remain a relatively infrequently experienced and ideal type of authority. On the other hand . . . written records of the major charismatic heroes tended to be utilized in support of more long-lasting patterns of authority vested in institutions. The ideal of divine charisma was appealed to in support of institutions which might otherwise remain weak and insecure."[6]

> Charismatic authority needed to be transformed, by the nature of its own unstable character, into a variety of forms of more traditional authority. The spoken word of the original prophet needed to become the meticulously preserved written word of the prophetic book. . . . The unique and transitory situation which the original prophet had encountered had to be set in a perspective that made it possible for the more enduring and practical needs of the community that respected him to be met. . . .[7]

From this point of view, the replacement of the unpredictable voice of prophecy with the more manageable one of scholarship and bureaucratic precedent was a good thing. Certainly it was so for the intellectuals and the politicians, to whom it opened up whole new avenues of advancement.[8] For the divine word had now to be interpreted, debated, and judi-

---

while Jews still recite prayers and scriptures in Hebrew even if they do not understand the language. The Samaritans still write the Pentateuch in a modified form of preexilic Hebrew script, which also occurs in the Dead Sea Scrolls (notably in the paleo-Hebrew Leviticus Scroll from Cave 11).

5. Weber, pp. 60-61.

6. Clements, p. 94.

7. Clements, p. 104.

8. Patricia Crone and Martin Hinds, *God's Caliph: Religious Authority in the First Centuries of Islam* (Cambridge: Cambridge University Press, 1986), show persuasively how the jurists and the theologians stripped the caliphate of any claim to genuinely religious (as

ciously applied. The essential task of theologians, as G. van der Leeuw notes, is to speak systematically or connectedly about the acts of God. Their obligation is to bring the revelation they have received to bear upon the history of their community, to deal with heresy and innovation, and to respond to the intellectual currents in which they find themselves and their tradition floating.[9]

"Theology," writes F. E. Peters, "discourse about God according to the principles of reason, was the invention of a people without benefit of revelation."[10] Peters is referring to the Greeks, and his statement is not quite as true, perhaps, as he intended it, for the Greeks were not without claimants to revelation (including Socrates and his *daimon*). Still, theology tames prophecy, manages it, and most often, worships at its tomb. At Delphi official interpreters stood near the oracle of Apollo to make sense of the enraptured statements of the prophetess. Plutarch called them *theologians,* and felt that they did not do justice to the oracle's pronouncements.[11] Muhammad might have felt much the same about his own interpreters.

But the Prophet was by no means eclipsed within Islam. He could not have been. For Muhammad's personal life shows up, from time to time, in the pages of the Qur'an, where even rather ordinary domestic situations are now memorialized forever in Islamic scripture. There was the time, for example, when Muhammad took a Coptic Christian slave girl named Mariya as his concubine. His other wives became extremely and overtly jealous of her when he began to spend a great deal of time with her. In response he moved her farther away, but then continued to visit her both by day and by night, now taking even more time away from the other wives because of the increased distance he had to travel to reach her. Retaliating, several of his wives began to make his life thoroughly miserable, and he finally swore that he would visit the beautiful Copt, Mariya, no longer.

Amidst these very personal unpleasantnesses came a revelation now known as Surat al-Tahrim, "The Chapter of Prohibition": "O Prophet!" it

opposed to political) authority, and did so with such astonishing effectiveness that it has been virtually forgotten that the caliphs ever asserted such a claim. Ringgren, pp. 173-74, briefly discusses the replacement of prophets by lawyers in postexilic Judaism, which, although celebrated by the lawyers, did not altogether destroy the hope that prophecy would return.

9. See van der Leeuw, pp. 761-62.
10. Peters, *Children of Abraham*, p. 156.
11. Plutarch, *On the Cessation of the Oracles* 15.417f.

begins. "Why have you prohibited that which God has made lawful to you? You seek to please your wives. But God is forgiving and compassionate."[12] Then the revelation turns to address the wives: "It may be, if he divorced you all, that his Lord would give him better wives than you in exchange — submissive, believing, devout, repentant, worshipful, given to fasting, previously married or virgins."[13] The revelation closes with a contrast between two pairs of women from sacred history. The wife of Noah and the wife of Lot betrayed their husbands, and both accordingly were condemned to the flames of hell. By contrast the Qur'an points to the wife of Pharaoh, who, it says, listened to and received the message of the prophet Moses, and also to Mary, the daughter of Imran, who preserved her chastity and became the virgin mother of Jesus, the Messiah.[14]

Muhammad thereupon avoided his wives for the next month. At the end of it, though, he went first to A'isha and recited to her a new Qur'anic revelation:

> O Prophet! Say to your wives, "If you desire the life of this world and its adornment, come! I will provide for you and will set you free in a pleasant manner.
>
> "But if you desire God and his messenger and the abode of the hereafter, God has prepared a great reward for those among you who do good."
>
> O women of the Prophet! Whoever among you commits manifest uncleanness, her punishment will be doubled. That is an easy thing for God.
>
> And whoever among you is obedient to God and his messenger and works righteousness, we shall grant her reward twice, and we have prepared a noble sustenance for her.

12. Q 66:3.

13. Q 66:5.

14. See Q 66:10-12. Western scholars of Islam have often pointed to the information mentioned here about "Mary, the daughter of Imran," as evidence that Muhammad had confused Mary, the mother of Jesus, with Miriam, the daughter of Amiram and the sister of Moses and Aaron. Both names would occur in Arabic as Maryam. According to early Christian tradition, the father of the Virgin Mary was named Joachim. See, for example, the second-century *Protevangelium of James* 1–5, conveniently available in J. K. Elliott, *The Apocryphal New Testament: A Collection of Apocryphal Christian Literature in an English Translation* (Oxford: Clarendon, 1993), pp. 57-59.

O women of the Prophet! Do not be like one of the [other] women, if you fear God. Do not be [too] compliant in your speech, so that one with a diseased heart desires [you], but speak honorably.

And remain in your houses, and do not ornament yourselves ostentatiously in the manner of the time of ignorance [*al-jahiliyya*]. Establish prayer and give alms, and obey God and his messenger. God only wants to remove abomination far from you, O people of the house [*ahl al-bayt*], and to purify you.[15]

When the choice was presented to her, A'isha did not hesitate to choose God and his messenger over divorce and a generous settlement. The other wives, too, in their turn, repented and pledged their fidelity to Muhammad anew.

The personal life of the Prophet also became a source of legal and theological precedent for the rising Muslim community. One day, for instance, Muhammad went to the house of his adopted son Zayd to speak with him. Zayd, however, was not at home, and the door was opened by his wife, Zaynab. She was roughly forty years old but was still, as most of the accounts agree, a woman of remarkable beauty.[16] It was as if she and the Prophet had never previously laid eyes on one another. Instantly Muhammad knew that he was in love with her and that she was in love with him. He hurriedly turned and walked away, but Zaynab heard him say to himself, "Glory be to the Most High God! Glory be to the One who disposes men's hearts!" When Zayd returned home, his wife told him of her strange encounter with the Prophet. Zayd instantly divined what was going on and went to Muhammad, offering to yield up his wife to the Prophet if the Prophet so desired. "Keep your wife," the Prophet responded, "and fear God." Muhammad was very much opposed to divorce, saying that, of all legal things, it was the most hateful in the sight of God. But Zayd returned the following day with the same offer. Again Muhammad refused the proposal, but Zayd now divorced Zaynab, making her thereby available to marry the Prophet.

But not really. Marrying her was still not an option open to Muham-

---

15. Q 33:28-33.

16. Watt, p. 158, rather unchivalrously observes that the story of Muhammad's enchantment with Zaynab's beauty does not occur in the earliest source, and points out that she was quite old by ancient Arabian standards.

mad, for two quite different reasons. First of all, he already had four wives, and four was the maximum number permitted under Qur'anic revelation.[17] Furthermore, the Qur'an forbade men to marry the wives of their sons, and Arabian tradition considered adoptive sonship to be just as real as literal genetic descent. However, a revelation came to Muhammad several months later that solved the problem for him:

> Lo, you say to him whom God and you have favored [i.e., Zayd], "Keep your wife, and fear God." And you hide in your soul what God has made manifest, and you fear the people. But God is more deserving of fear. So when Zayd divorced her, we gave her in marriage to you so that there would not be a restriction for the believers regarding the wives of their adopted sons if they have divorced them. And God's command is to be carried out.
>
> There is no restriction for the Prophet in what God has stipulated for him . . .
>
> Muhammad is not the father of a single one of your men, but he is the messenger of God and the seal of the prophets. And God knows all things.[18]

When Muhammad emerged from the revelatory state, he said to those nearby, "Who will go to Zaynab, and tell her of the good news that God has given her to me in marriage?" He had been granted an exception to the limit of four wives, to marry Zaynab. The implications of the revelation went far beyond the personal circumstances of these two Arabians, however. In effect it undercut the entire notion of adoption in all of subsequent Islamic history. The revealed dictum that "Muhammad is not the father of a single one of your men" meant that Zayd, despite Muhammad's formal adoption of him, was not to be considered Muhammad's son. In the future, Muslims concluded, adopted sons should continue to be named after their literal fathers, and not after their adoptive ones. Thus, although Zayd had been known for nearly four decades as Zayd b. Muhammad, his name now reverted to Zayd b. Haritha, after his biological father. Practically speaking, adoption was no longer a viable or desirable option.

Another incident from Muhammad's personal life that proved im-

17. Q 4:3.
18. Q 33:37-38, 40.

portant for subsequent Muslim religious practice involved an onyx necklace that belonged to his beloved wife A'isha. One day while traveling with the Prophet during a military expedition, A'isha's necklace somehow came loose and fell from her neck, although she did not notice that it was missing for some time. The necklace was very precious to her because it had been given to her on her wedding day. The place where the travelers had stopped was a waterless one, and the intention had been to rest there for only a few moments. Now, however, in deference to his wife and her distress at the loss of her necklace, the Prophet announced that they would camp there until the next morning. It did not take long before the reason for their prolonged stay became general knowledge throughout the army, and needless to say, more than a few of the men were highly indignant that they were being required to stay in an unpleasant place, without water, for the sake of a necklace and a young woman's apparent carelessness. Some of the soldiers, confident that they would soon be arriving at a well-watered campsite, had taken no special care to conserve their personal water supplies, and now they were in somewhat uncomfortable straits. Abu Bakr, A'isha's father, was extremely embarrassed.

But embarrassment and discomfort were not the only problems. Without water, the Muslims would not be able to pray the dawn prayer, for they would be unable to make the required ritual ablutions. In answer to this problem, though, in the hours just before the dawn, God spoke to his prophet, revealing what has been called "the verse of earth-purification." If you are traveling, the Qur'an now informs believers, "and you do not find water, take good sand [or dirt] for yourself and with it rub your faces and your hands."[19] As to the necklace, when day had broken and further searching had still not found the missing object, the expedition prepared to set out. But when A'isha's camel rose from the spot where it had been kneeling, there was the necklace.

However, that piece of jewelry was destined to play yet another important role in the development of Islamic practice and law. Later during the same journey, A'isha lost her necklace again. She was already seated in her howdah, the canopied and enclosed seat that was to be placed on her camel, with her curtains closed, and the order to commence the day's travel had already been given, when she suddenly realized that, once more, her necklace had slipped from her. Without saying a word to anyone — she

19. Q 4:43.

was still quite young, only fourteen[20] — she slipped from the howdah to find the missing ornament. When the men came to place the howdah on the camel, they apparently did not notice that it was even lighter than normal. (A'isha was very small even for her age.) When A'isha returned from a successful search for the necklace, the camp was deserted. The caravan had proceeded on its way, never imagining that the Prophet's wife was not in the howdah where she belonged. There was nothing for her to do except to sit down in the abandoned campsite and wait for a search party to return for her when she was missed. In the heat of the Arabian day, however, she fell asleep.

When she awoke, a young man by the name of Safwan b. Mu'attal was standing over her. He had fallen behind the main body of the expedition for some reason or other, and had not spent the night with them in the camp. While attempting to catch up with them, he had noticed a young girl asleep, all alone in the wilderness, and when he investigated had recognized her as the wife of Muhammad. (The veil had only recently been imposed on the wives of the Prophet, so he knew what she looked like.) A'isha immediately drew her veil over her face. Safwan naturally offered her a ride on his camel as he sought to overtake the other Muslims. He led the camel on foot. Meanwhile the main expedition did not notice her absence for a surprisingly long time. Even after they had arrived at the next halt and had placed her howdah on the ground, they were not surprised that she did not emerge from it. The warmth of such an enclosure and the rhythmic, monotonous motions of the supporting camel were quite likely to put its occupant to sleep, and nobody — certainly no other man — would have dreamed of invading the privacy of one of the wives of the Prophet in order to check on her, even had they suspected something amiss. So everyone was surprised when, toward the end of their rest, A'isha came riding into their midst on a camel led by the young Safwan.

But that was far from the end of the story. Suspicions soon began to circulate among the travelers, and then, upon their return to Medina,

20. At almost precisely this time, and indeed, in connection with the event being narrated here, A'isha's maidservant told Muhammad that the one complaint she could think of against her mistress was that she was just a young girl. When she was kneading dough, she explained, and, having an errand elsewhere, she asked A'isha to watch it, the girl would sometimes fall asleep. And then her pet lamb would come and devour the undefended dough.

throughout the Muslim community, that something untoward had occurred between the Prophet's teenage wife and Safwan. Before long, although presumably not everyone believed the rumors, they were on every
tongue. Only A'isha herself seemed to be ignorant of the circulating rumors, although she eventually became aware of a certain coolness and distance on the part of her husband, the Prophet. Naturally, Ibn Ubayy and
the others known in the traditional Muslim accounts as the "hypocrites"
were among the most vocal and insistent in the matter. But Ali too believed
A'isha guilty of misbehavior in the case, and the rift that his suspicions created between them had fateful consequences for the Islamic empire in the
years after Muhammad's death. Disputes about A'isha's chastity, between
those who doubted it and those who sought to defend her honor, eventually threatened even to become violent.

When A'isha finally realized what was being said about her, she was
horrified. And she was deeply distressed to hear that her husband, Muhammad, was asking questions about her and seeking to make up his mind
whether or not to believe in her fidelity to him. He eventually came to the
conclusion that he could trust her, but the community at large remained
divided on the issue, and it was easy to dismiss Muhammad's confidence in
A'isha as nothing more than the wishful thinking of a doting husband. But
after a month of doubts and anguish, a revelation on the subject finally
came to Muhammad assuring him of her innocence.

> Truly, those who brought forth the lie are a party among you. Do not
> think it an evil to you, but rather a good to you. Every man among
> them will receive what he earned of sin, and he among them who took
> the lead in it will receive a great punishment.
>
> Why, when they heard it, did the believers — both men and women
> — not think good within themselves, and say, "This is a manifest lie"?
>
> Why did they not bring forward four witnesses? So, since they have
> not brought forward such witnesses, these people, in the view of God,
> are the liars.
>
> Had it not been for the favor and mercy of God upon you in this
> world and the next, there would have come upon you a grievous pun-
> ishment for that which you rushed into here.
>
> When you took it upon your tongues and said something with your
> mouths about which you had no knowledge, you thought it a small
> thing, but with God it was an enormity.

And when you heard it, why did you not say, "We have no business speaking of this. Glory be to Thee! This is a monstrous slander"?

God admonishes you that you never repeat such conduct, if you are believers.[21]

Thus, in the future, allegations of adultery against a woman were to be supported by the testimony of four witnesses (which makes such accusations virtually impossible to prove). Moreover, the penalty for those who brought false accusations against chaste and honorable women was that they be scourged. The sentence was actually carried out against some of the most outspoken bearers of the rumor, but, perhaps for political reasons, the "hypocrites" (along with Ali, of course) escaped earthly punishment. A'isha, in the meantime, was not only fully vindicated in the minds of the faithful, but was astonished, unimportant as she thought herself, to figure in a revelation from the throne of God.

Muhammad's importance as a guide to Muslim belief and practice is, however, by no means limited to his appearances in the holy book. As Islam spread, it encountered new situations and questions for which the Qur'an provided no direct answer. Devout Muslims, therefore, earnestly sought for whatever guidance they could find. And they found it in the life of the Prophet, or at least in accounts of his life and actions and sayings that were compiled to meet their needs. If anyone had ever understood the principles of Islam and their proper application, it was felt, that person would be the Prophet, through whom they were revealed. Thus Muhammad himself became a kind of revelation of the divine will, and narrations of his deeds, of what he said, of what he approved and disapproved were eagerly sought for by jurists and theologians — and in many cases perhaps created by them. (In the matter of these narratives — called hadith — as in economics, demand seems to have called forth supply.) Muhammad's primary distinction lies in his being the conduit through whom the divine message came that is contained in the Qur'an. But the Muslim profession of faith, the *shahada* or "testimony," quite aptly refers both to God and to the Prophet: "I testify that there is no god but God, and that Muhammad is the Messenger of God."

F. E. Peters compares Muhammad's sunna, his paradigmatic behavior and commentary, and the consensus of the *umma*, or community, that

21. Q 24:11-17.

also went into forming the overall Islamic sunna, with the "tradition" of the Mishnah in Judaism.[22] Ronald Clements sees the shaping and choosing of the prophetic literature in the Hebrew Bible as reflecting "a work of interpretation and routinization that endeavored to make the insights and messages of the great prophets applicable to the ongoing needs of a larger world of followers."[23] In other words, there was a dynamic relationship between the community and the sacred traditions upon which it was built. Each shaped the other. Much the same could be said of the legacy of the Prophet of Islam. G. van der Leeuw makes the point (and, with the aid of G. K. Chesterton, makes it wittily) that a scripture means everything with but nothing without the help of a living interpretive community. In Islam, that community has built its interpretation largely upon the hadith.[24]

Max Weber identified two types of prophets. One, the "exemplary prophet," is someone "who, by his personal example, demonstrates the way to religious salvation." "The preaching of this type of prophet," writes Weber, "says nothing about a divine mission or an ethical duty of obedience, but rather directs itself to the self-interest of those who crave salvation, recommending to them the same path as he himself traversed." The paradigmatic exemplary prophet, according to Weber, is the Buddha, and Weber sees the phenomenon as especially characteristic of India — although he will admit that it has also manifested itself in China (e.g., in Lao Tzu) and in the Near East. The other type of prophet, the "ethical prophet," is to be found, in Weber's view, only in the Near East, and he finds especially clear illustration of it in the lives of Zoroaster and Muhammad. In this understanding of prophecy the prophet is a messenger, "an instrument for the proclamation of a god and his will, be this a concrete command or an ab-

22. Peters, *Children of Abraham,* p. 89.

23. Clements, p. 105.

24. Van der Leeuw, pp. 501-2. Van der Leeuw writes of "the terrible problem of *interpretation*" (emphasis in original, here and below). "What does the Bible say? Everything and nothing. 'When will people understand that it is useless for a man to read his Bible unless he also reads everybody else's Bible? A printer reads a Bible for misprints. A Mormon reads his Bible and finds polygamy; a Christian Scientist reads his and finds we have no arms and legs.' The Bible must be *interpreted.* But how, and by what authority? A not inconsiderable portion of the most important questions that have agitated Christendom in the course of its history have their origin in these difficulties. In Islam, moreover, it was precisely the same." I have taken the original English of the Chesterton passage that van der Leeuw cites from G. K. Chesterton, *The Innocence of Father Brown* (Harmondsworth: Penguin Books, 1950), p. 226.

stract norm. Preaching as one who has received a commission from god, he demands obedience as an ethical duty." Such prophecy was absent from East Asia and the Indian subcontinent, says Weber, because of the "absence," in those places and their cultures, "of a personal, transcendental, and ethical god." In the Near East, by contrast, the concept of such a god was present because it had grown out of the real-world notion of "an all-powerful mundane king with his rational bureaucratic regime."[25] The Muhammad of the Qur'an is clearly a case of the "ethical prophet." But the Muhammad depicted and remembered in the vast, canonical hadith collections is not so easily distinguished from Weber's "exemplary prophet."

Muhammad himself might not have been altogether surprised or dismayed by the role he assumed in later Islam. He was made deeply conscious, by the revelations he received, of the gap that separated him from ordinary men. The later revelations, in fact, spoke not merely of obedience to God, but of deference to "God and his messenger." Others were not to address him by name in the normal, everyday way. Unlike him, they were limited to four wives. His wives, however many there might be, bore the title "mothers of the believers," and they were never to marry another after him. If one of the believers sought their intercession, that person was to speak with them from behind a curtain:

> It is not for any male or female believer, if God and his messenger have decided a matter, to have any option in the matter. And whoever rebels against God and his messenger has clearly erred. . . .
>
> O you who believe! Do not enter the houses of the Prophet unless permission is granted to you — for a meal, not waiting for it, but when you are invited, enter. And when you have eaten, disperse, without seeking familiar conversation. Such behavior annoys the Prophet. He hesitates to send you away, but God does not hesitate to tell you the truth. And when you ask his wives for anything, ask them from behind a curtain. That is purer for your hearts and for their hearts. Nor should you annoy the messenger of God, nor marry his wives after him. Indeed, such a thing, with God, would be a terrible wrong.[26]

25. Weber, pp. 55-56. However, since India and certainly China also enjoyed such earthly kings and their courts, it is not clear that Weber's comments on the Near East possess much real explanatory power.

26. Q 33:36, 53.

And the believers, too, treated him as their superior. When an unbeliever, at one point, engaged him in earnest conversation and, as was sometimes done, took hold of his beard while addressing him, a Muslim bystander offered to remove the man's hand with a sword if he did not let go of the Prophet's beard. That same unbeliever later reported to the Quraysh that he had never seen anyone who could claim such complete loyalty and veneration from his followers as could Muhammad. They vied with one another, he said, in their eagerness to fulfill his every wish. When he spoke, they were quiet and reverent in his presence, and they lowered their eyes while speaking with him, as if to look him straight in the face were to commit a kind of sacrilege. In fact, he said, perhaps exaggerating, they even fought for the water that he discarded after his ritual ablutions.[27]

The believers' veneration of Muhammad sought to attribute to him all possible perfections. Although, for example, he never claimed to have performed any miracle other than the supreme feat of bringing the Qur'an, Muslim tradition soon ascribed to him a wide variety of miracles. "This," writes David Noel Freedman of miracle working among the biblical prophets,

> was a distinctive aspect of prophetic behavior in certain cases only, and it is not clear whether it was regarded as important for a prophet to demonstrate such powers, or whether these were more or less incidental and associated with certain charismatic personalities. Thus, miracles are clearly and strongly associated with prophets such as Moses, Samuel, and especially Elijah and Elisha, as well as with Isaiah among the so-called writing prophets; however, there are many prophets with little or no such connection, for example, Jeremiah, Amos, Hosea, and Micah. . . . Certainly they were not obligatory, and such miracles seem to be attached to unusual charismatic individuals who were also prophets, but not necessarily to the role or office of prophet.[28]

27. Perhaps he was not exaggerating. Abu Sufyan is said to have witnessed the same thing on the morning of his conversion, when the Muslims were about to enter Mecca. It was perhaps one of the factors in his conversion, for he sensed that such devotion could not easily be explained away and might indeed be evidence of a supernatural agency at work.

28. Freedman, "Between God and Man," p. 62. "With Ezekiel, strange things happen to the prophet and he has extraordinary extra-sensory experiences, but these are hardly in the same category with the popular healing and feeding miracles associated with Moses and the period of the Exodus-wanderings or with Elijah and Elisha at a later time." As Freedman

But it was precisely such prophets as Moses and Samuel and Elijah and Elisha who were likely to live on in the folklore of the Arabian Jews and their pagan neighbors, and it is such figures who appear in the pages of the Qur'an. (By contrast, Jeremiah, Amos, Hosea, and Micah are virtually if not completely invisible in the Muslim tradition.) And they served as the models against which the story of Muhammad would be judged, both by Muslims and by the Christians and Jews whom they sought to convince.

For many centuries and still today, Muhammad has been and is the ideal model of masculine beauty, the paradigm of pure spirituality. For the Muslim mystics known as the *Sufis,* Muhammad or the "Light of Muhammad" is the first creation of God. His birthday is celebrated annually with lights and delicious desserts, and he is praised in poems and folk songs across the Islamic world.[29]

Speaking in regard to ancient Israel, David Noel Freedman mentions, besides the prophet's primary role as a messenger of and a spokesman for God, his role as an intercessor with God on behalf of his people. This is not the case — or, at least, not expressly so — with every biblical prophet. In fact, as Freedman points out, Jeremiah mentions two prophetic intercessors, Moses and Samuel, with the explicit admission that such a role has been divinely denied to him.[30] Freedman is willing to add to this very short list the names of Amos and, less confidently, Abraham.[31]

Is Muhammad an intercessor? Emphatically yes, and his intercession is eagerly sought, for it is thought to extend even beyond the gates of death. One of the most offensive aspects of Muhammad's preaching, in the minds of his pagan hearers, was its condemnation of their venerated ancestors to

---

notes on p. 57, biblical prophets were both "foretellers and forthtellers." So was Muhammad, but the emphasis must clearly be overwhelmingly on the latter role.

29. Excellent discussions of this subject and of the general subject of this section include Annemarie Schimmel, *And Muhammad Is His Messenger: The Veneration of the Prophet in Islamic Piety* (Chapel Hill and London: University of North Carolina Press, 1985); Tor Andrae, *Die Person Muhammads in Lehre und Glaube seiner Gemeinde* (Stockholm: P. A. Vorstedt og söner, 1918); Rodinson, pp. 302-11.

30. Jer. 15:1.

31. Freedman, "Between God and Man," pp. 70-71. For Moses' intercessory role, see the story of the Golden Calf as recorded in Exod. 32. For Samuel see 1 Sam. 15:10-34 — where he is actually unsuccessful in his attempt to mediate between God and Saul. Amos's intercession is described in Amos 7:1-6, while Abraham appears as a mediator or intercessor in Gen. 18:16-33; 20:7, 17. For general remarks on the figure of the mediator, see van der Leeuw, pp. 764-67.

everlasting torment in the flames of hell. But Muhammad played no favorites in the matter. The story is related that, soon after his conquest of Mecca, the Prophet was seen lying prostrate on an unkept grave, weeping. When Umar asked him the cause of his sorrow, Muhammad explained that this was the grave of his mother. He had, he said, sought from God the privilege of visiting his mother's grave before he died, and that had been granted. But his request that she be forgiven for her pagan polytheism had been denied. Later, though, the tradition arose that, because of the Prophet's intercession, God in his mercy had miraculously permitted both Muhammad's mother and his father a brief revivification from the grave so that their son might preach Islam to them and, thus, save their souls.[32]

The Qur'an would not seem, at first glance, to offer much support for such a notion. But there is no underestimating the ingenuity of lawyers and theologians. When Muhammad's dear and supportive uncle Abu Talib lay on his deathbed, Muhammad went to him and implored him to accept Islam before it was too late. But two of the Prophet's most implacable enemies had already visited the old man and convinced him that it would be terribly wrong to abandon the faith of his ancestors, and his dying words to Muhammad were "I hold to the faith of Abd al-Muttalib." When he finally died, still a pagan, it is said that the Prophet locked himself in his house for several days, praying for Abu Talib's soul. But then the angel Gabriel came to him, bringing a revelation that reads, in part:

> It is not for the Prophet and those who believe to seek forgiveness for polytheists, even if they are close kin, after it has become clear to them that they are people of hell [i.e., after they have died?].
>
> Abraham would not have prayed for his father except for a promise that he had made to him. But when it became clear to him that he was an enemy to God, he dissociated himself from him. Truly, Abraham was compassionate, kind.[33]

This would seem definitively to close off the hope of postmortem salvation for idolaters and unbelievers. But the theologians argued, from an early time, that the revealed declaration that "It is not for the Prophet and those who believe to seek forgiveness for polytheists" really means "It is not for

---

32. Andrae, *Mohammed*, pp. 36-37, relates the stories and supplies the references.
33. Q 9:113-14.

the Prophet and those who believe to seek forgiveness for polytheists except insofar as God grants him permission to do so."[34]

Western skeptics have been disturbed by what seems like apparent cruelty on the part of Muhammad. We have tried to set such acts as the extermination of Banu Qurayza and the assassinations of various poets in the context of their time. But it should also be noted that the traditional accounts portray a man who was, on most occasions, very far from cruel. He was an entirely human prophet. At one point the sources depict him pulling up the hem of his robe and running a footrace with his young wife A'isha. He was also tender toward children. He adored his grandchildren, including Hasan and Husayn, whom his daughter Fatima frequently brought to see him. We read of him performing the canonical prayers, the five daily prostrations, with one or the other of the boys climbing on his back. And his granddaughter Umama would come with her mother, his daughter Zaynab, to visit. A few times the Prophet took the little girl with him to the mosque, where he would recite from the Qur'an while she sat on his shoulders.

All accounts agree that Muhammad was a man of what we would today call unusual charisma. He was a marvelous conversationalist, who could make anyone feel that all his attention and time were reserved for just that individual. When he shook hands, he was never the first to release his grip. Perhaps his abilities as a listener gave him what seemed to his contemporaries to be uncanny discernment. Some, like his uncle Abbas, are said to have been astonished at his supernatural ability to know of private thoughts and confidential acts. Muhammad was notably kindhearted toward animals. The traditional sources about his life tell, for example, of an incident when one of his disciples brought a baby bird into camp, and suddenly one of the baby's parents hurled itself at the hands of the man. The bystanders were surprised at the adult bird's behavior, but Muhammad asked them what else they were to expect, seeing that the man had seized the bird's baby. He used the occasion to teach his disciples about the mercy of God, which, he said, far exceeded even the self-sacrificing mercy demonstrated by the older bird. And he directed his followers to put the young bird gently back in its nest. On another occasion, during the final march against Mecca, the Prophet saw a mother dog lying beside the road nursing her newborn pups. Concerned lest the passing army disturb her or some

---

34. Andrae, *Mohammed*, pp. 39-40; compare Schimmel, pp. 81-104.

member of the army feel disposed to molest her, he set one of his followers beside her as a guard until the entire army of ten thousand had moved on. At yet another time, the Prophet rebuked a man for mistreating a donkey.

And what of his appetites for women and food? For many years anti-Muslim polemics have delighted in portraying Muhammad as a lustful debauchee. And it is true that, although he certainly fasted and prayed and encouraged abstinence from unlawful pleasures and even from lawful pleasures at certain times, Muhammad was not an ascetic, nor did he encourage asceticism in others. While, he said, he loved the "coolness" that came to him in prayer — an interesting word, and no doubt a significant one in the extreme heat that often afflicts Arabia — Muhammad is also said to have declared, without any sense of embarrassment or impropriety, his love for perfume and women.[35] *La rahbaniyya fi al-Islam,* he announced: "There is no monasticism in Islam."

He zealously sought to wean his formerly-pagan followers from some of their rather depraved former practices, but he intended also to guard against the opposite extreme. One early convert to Islam, a certain Uthman b. Ma'zun (who is not to be confused with Uthman b. Affan, the man who would succeed Muhammad as the third caliph), was deeply inclined toward self-denial and ascetic behavior, and had been so since before his acceptance of Islam. Once he had moved to Medina, his ascetic impulse grew so strong that he even sought the Prophet's permission to make himself a eunuch, and then to spend the remainder of his life as a wandering mendicant. Muhammad refused his request. "Do you not have a fair example in me?" the Prophet asked. "And I go in to women, and I eat meat, and I fast, and I break my fast. Whoever makes men eunuchs or makes himself a eunuch is not of my community." On another occasion Muhammad again addressed Uthman, who, it would seem, had not fully aban-

---

35. Muhammad seems to have been quite sensitive to odors of any kind, both pleasant and unpleasant. He was especially offended by bad breath. (Although he is also said to have commented that the breath of those who were fasting is sweet like the breezes of paradise.) He discouraged Muslims from eating foods that were excessively flavored with onion or garlic, particularly before going to the mosque for prayer. His wife A'isha recalled that the very first thing he did whenever he returned to his house was to seek a "tooth-stick," made from green palm wood, that he used for oral hygiene. His followers always made sure that such a stick was available for him during journeys as well. His use of the tooth-stick became a precedent for his "companions" and for subsequent generations of Muslims, who also followed his practice of rinsing his mouth after every meal.

doned his desire to go beyond normal Islamic observance in his zeal for the next world: "Do you not have in me an example?" the Prophet again demanded. Uthman enthusiastically agreed that indeed he did, and asked to know what might be wrong that provoked such a question. "You fast every day," Muhammad responded, "and you keep a prayer vigil every night." Yes, Uthman replied, perhaps not yet understanding what the problem might be, since Muhammad had often commended the virtues of fasting and of prayer in the watches of the night. "Do not do so," said the Prophet. "For, truly, your eyes have their rights over you, and your body has its rights, and your family have their rights. So pray, and sleep, and fast, and break your fast." While Muhammad was no ascetic, he was also, by the frank and earthy standards of his time and culture, no lustful epicure.

How should non-Muslims view Muhammad? There are few Western scholars today, if any, who doubt that the Prophet of Islam was honest and was genuinely convinced that his revelations came from a source outside himself that he identified with God or with Gabriel. Even the French Marxist Maxime Rodinson is more than willing to grant Muhammad's sincerity, although he is firmly convinced that the Prophet was hallucinating and that the Qur'an was a product of Muhammad's unconscious mind.[36] A touching story from the period immediately following the Khaybar campaign illustrates the Prophet's honesty. After the successful siege, one of the pieces of plunder that was taken was a camel's skin full of jewels and ornaments. Before the booty was divided, Muhammad took a pearl necklace from this treasure to A'isha. But he could not sleep that night because of his acute awareness that, in removing an item from the spoils before they were divided, he had taken more than he was legitimately entitled to take. However, in the morning when he asked A'isha to return the necklace, he learned that she had already given the pearls to the poor. As Tor Andrae writes, "The frankness with which this error is acknowledged does credit both to Mohammed and to the Moslem tradition."[37]

Muhammad remains, today, a challenge for interpretation, a complex but commanding figure — much as he was for his own contemporaries.

36. Rodinson, pp. 75-81, 218-20, 300.
37. Andrae, *Mohammed*, p. 162.

Bibliography

Al-Tabari, *The History of al-Tabari [Ta'rikh al-rusul wa'l-muluk]*, vol. 6. Trans. W. Montgomery Watt and M. V. McDonald. Albany: State University of New York Press, 1988.

Andrae, Tor. *Mohammed: The Man and His Faith*. Trans. Theophil Menzel. New York: Harper & Row, 1960.

Guillaume, A. *The Life of Muhammad: A Translation of Ibn Ishaq's "Sīrat Rasūl Allāh."* Karachi: Oxford University Press, 1967.

Lewis, Bernard. *The Arabs in History*. Rev. ed. New York: Harper & Row, 1967.

Lings, Martin. *Muhammad: His Life Based on the Earliest Sources*. New York: Inner Traditions International, 1983.

Morony, Michael G. *Iraq after the Muslim Conquest*. Princeton: Princeton University Press, 1984.

Peters, F. E. *Muhammad and the Origins of Islam*. Albany: State University of New York Press, 1994.

Rodinson, Maxime. *Mohammed*. Trans. Anne Carter. Harmondsworth: Penguin Books, 1971.

Schimmel, Annemarie. *And Muhhamad Is His Messenger: The Veneration of the Prophet in Islamic Piety*. Chapel Hill and London: University of North Carolina Press, 1985.

Sergeant, R. B. *Studies in Arabian History and Civilization*. London: Variorum Reprints, 1981.

Watt, W. Montgomery. *Muhammad: Prophet and Statesman*. London: Oxford University Press, 1974.

Widengren, Geo. *Muhammad, the Apostle of God, and His Ascension*. Uppsala and Wiesbaden: A.-B. Lundequistska Bokhandeln and Otto Harrassowitz, 1955.

Index of Names and Subjects

Index of Qur'anic Citations